INSIDE ALGEBRA

INTERACTIVE TEXT

Larry Bradsby

Cambium LEARNING® Group | Voyager

Printed in the United States of America

Published and distributed by

4093 Specialty Place • Longmont, CO 80504 • (303) 651-2829
www.voyagerlearning.com

TABLE OF CONTENTS

Variables and Expressions

In this chapter, we are learning about expressions. We work with verbal and mathematical expressions and use order of operations. We also learn to evaluate expressions and check if an expression is true, false, or open. Variables are introduced throughout the chapter and help us understand expressions, properties, and basic identities.

Objective 1
Translate verbal expressions into mathematical expressions and vice versa.

Objective 2
Evaluate expressions using the order of operations.

Objective 3
Solve open sentences by performing arithmetic operations.

Objective 4
Use mathematical properties to evaluate expressions.

Chapter 1
VOCABULARY

algebraic expression An expression that includes variables

$9 - 2y$

---

cube A number or variable raised to the third power

x^3 or 2^3

---

false The statement is always incorrect

Five added to six is ten.

or $3 \cdot 8 = 16$

---

open The truth of the statement cannot be determined without further information

An unknown number multiplied by six is thirty-six.

or $n(n + 3) = 40$

power A number or variable that indicates repeated multiplication; x^y is the product of y copies of x

$a^2 = a \cdot a$ or $4^5 = 4 \cdot 4 \cdot 4 \cdot 4 \cdot 4$

---

square A number or variable raised to the second power; the product of two equal factors

b^2 or $49 = 7 \cdot 7$

---

true The statement is always correct

Twenty-seven divided by nine is three.

or $2 \cdot 8 = 16$

---

variable A letter or symbol used to represent a value or set of values

x, y, a, b, n, or π

EXPRESSIONS 1

Mathematical Expression	Example Equivalent Verbal Expression
$3 + 9$	three plus nine
$7 \cdot 52$	seven times fifty-two
$18 - 3$	the difference of eighteen and three
$\left(\frac{1}{2}\right) + \left(\frac{3}{4}\right)$	one-half increased by three-fourths
$5\% \cdot 12$	five percent of twelve
$29 - 17$	twenty-nine minus seventeen
$25 + 13$	the sum of twenty-five and thirteen
$5 \cdot (-45)$	the product of five and negative forty-five
$84 - 33$	eighty-four reduced by thirty-three
$9 + 5$	the addends nine and five
$10 - 6$	six less than ten
$21 + 43$	forty-three more than twenty-one
$27 \cdot 86$	twenty-seven multiplied by eighty-six
$7 - 13$	thirteen subtracted from seven
$9 + 5$	five added to nine
$23 - (-4)$	twenty-three subtract a negative four

CONCEPT DEVELOPMENT

EXPRESSIONS 2

Mathematical Expression	Example Equivalent Verbal Expression
$9 - 2x$	two times x subtracted from nine two times x less than nine nine subtract the product of two and x
$3x - (x - 2)$	the product of three and x reduced by the quantity x decreased by two the quantity x minus two subtracted from three times x three multiplied by x subtract the quantity x reduced by two
$(x + 3)(x - 3)$	the quantity x increased by three multiplied by the quantity x decreased by three the quantity x plus three times the quantity x minus three the product of the quantity three added to x and the quantity three subtracted from x
$(5\%)(9 + 4)$	five percent of the quantity nine increased by four the product of five percent and the quantity nine plus four five percent of the quantity nine plus four
$3(x - 7) - 4$	three times the quantity x reduced by seven, minus four the product of three and the quantity x minus seven, subtract four the difference of three times the quantity x minus seven and four
$x - 3(x + 1)$	three times the quantity x plus one subtracted from x x minus three times the quantity x increased by one three times the quantity x plus one, less than x

Name_____ Date_____

MATCHING VERBAL AND MATHEMATICAL EXPRESSIONS—PARTS 1 AND 2

Match each mathematical expression with the correct verbal expression.

Verbal Expression

Mathematical Expression

1. three times nineteen _____

2. the product of x and five plus four _____

3. the product of x and the quantity five increased by four _____

4. x plus five times x minus five _____

5. nine plus eleven minus four _____

6. five hundredths of seventeen _____

7. x plus two squared _____

8. x plus y, the quantity cubed _____

9. five dollars increased by one and ninety-five hundredths dollars _____

10. two plus five, the quantity squared _____

11. four-tenths of x, minus nine _____

12. the product of the quantity x plus five and the quantity x minus five _____

13. eighteen _____

14. nine decreased by seventeen _____

15. one-fifth of seventy-five percent _____

16. the product of seven-hundredths and nine-hundredths _____

17. seven-hundredths percent times nine percent _____

18. seventy-nine hundredths minus the quantity of nine times five hundred forty-five thousandths _____

19. five-ninths of the quantity F minus thirty-two _____

20. x plus two, the quantity squared _____

a. $9 - 17$

b. $\left(\frac{5}{9}\right)(F - 32)$

c. $(7\%)(\$29.45)$

d. $(5\%)(17)$

e. $(x + 5)(x - 5)$

f. $x + 5x - 5$

g. $(0.07\%)(9\%)$

h. 16

i. $0.4(x - 9)$

j. $5x + 4$

k. $\left(\frac{1}{2}\right)(33\%)(120)$

l. $9 + \left(\frac{1}{2}\right)9$

m. $0.07(0.09)$

n. $-9 - 9$

o. $x + 5(x + 5)$

p. $\$5.00 + \$1.95$

q. $3x - 4$

r. $\left(\frac{9}{5}\right)C + 32$

s. $-9 - (-9)$

t. $4 - 4$

Name_____ Date_____

MATCHING VERBAL AND MATHEMATICAL EXPRESSIONS—PARTS 1 AND 2 *(continued)*

Verbal Expression

Mathematical Expression

21. x plus five times the quantity x plus five _____

22. negative nine decreased by nine _____

23. three times the quantity x minus four _____

24. four decreased by four _____

25. fifty percent of one-half _____

26. five percent of seventeen _____

27. sixteen _____

28. nine increased by half of that same number _____

29. zero divided by nine _____

30. seven percent of twenty-nine and forty-five hundredths dollars _____

31. nine-fifths of C increased by thirty-two _____

32. half of x plus three subtract half of x subtract three _____

33. negative nine minus negative nine _____

34. four-tenths of the quantity x minus nine _____

35. one-half of the sum of eleven, twelve, and thirteen _____

36. one-third of x increased by thirteen _____

37. half of the quantity x plus three, decreased by half of the quantity x minus three _____

38. half of thirty-three percent of one hundred twenty _____

39. zero _____

40. three times x minus four _____

u. $0.05(17)$

v. $0.79 - 9(0.545)$

w. $x(5 + 4)$

x. 0

y. $x + 2^2$

z. $9 + 11 - 4$

aa. $3(19)$

bb. $(2 + 5)^2$

cc. $\left(\frac{1}{2}\right)(x + 3) - \left(\frac{1}{2}\right)(x - 3)$

dd. $\left(\frac{1}{2}\right)x + 3 - \left(\frac{1}{2}\right)x - 3$

ee. $(x + y)^3$

ff. $3(x - 4)$

gg. $(x + 2)^2$

hh. $0.4x - 9$

ii. 18

jj. $\frac{0}{9}$

kk. $\left(\frac{1}{5}\right)75\%$

ll. $\left(\frac{1}{2}\right)(11 + 12 + 13)$

mm. $\left(\frac{1}{3}\right)x + 13$

nn. $50\%\left(\frac{1}{2}\right)$

WRITING VERBAL AND MATHEMATICAL EXPRESSIONS

Write the equivalent verbal or mathematical expressions in the corresponding spaces.

Verbal Expression   **Mathematical Expression**

1. _____ $0.07(x + 1)$

    _____

2. the product of twenty-nine and x increased by the   _____
quantity x plus seven

3. _____ $17 - 3x - (3 - x)$

    _____

4. the product of seven-hundredths and x reduced   _____
by five

5. _____ $(x - 7)(3x + 4)$

    _____

6. x times y times z minus the quantity nine   _____
minus seven

7. _____ $17 + 9 - x - 3x$

    _____

8. the quantity x minus five multiplied by the quantity   _____
x plus five

9. _____ $x - 5x + 5$

    _____

10. seventeen reduced by the product of six and x _____

11. _____ $43 - 9$

    _____

12. nine times x minus seventeen plus three   _____

13. _____ $9x - 17(x + 3)$

    _____

APPLY SKILLS 1

Write the equivalent mathematical expression for the given verbal expression.

Verbal Expression	Mathematical Expression
1. seven plus three	_____
2. six subtracted from nine	_____
3. the product of two and seven	_____
4. ten increased by seven	_____
5. five plus two times nine	_____
6. four times seven minus twenty	_____
7. five times the quantity three plus one	_____
8. x increased by three	_____
9. six subtracted from y	_____
10. the product of two and a	_____
11. x added to seven	_____
12. five plus two times y	_____
13. four times x minus twenty	_____
14. five times the quantity x plus one	_____
15. the quantity x plus four multiplied by eight	_____
16. the sum of seven and nine times x	_____
17. the quantity of x minus two times the quantity of x plus one	_____
18. six plus four times x minus seventeen	_____

APPLY SKILLS 2

Write an equivalent verbal expression for the given mathematical expression.

Mathematical Expression	Verbal Expression
1. $7 + 8$	_____
2. $2x$	_____
3. $2 \cdot 3 + 1$	_____
4. $3 \cdot 6 - 1$	_____
5. $5x - 4$	_____
6. $3x^2$	_____
7. $3(x + 1)^2$	_____
8. $2^2 - 4$	_____
9. $(x + 2)^2$	_____
10. $x + 2^2$	_____
11. $5x - 9$	_____
12. $x^2 + y^2$	_____
13. $(x + y)^2$	_____
14. $7x^2 + 2x + 3$	_____
15. $3x^2 + 4y - 5$	_____

APPLY SKILLS 3

Fill in the missing equivalent verbal or mathematical expressions.

Verbal Expression	Mathematical Expression
1. thirteen increased by the factors two and two	_____
2. _____	$(5 + 2^3)2 - 5$
3. five percent of seven percent of thirteen	_____
4. _____	$7(3) - 4$
5. the product of nine and seven, the quantity squared	_____
6. _____	$3^2 - 17(-2)$
7. the difference between the sum of seven and nine and the sum of nine and eleven	_____
8. _____	$(5 - 7)2$
9. fifty-two thousandths times nine and ninety-eight hundredths dollars	_____
10. _____	$(7.5\%)(\$1.95)$
11. the product of three and seven increased by nine	_____
12. _____	$3(7 + 9)$
13. two cubed minus seven squared	_____
14. two cubed minus seven, the quantity squared	_____

NO PARENTHESES

Find the correct value for each expression.

Incorrect Values   **Correct Values**

1. $2 \cdot 9 + 6 = 30$ _____

2. $6 + 2 \cdot 5 + 9 = 49$ _____

3. $3 - 2 \cdot 5 + 9 = -4$ _____

4. $5 + 1 \cdot 2 + 4 = 36$ _____

5. $2 + 3 \cdot 3 + 4 \cdot 4 + 5 = 65$ _____

6. $4 + 3 \cdot 3 + 5 \cdot 4 = 41$ _____

7. $1 + 2 \cdot 3 + 4 \cdot 5 + 6 = 35$ _____

8. $7 \cdot 2 - 6 \cdot 2 + 4 = 20$ _____

9. $6 - 4 + 8 \cdot 2 + 3 - 7 = 16$ _____

10. $7 - 2 + 5 \cdot 3 = 0$ _____

11. $5 \cdot 3 - 2 + 7 = 12$ _____

12. $6 \cdot 2 \cdot 4 - 7 = 6$ _____

13. $9 - 7 + 4 \cdot 7 = 42$ _____

14. $6 + 3 \cdot 4 - 4 \cdot 2 = 28$ _____

15. $6 \cdot 5 - 8 + 3 \cdot 4 = 100$ _____

Name_____ Date_____

APPLY SKILLS 1

Evaluate the expressions using the order of operations.

Example:
11 − 2 · 3 = ___5___

1. 3 · 6 − 2 = _____

2. 5^2 + 9 = _____

3. 5 + 4 · 6 = _____

4. 18 − 7 · 2 + 7 = _____

5. 3 · 6 + 9 · 4 = _____

6. 8 + 3 + 6 · 2 = _____

7. 17 − 3 · 5 = _____

8. 28 − 6 · 4 + 5 = _____

9. 3.6 · 4 − 6.2 = _____

Evaluate the expressions.

Example:
(2 · 3) + 9 = ___15___

10. 7 + (2 · 6) = _____

11. (9 − 4) + (4 · 3) = _____

12. 15 − 7 + (6 · 2) = _____

13. 6 · (7 − 4) + 12 = _____

14. (3 + 7) · (9 − 3) = _____

15. 7 + (12 − 4) − 2 = _____

16. 35 · (17 − 7) + 13 = _____

17. 40 − 11 · 3 = _____

18. 42 − 6 · 2 + 7 = _____

19. 14 + 3 · (6 − 4) = _____

20. 3.8 · 4 − 1.6 = _____

APPLY SKILLS 2

Evaluate each expression using the order of operations.

Example:
$6 \cdot (7 - 3) + 4 =$ ____28____
$6 \cdot 4 + 4$
$24 + 4$

1. $11 - 4 \cdot 2 =$ _____

2. $(15 - 4) \cdot 6 =$ _____

3. $3 + 12 - 3^2 =$ _____

4. $8^2 - (4 \cdot 8) =$ _____

5. $8 + 4 \cdot 3 - 5 =$ _____

6. $27 - (6 + 8) =$ _____

7. $(3 + 8)(9 - 4) =$ _____

8. $6 \cdot (4 - 2) + 5 =$ _____

9. $8^2 + 2 \cdot 5 - 8 =$ _____

10. $(3 + 7)^2 =$ _____

11. $(6 + 3)(6 - 3) =$ _____

12. $4 + (7 - 2)^2 + 3 =$ _____

13. $(6 + 3)^2 - (6 - 3)^2 =$ _____

14. $8 \cdot (11 - 7) \cdot (3 + 4) =$ _____

15. $3^2 + 17 - 4 \cdot 3 =$ _____

16. $8 + 4^2 - 3^2 =$ _____

17. $5 \cdot 3^2 + (17 - 15)^3 =$ _____

Name_____ Date_____

APPLY SKILLS 3

Find the value of each expression if $x = 2$, $y = 6$, and $z = 4$.

Example:

$(x + y)z =$ ___32___
$(2 + 6)4$

1. $xy =$ _____

2. $2x + y =$ _____

3. $6 + xz =$ _____

4. $xy - z =$ _____

5. $4 + x(y - z) =$ _____

6. $\frac{1}{2}(2x + z) =$ _____

7. $xyz =$ _____

8. $(6 + x)x - z =$ _____

9. $x^2 + y^2 =$ _____

Find the value of each expression if $a = 3$, $b = 6$, and $c = 4$.

Example:

$2b - 4 =$ ___8___
$2 \cdot 6 - 4$

10. $8 - 2a =$ _____

11. $16 - a^2 + c =$ _____

12. $ab - 4 =$ _____

13. $7 - b \div a + c =$ _____

14. $b - 2a + 7 =$ _____

15. $3b - 4c =$ _____

16. $\frac{b + 3c}{a} =$ _____

17. $(a + c)^2 =$ _____

18. $a + b + c - 2a =$ _____

19. $(b - c) \cdot a =$ _____

20. $3(b - a) + 12 =$ _____

DECIDING WHETHER A STATEMENT IS TRUE, FALSE, OR OPEN—PART 1

Identify each statement as True, False, or Open.

- True: The statement is true.
- False: The statement is false.
- Open: The truth value of the statement cannot be determined without further information; hence, the statement is open.

Statements:

1. William Jefferson Clinton is now president of the United States of America. _____

2. He is a 12-year-old student. _____

3. Thanksgiving is always on a Thursday in the United States. _____

4. George W. Bush is a former governor of Texas. _____

5. He was in the oil business. _____

6. Today's date is January 24, 2001. _____

7. It is a Wednesday. _____

8. Ford is the name of an automobile manufacturing company. _____

9. The company is based in this country. _____

10. Benjamin Franklin, the founding father who signed the Declaration of Independence, was also once president of the United States. _____

11. He was a printer. _____

12. Five added to seven is thirteen. _____

13. It is twelve. _____

14. The square of twenty-five is six hundred twenty-five. _____

15. Labor Day is always celebrated in the spring in the United States. _____

CONCEPT DEVELOPMENT

DECIDING WHETHER A STATEMENT IS TRUE, FALSE, OR OPEN—PART 2

Identify each statement as True, False, or Open.

- True: The statement is true.

- False: The statement is false.

- Open: The truth value of the statement cannot be determined without further information; hence, the statement is open.

Statements:

1. Nine increased by seven is twenty-two. _____

2. When an unknown number is reduced by five, the result is one hundred seven. _____

3. The square of twenty is four hundred. _____

4. Five multiplied by the quantity of seven plus two is forty-five. _____

5. $x + 7 = 13$ _____

6. $5 = 6$ _____

7. $a(b + 4) = 29$ _____

8. $0.5(9 + 7) = 8$ _____

9. $x + 5 = x + 3 + 2$ _____

10. Three plus five times seven is fifty-six. _____

11. Three plus five times seven is thirty-eight. _____

12. $3 + (5)(2) + 4 = 34$ _____

13. It should be seventeen. _____

14. $(2)(2)(2) > 7$ _____

15. $2 + (2)(2) > 7$ _____

APPLY SKILLS 1

Determine if each given statement is True, False, or Open. Place an X in the correct column.

Statement	True	False	Open
1. It is behind the barn next to the tractor.			
2. In the order of the days of the week, Thursday always comes after Wednesday and before Friday.			
3. When x is added to twenty-seven, the sum can be thirty.			
4. When twenty-seven is added to three, the sum can be forty.			
5. George Washington was the first president of the United States of America.			
6. He lived in South Carolina.			
7. For any real number x, $x > 5$.			
8. For any real number x, $x + 5 = 22$.			
9. For any real number x, if $x = 7$, then $x + 5 = 12$.			
10. $2(5 + 4) - 7 = 7$			
11. $3(4 - 3) + 6 = 9$			
12. For any real number called x, $3(x + 5) = 3x + 15$.			
13. For any real number called x, $5(x + 7) = 5x + 12$.			
14. $[2 + 6(9 - 7)2^2]3 + 3 = 51$			
15. $[2 + 6(9 - 7)2^2]3 + 3 = 153$			
16. Now is the time for a man to come to the aid of his country.			
17. Tom Cruise is a movie star.			
18. He starred in more than five movies.			
19. Tom is not married.			

APPLY SKILLS 2

Label the statement as True, False, or Open when each of the values is used for the variable.

Statement	$x = 2$	$x = 3$	$x = 5$
1. William Jefferson Clinton had x terms as president of the United States of America.			
2. $x - 3 = x - 3$			
3. $x + 5 = x + 7$			
4. $x + 7 = 2x + 5$			
5. $3(x + 2) = 3x + 6$			
6. $x - 5 = 0$			
7. TV programs can be received on channel x in this city.			
8. $x + 7 < 2x + 9$			
9. $x\left(\dfrac{1}{x}\right) = 1$			
10. $x + x + x = 0$			
11. $(x - 5)(2x) = 0$			
12. A triangle has x sides.			
13. $3^x = 27$			
14. $3x + 18 = 11x + 2$			
15. $2x - 7 = x + 2$			
16. x subtracted from 13 is 8.			
17. The product of the quantities $x + 2$ and $x - 2$ is zero.			

Name_____ Date_____

APPLY SKILLS 3

Use substitution to find the solution for each formula.

Example:

$P = 2l + 2w$

$l = 14$ ft., $w = 8$ ft.

$P = 2(14) + 2(8)$

$P = \underline{\quad 44 \text{ ft.} \quad}$

1. $A = \frac{1}{2}(b_1 + b_2) \cdot h$

$b_1 = 9$, $b_2 = 11$, $h = 6$

$A = \underline{\quad\quad}$

2. $y = x^2 + 3x + 1$

$x = 4$

$y = \underline{\quad\quad}$

3. $V = \pi r^2 h$

$\pi = 3.14$, $r = 6$, $h = 5$

$V = \underline{\quad\quad}$

4. $C = \frac{5}{9}(F - 32)$

$F = 77$

$C = \underline{\quad\quad}$

5. $y = \frac{a^2 - b^2}{a - b}$

$a = 6$, $b = 1$

$y = \underline{\quad\quad}$

6. $y = (x + 3)^2$

$x = 5$

$y = \underline{\quad\quad}$

7. $P = (5\%)(3)(400)$

$P = \underline{\quad\quad}$

8. $y = 2x + 6 - x$

$x = 11$

$y = \underline{\quad\quad}$

Name_____ Date_____

CONVERTING CELSIUS TO FAHRENHEIT TEMPERATURES

Most European countries and most of the world use the Celsius scale for measuring temperature. When Americans are traveling outside of the United States, they will get the weather forecast in Celsius. In order to understand the Celsius temperature, it is helpful to convert the temperature to our Fahrenheit scale.

The formula for conversion from Celsius (C) to Fahrenheit (F) is $F = \frac{9}{5}C + 32$

Use the formula to convert each temperature.

Example:

If the temperature is 30° Celsius, what is the equivalent Fahrenheit temperature?

$F = \frac{9}{5}(30) + 32$

$F = 54 + 32 = 86$

86°F

1. The temperature in Paris is reported at 15° Celsius. What is the equivalent Fahrenheit temperature?

_____

_____

_____

2. The winter temperature in London is 5° Celsius. What is that in Fahrenheit?

_____

_____

_____

3. What is the Fahrenheit temperature for −5° Celsius?

_____

_____

_____

4. What Celsius temperature would be a comfortable room temperature? Most Americans keep their room temperature between 68° and 75° Fahrenheit.

_____

_____

_____

CONVERTING CELSIUS TO FAHRENHEIT TEMPERATURES *(continued)*

5. If the temperature in Berlin is 0° Celsius, what is that in Fahrenheit?

_____

_____

_____

6. What would be the Fahrenheit temperature for 100° Celsius?

_____

_____

_____

7. Dublin reported a reading of 25° Celsius. What is that in Fahrenheit?

_____

_____

_____

8. A temperature of 35° Celsius was reported in Lisbon. How hot is that in Fahrenheit?

_____

_____

_____

9. How cold in Fahrenheit is a temperature of −25° Celsius?

_____

_____

_____

10. About what temperature in Fahrenheit is 14° Celsius?

_____

_____

_____

PROBLEM SOLVING

Name_____ Date_____

IDENTIFYING PROPERTIES

Identify each instance of a mathematical property by name and formula statement, and give the corresponding values of the variables in the formula statement. Use *a*, *b*, and *c* as the variables, and use · as the symbol for multiplication. See the first entry for an example. Some properties will not use all three variables.

Problem	Name of Property	Formula of Property	Values of the Variables		
			a	*b*	*c*
Example: $3(0.5 + 7) = 3(0.5) + 3(7)$	Distributive	$a \cdot (b + c) = a \cdot b + a \cdot c$	3	0.5	7
1. $137(5\%) = (5\%)(137)$					
2. $12 + 0 = 12$					
3. $\frac{4}{3}\left(\frac{3}{4}\right) = 1$					
4. $(7 \cdot 4) \cdot 5 = 7 \cdot (4 \cdot 5)$					
5. $173(1) = 173$					
6. $1.05 + 2.23 = 2.23 + 1.05$					
7. $973 \cdot 0 = 0$					
8. $(1 + 2) + 3 = 1 + (2 + 3)$					
9. $19.98 + 0 = 19.98$					
10. $1.79 + 2.19 = 2.19 + 1.79$					
11. $(0.2 \cdot 0.4)6 = 0.2(0.4 \cdot 6)$					
12. $4{,}972.03 \cdot 0 = 0$					
13. $30.33 \cdot 0.76 = 0.76 \cdot 30.33$					

Name_____ Date_____

IDENTIFYING PROPERTIES (*continued*)

Problem	Name of Property	Formula of Property	Values of the Variables		
			a	b	c
14. $13(5 + 2) = 13 \cdot 5 + 13 \cdot 2$					
15. $(2 + 3) + 9 = 2 + (3 + 9)$					
16. $3.14159 \cdot 1 = 3.14159$					
17. $13 + 0 = 13$					
18. $29 \cdot 0 = 0$					
19. $75 \cdot 1 = 75$					
20. $(2 \cdot 7) \cdot 5 = 2 \cdot (7 \cdot 5)$					
21. $(2 \cdot 7)5 = 2(7 \cdot 5)$					
22. $2(0.5) = 1$					
23. $0.5(2) = 2(0.5)$					
24. $2(5 + 3) = 2(5) + 2(3)$					
25. $4.98 + 2.673 = 2.673 + 4.98$					
26. $5(7 + 6) = (7 + 6)5$					
27. $3 \cdot 17 = 3 \cdot 10 + 3 \cdot 7$					
28. $(5\% \cdot 275) \cdot 1 = (5\%)(275)$					
29. $(a + b)c = c(a + b)$					

CONCEPT DEVELOPMENT

Name_____ Date_____

PROPERTIES

Write a numerical example of each property.

1. $a + 0 = a$

2. $a \cdot 1 = a$

3. $a \cdot 0 = 0$

4. $\dfrac{a}{b} \cdot \dfrac{b}{a} = 1$

$a \neq 0,\ b \neq 0$

5. $a \cdot (b + c) = a \cdot b + a \cdot c$

6. $a + b = b + a$

7. $a \cdot b = b \cdot a$

8. $(a + b) + c = a + (b + c)$

9. $(a \cdot b) \cdot c = a \cdot (b \cdot c)$

APPLY SKILLS 1

Rewrite each mathematical expression so it will be easy to compute, then compute the answer.

Example:
$(5 \cdot 53) \cdot 20 = (5 \cdot 20) \cdot 53 = 100 \cdot 53 = 5{,}300$

1. $(16 + 37) + 4 =$ _____

2. $\frac{3}{4} \cdot \left(\frac{2}{5} \cdot \frac{4}{3}\right) =$ _____

3. $35 + 22 + 5 + 8 =$ _____

4. $47 \cdot 69 \cdot 0 \cdot 97 =$ _____

5. $(14 \cdot 7) + (14 \cdot 3) =$ _____

6. $(17 + 8) \cdot (5 + 5) =$ _____

7. $4 \cdot (51 \cdot 25) =$ _____

8. $2.4 + 7.7 + 5.6 + 0.3 =$ _____

9. $\frac{3}{4} \cdot (17 \cdot 4) =$ _____

10. $\frac{5}{8} + \left(\frac{2}{9} + \frac{3}{8}\right) =$ _____

11. $(9 \cdot 67) \cdot (12 \cdot 0) =$ _____

12. $(6 + 17) + (4 + 3) =$ _____

13. $(2 \cdot 8) \cdot 5 =$ _____

14. $\frac{3}{8} \cdot \left(15 \cdot \frac{8}{3}\right) =$ _____

15. $17 + (83 + 68) =$ _____

APPLY SKILLS 2

Compute the answers using properties to make the computation easier.
Name one property you used.

Problem   **Property Used**

1. $(15 \cdot 7) \cdot 0 = $ _____   _____

2. $\frac{5}{8} \cdot \left(19 \cdot \frac{8}{5}\right) = $ _____   _____

3. $(47 + 3) + (-3) = $ _____   _____

4. $(8 \cdot 7) + (8 \cdot 3) = $ _____   _____

5. $20 + 7.4 + 80 = $ _____   _____

6. $(29 + 17) + (13 + 21) = $ _____   _____

7. $25 \cdot (17 - 6) \cdot 4 = $ _____   _____

8. $40 \cdot (11 \cdot 5) = $ _____   _____

9. $\frac{5}{6} + \left(\frac{1}{7} + \frac{1}{6}\right) = $ _____   _____

10. $(16 \cdot 7) \cdot (12 \cdot 0) = $ _____ _____

11. $9 + 7 + 3 + 8 + 1 + 2 = $ _____   _____

12. $5 \cdot (37 \cdot 2) = $ _____   _____

13. $5 \cdot 40 \cdot 1 = $ _____   _____

14. $44 + 17 + 56 + 83 = $ _____   _____

Name_____ Date_____

APPLY SKILLS 3

Each of the equalities illustrates a mathematical property. Name the property.

1. $(x + 2) + 0 = (x + 2)$

_____

2. $(\$4.98)1 = \$4.98$

_____

3. $(7x)9 = 7(x9)$

_____

4. $(589\%)(0) = 0$

_____

5. $\left(\dfrac{x + 2}{9}\right)\left(\dfrac{9}{x + 2}\right) = 1$, when $x \neq -2$

_____

6. $3(x^2 + 2x + 7) = (x^2 + 2x + 7)3$

_____

7. $(x + 5)(x + 9) = (x + 5)x + (x + 5)9$

_____

8. $(x + 7) + 5 = x + (7 + 5)$

_____

9. $x + (7 + 5) = (7 + 5) + x$

_____

10. $29(x + 4) = (x + 4)29$

_____

11. $(x - 5)x = x(x - 5)$

_____

12. $x(x + 9) = x^2 + x9$

_____

APPLY SKILLS 3 (*continued*)

Each of the equalities is the result of applying more than one mathematical property. Name, in order, all the mathematical properties used to transform the left-hand side of the equality into the right-hand side of the equality.

13. $x(x + 7) = x^2 + 7x$

_____

_____

_____

_____

14. $5 + x(x + 2) = x^2 + 2x + 5$

_____

_____

_____

_____

15. $(5 - 5)\left(\dfrac{1}{2}\right) = 0$

_____

_____

_____

_____

16. $x(2x + 3x + 7 + 2) = 5x^2 + 9x$

_____

_____

_____

_____

Name_____ Date_____

OBJECTIVE 1

Write a mathematical expression for each written expression.

1. The product of six and fifteen _____

2. The sum of twelve and three times seven _____

Write a verbal expression for each mathematical expression.

3. $17 - 4 \cdot 2$

    _____

    _____

4. $3^2 + 9$

    _____

    _____

OBJECTIVE 2

Find the value of each mathematical expression.

5. $7 + 2 \cdot 5 - 3 =$ _____

6. $12 - 5 + 6 - 3 =$ _____

7. Evaluate $6 + b \cdot 3$ when $b = 5$.

    _____

8. $40 - (5 + 3) \cdot 3 =$ _____

Name_____ Date_____

OBJECTIVE 3

Solve.

9. True or false: $5x - 6 = 14$ if $x = 5$?

_____

10. Find A if $A = \frac{1}{2}bh$ and $b = 7$ and $h = 6$. _____

11. Find x if $x = y^2 + y + 2$ and $y = 4$.

_____

12. What number for x makes $x - 9 = 3$ true? _____

OBJECTIVE 4

Evaluate the mathematical expressions by using properties to make the computation as easy as possible.

13. $(19 + 30) + 70 =$ _____

14. $(6 \cdot 8) + (6 \cdot 22) =$ _____

15. $(40 + 38) + (60 + 2) =$ _____

16. $28 + 17 - 8 =$ _____

Inside Algebra

Exploring Rational Numbers

In this chapter, we learn about the properties of rational numbers and how they relate to integers. We use these properties to add, subtract, multiply, and divide rational numbers, and we also use a number line to compare rational numbers and put them in order. Finally, we learn to find square roots and to identify the principal square root of a number.

Objective 1
Graph rational numbers on the number line.

Objective 2
Add and subtract rational numbers.

Objective 3
Compare and order rational numbers.

Objective 4
Multiply and divide rational numbers.

Objective 5
Find the principal square root of a number.

Chapter 2
VOCABULARY

absolute value The distance of a number from zero on the number line; it is always a positive number

$$|-3| = 3 \text{ or } |9| = 9$$

average The sum of the values in a set, divided by the number of values in the set

The average of the numbers 7, 19, 26, 31, and 42 is 25.

finite A set that contains a specific number of values

infinite A set that goes on forever

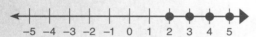

integer The set of whole numbers and their opposites

$$\{...-2, -1, 0, 1, 2...\}$$

inverse operations Pairs of operations that undo each other and share an inverse relation

irrational number A number that cannot be expressed as the ratio of two integers

$$\sqrt{2} = 1.414213...$$

median The center value in a set when all values are ordered by size

The median of the numbers 21, 18, 25, 26, and 17 is 21.

mode The value in a set that appears most

The mode of the numbers 29, 27, 23, 29, 26, and 25 is 29.

number line A tool used to represent numbers in graphic form

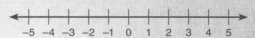

principal square root The positive square root of a number

$$\sqrt{81} = \sqrt{9 \cdot 9} = 9$$

radical A symbol that indicates that one is to determine the square root

rational number A number that can be expressed as the ratio of two integers

$$\frac{1}{8} \text{ or } -0.5$$

reciprocal The reciprocal of a number a is a number b such that $a \cdot b = 1$

The reciprocal of $\frac{5}{2}$ is $\frac{2}{5}$.

square root One of two equal factors of a given number

$$5 = \sqrt{5 \cdot 5} = \sqrt{25}$$

zero pair A positive value and a negative value of equal magnitude that together equal zero

$$+4 + (-4) = 0 \text{ or } +103 + (-103) = 0$$

Name _____   Date _____

APPLY SKILLS 1

Use the number lines to solve each problem.

1. Using the number line below, put a dot on the following rational numbers: −3, 1, 5, −5, and 3.

    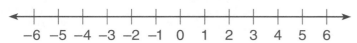

2. How many numbers did you graph? _____

3. Is the set finite or infinite? _____

4. Express the numbers as a set. _____

5. Using the number line below, graph this set of numbers: {−4, −3, −2, −1, . . .}.

    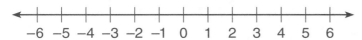

6. How many integers did you graph? _____

7. Does the graphed set of numbers stop or continue on indefinitely?

    _____

8. Is the graphed set an infinite set or a finite set? _____

9. Using the number line below, graph this set of numbers: {−6, −4.9, −3$\frac{1}{2}$, −1.75, 0, $\frac{1}{2}$, 2, 3.4, 5}.

10. Using the number line below, graph this set of numbers: {integers between −5 and 6}.

    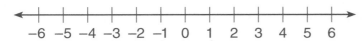

APPLY SKILLS 2

Graph the following sets on the given number lines.

Example:

{−3, −1, 0, 2, 3}

1. {−2, 1, 2, 3}

2. {−7, 4, 9, 0, −3}

3. {−2.5, −0.5, 1.5, 2.8}

4. {−8, −1$\frac{1}{2}$, 5$\frac{1}{2}$, −6$\frac{3}{4}$, 8}

5. {integers between −3 and 3}

6. {integers greater than −2}

7. {integers less than 2}

8. {0.6, −0.2, 0.25, −0.4, 0.9}

Write in set notation the sets that are graphed in Problems 9–15.

9.

10.

11.

12.

13.

14.

15.

Name _____ Date _____

APPLY SKILLS 3

Label the number lines so you can graph each set, then graph the following sets on the given number lines.

Example:

{integers between −4 and 4}

−5 −4 −3 −2 −1 0 1 2 3 4 5

1. {integers less than 12}

2. {integers greater than −30}

3. {−3, 0, 3, 4}

4. {−400, −100, 0, 200, 300}

5. $\left\{-2\frac{1}{2}, -\frac{4}{5}, 0, 1.8, 2.5\right\}$

6. {even integers from −4 to 4}

7. {odd integers from −3 to 3}

8. $\left\{\frac{1}{2}, 1, -0.7, -0.1, \frac{3}{4}\right\}$

9. {negative integers}

10. {integers}

11. $\left\{-2\frac{1}{2}, -1\frac{1}{2}, 0, 1\frac{1}{2}, 2\frac{1}{2}\right\}$

12. {−0.4, −0.2, 0, 0.1, 0.3}

13. {even nonpositive integers}

14. {−20, 10, 30, −10, 5}

Name_____ Date_____

FOOTBALL RUNNING BACK

The following are possible results of a running back's attempts to gain yardage.

- **a.** gain of 1 yard
- **b.** gain of 2 yards
- **c.** gain of 3 yards
- **d.** gain of 5 yards
- **e.** gain of 8 yards
- **f.** gain of 9 yards
- **g.** loss of 1 yard
- **h.** loss of 3 yards
- **i.** loss of 5 yards

Use the gains and losses to complete the following steps for each series.

- Translate each series of four tries (downs) into an addition problem.
- Calculate the result as a positive or negative number.
- Answer the question: "Did the running back gain a first down?" (This means gaining 10 yards or more.)

Example:

a, c, d, h $(\underline{+1}) + (\underline{+3}) + (\underline{+5}) + (\underline{-3}) = \underline{+6}$ Answer __no__

1. b, c, h, d $(\underline{\quad}) + (\underline{\quad}) + (\underline{\quad}) + (\underline{\quad}) = (\underline{\quad})$ Answer _____

2. e, i, g, f $(\underline{\quad}) + (\underline{\quad}) + (\underline{\quad}) + (\underline{\quad}) = (\underline{\quad})$ Answer _____

3. g, d, b, d $(\underline{\quad}) + (\underline{\quad}) + (\underline{\quad}) + (\underline{\quad}) = (\underline{\quad})$ Answer _____

4. f, i, h, e $(\underline{\quad}) + (\underline{\quad}) + (\underline{\quad}) + (\underline{\quad}) = (\underline{\quad})$ Answer _____

5. e, h, g, d $(\underline{\quad}) + (\underline{\quad}) + (\underline{\quad}) + (\underline{\quad}) = (\underline{\quad})$ Answer _____

6. f, i, b, e $(\underline{\quad}) + (\underline{\quad}) + (\underline{\quad}) + (\underline{\quad}) = (\underline{\quad})$ Answer _____

7. e, g, h, i $(\underline{\quad}) + (\underline{\quad}) + (\underline{\quad}) + (\underline{\quad}) = (\underline{\quad})$ Answer _____

WINTER TEMPERATURE CHANGES

Use the table to solve each problem. Show the change in temperature as positive or negative numbers.

Winter Temperature Changes		
Day	**High Temp.**	**Low Temp.**
1	25°F	5°F
2	20°F	−3°F
3	10°F	−11°F
4	−4°F	−15°F
5	33°F	16°F
6	50°F	22°F
7	20°F	4°F
8	12°F	−12°F

WORK SPACE

1. Find the change in temperature _____
   from the high of Day 2 to the
   low of Day 2.

2. Find the change in temperature _____
   from the high of Day 3 to the
   low of Day 3.

3. Find the change in temperature _____
   from the high of Day 1 to the
   low of Day 4.

4. Find the change in temperature _____
   from the high of Day 5 to the
   low of Day 8.

5. Find the change in temperature _____
   from the high of Day 8 to the
   low of Day 8.

6. Find the change in temperature _____
   from the low of Day 4 to the
   high of Day 5.

APPLY SKILLS 1

Evaluate the problems as in the example.

Example:

$+8 + (-3) =$ __(+5)__   =   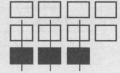   ___+5___

1. $-4 + (+6) =$ _____

2. $+9 + (-5) =$ _____

3. $-9 + (+5) =$ _____

4. $-9 + (-5) =$ _____

5. $-8 + (+8) =$ _____

6. $+8 + (-3) =$ _____

7. $-6 + (-12) =$ _____

8. $+38 + (-17) =$ _____

9. $-16 + (-4) =$ _____

10. $-14 + (-7) =$ _____

11. $-4 + (+14) =$ _____

12. $+11 + (-16) =$ _____

13. $+14 + (-18) =$ _____

14. $+6 + (-12) =$ _____

15. $0 + (+11) =$ _____

16. $-14 - (+11) =$ _____

17. $+11 - (-14) =$ _____

18. $-234 + (+188) =$ _____

19. $+5 + (+28) =$ _____

20. $-17 + (+12) =$ _____

21. $+1,246 - (+1,418) =$ _____

PROGRESS MONITORING

Name_____ Date_____

APPLY SKILLS 2

Study the two examples, then complete the remainder of the subtraction problems.

Example:	*Example:*
$4 - (-3) = \underline{\ 4 + (+3)\ } = \underline{\ \ 7\ \ }$	$-5 - (-2) = \underline{\ -5 + (+2)\ } = \underline{\ -3\ }$

1. $-3 - (-5) = -3 + (+5)$ $\qquad = \underline{\quad\quad}$

2. $-3 - (+5) = -3 + \underline{\quad\quad}$ $\qquad = \underline{\quad\quad}$

3. $15 - (-15) = \underline{\hspace{4cm}} = \underline{\quad\quad}$

4. $-15 - (-15) = \underline{\hspace{4cm}} = \underline{\quad\quad}$

5. $-15 - (+15) = \underline{\hspace{4cm}} = \underline{\quad\quad}$

6. $15 - (+15) = \underline{\hspace{4cm}} = \underline{\quad\quad}$

7. $25 - (-11) = \underline{\hspace{4cm}} = \underline{\quad\quad}$

8. $-25 - (-11) = \underline{\hspace{4cm}} = \underline{\quad\quad}$

9. $-25 - (+11) = \underline{\hspace{4cm}} = \underline{\quad\quad}$

10. $25 - (+11) = \underline{\hspace{4cm}} = \underline{\quad\quad}$

11. $13 - (-12) = \underline{\hspace{4cm}} = \underline{\quad\quad}$

12. $-13 - (-12) = \underline{\hspace{4cm}} = \underline{\quad\quad}$

13. $-13 - (+12) = \underline{\hspace{4cm}} = \underline{\quad\quad}$

Name_____ Date_____

APPLY SKILLS 2 (*continued*)

Solve these addition and subtraction problems.

Example:

$-3.7 - (-5.4) = $ ___+1.7___

$-3.7 + (+5.4)$

Example:

$-3\frac{1}{2} - \left(-2\frac{1}{2}\right) = $ ___−1___

$-3\frac{1}{2} + \left(+2\frac{1}{2}\right)$

14. $-11 + (-12) = $ _____

15. $-12 - (+20) = $ _____

16. $12 + (-37) = $ _____

17. $3.7 + (-5.4) = $ _____

18. $3.7 - (+5.4) = $ _____

19. $4\frac{1}{4} + \left(-2\frac{1}{2}\right) = $ _____

20. $7 - \left(-2\frac{1}{2}\right) = $ _____

21. $2\frac{1}{4} - \left(-\frac{1}{2}\right) = $ _____

Name_____ Date_____

APPLY SKILLS 3

Use the number lines to find the answer to each problem.

Example:

6 + (−3) = ___+3___

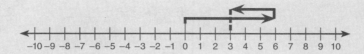

1. +4 + (+5) = _____

2. +4 + (−2) = _____

3. −6 + (+4) = _____

4. +6 − (+2) = _____

5. +8 − (+6) = _____

6. −10 + (+12) = _____

7. −3 − (+4) = _____

8. +5 − (+5) = _____

9. +7 − (−3) = _____

10. −3 − (−4) = _____

11. −8 − (−5) = _____

12. +6 − (−2) = _____

APPLY SKILLS 4

Find the solutions to these addition and subtraction problems.

Example:
$+7 + (-5) = \underline{\quad +2 \quad}$

1. $+6 + (+9) = \underline{\qquad}$

2. $-8 + (-4) = \underline{\qquad}$

3. $+6 - (+8) = \underline{\qquad}$

4. $+3 - (-3) = \underline{\qquad}$

5. $-6 - (+4) = \underline{\qquad}$

6. $+11 - (+8) = \underline{\qquad}$

7. $-4 - (-12) = \underline{\qquad}$

8. $-3 - (+6) = \underline{\qquad}$

9. $+13 + (-10) = \underline{\qquad}$

10. $-4 + (+10) = \underline{\qquad}$

11. $-7 + (+7) = \underline{\qquad}$

PROGRESS MONITORING

APPLY SKILLS 4 (continued)

12. +2 + (−9) = _____

13. +3 − (−10) = _____

14. +16 + (−8) = _____

15. +67 + (+18) = _____

16. −61 + (−12) = _____

17. −24 + (+55) = _____

18. −13 − (−21) = _____

19. +12 − (−3.5) = _____

20. $-1\frac{1}{2}$ + (+17) = _____

21. $-2\frac{1}{4} + \left(+6\frac{1}{2}\right)$ = _____

22. −12.35 − (−13.22) = _____

23. +100 − (+14.3) = _____

PROGRESS MONITORING

Name _____   Date _____

USED BOOKSTORE

Jeff owns a used bookstore. He buys used books at half off the paid price. He sells the used books at a markup from the paid price. To keep track of his transactions, he records a purchase of a book as a negative number and a sale of a book as a positive number.

Listed below is one hour's worth of transactions. What was his final total for the hour?

Transaction	Ledger
Example: Purchased a book for $5.00	−5
Example: Sold a book for $7.00	+7
Sold a book for $3.00	
Purchased a book for $6.00	
Sold a book for $11.00	
Sold a book for $9.00	
Sold a book for $10.00	
Purchased a book for $6.00	
Purchased a book for $7.00	
Sold a book for $9.00	
Purchased a book for $5.00	
Purchased a book for $6.00	
Sold a book for $8.00	
Sold a book for $8.00	
Sold a book for $7.00	
Purchased a book for $6.00	
Sold a book for $12.00	
Total:	

PROBLEM SOLVING

Name_____   Date_____

PROFITS AND LOSSES

Solve the problems using the table, which shows several days of profits and/or losses for a school store.

1. Fill in the blanks by writing each profit or loss as a positive or negative rational number.

Day	Profit or Loss Amount	Rational Number (+ or –)
1	Profit $5.55	
2	Loss $6.10	
3	Profit $3.45	
4	Loss $3.95	
5	Profit $7.00	
6	Loss $4.35	
7	Profit $2.25	
8	Profit $4.80	

2. Graph each rational number on the number line below.

−10 −9 −8 −7 −6 −5 −4 −3 −2 −1 0 1 2 3 4 5 6 7 8 9 10

3. Arrange the rational numbers from smallest (largest losses) to largest (largest profits).

_____

Name_____ Date_____

Solve.

1. Graph these integers on the number line below: 5, 0, –3, –1, –2, 4, 3.

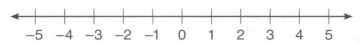

2. Rank the numbers in Problem 1 from smallest to largest.

    _____

3. Place the inequality symbol > or < between each pair of numbers to make a true sentence.

    a. 5 _____ 0   **b.** 0 _____ –3   **c.** –3 _____ –1

    d. –1 _____ –2   **e.** –2 _____ 4   **f.** 4 _____ 3

4. Place these low temperatures on the number line below.

    January 1   –10°   January 2   –12°
    January 3   –2°   January 4   5°
    January 5   12°   January 6   16°

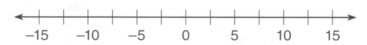

5. Rank the low temperatures from Problem 4 from smallest (or coldest) to largest (or warmest).

    _____

APPLY SKILLS 2

Rearrange each set of numbers from smallest to largest.

1. −5, 5, 10, −10, 9, −9, −3   _____, _____, _____, _____, _____, _____, _____

2. 3, 2, 0, −2, −3, 1   _____, _____, _____, _____, _____, _____

3. 1, −3, 5, −5, 3, −1   _____, _____, _____, _____, _____, _____

4. −100, −101, −99, 99, 100, −98   _____, _____, _____, _____, _____, _____

5. $-1\frac{1}{2}$, $1\frac{1}{2}$, 2, 1, −2, −1, 0   _____, _____, _____, _____, _____, _____

Place the symbol <, >, or = between each pair of numbers to make a true statement.

6. −1 _____ 1

7. −1 _____ 0

8. −1 _____ −2

9. −1 _____ $-1\frac{1}{2}$

10. −1 _____ $-\frac{1}{2}$

11. −1 _____ −1.1

12. −13 _____ −12

13. −13 _____ −14

14. 0.13 _____ 13.1

15. −0.13 _____ −13.1

16. −4 _____ −3

17. 4 _____ 3

18. 14 _____ 13

19. −14 _____ −13

20. −1 _____ 100

APPLY SKILLS 3

Rearrange the following numbers from smallest to largest.

1. −3, 5, −4, 4, −5

_____, _____, _____, _____, _____

2. $-\frac{1}{2}, \frac{2}{3}, -\frac{1}{4}, \frac{1}{2}$

_____, _____, _____, _____

3. 0.3, −0.1, −0.2, 0.2

_____, _____, _____, _____

4. $-4, -\frac{21}{5}, -3.95, -\frac{15}{4}$

_____, _____, _____, _____

5. $0, -\frac{5}{5}, \frac{5}{5}, -\frac{10}{5}, \frac{10}{5}$

_____, _____, _____, _____, _____

Place the symbol <, >, or = between each pair of numbers to make a true statement (calculator may be used).

6. −4 _____ $-\frac{15}{4}$

7. −3.95 _____ −4

8. 0 _____ −1

9. 4 _____ $\frac{16}{4}$

10. $-\frac{1}{2}$ _____ $-\frac{1}{4}$

11. $\frac{1}{2}$ _____ $\frac{1}{4}$

12. −3 _____ −4

13. 0.30 _____ 0.4

14. 0 _____ $-\frac{1}{4}$

15. $-\frac{1}{4}$ _____ $-\frac{4}{16}$

16. $\frac{5}{16}$ _____ $\frac{3}{8}$

17. $-\frac{1}{2}$ _____ $-\frac{7}{16}$

Solve.

18. Place these profits or losses on the number line below: loss of $10.50, profit of $5.75, loss of $7.25, loss of $6.75, profit of $4.50.

19. Rank the five numbers in Problem 18 from smallest to largest.

_____

_____

20. Was the total of all five numbers a profit or a loss? Of how much? (Express as a rational number.)

_____

Name_____ Date_____

CLOSER

Finish the table.

	Fraction	Find a Fraction Closer to:	Answer
1.	0.85	1	
2.	$\frac{1}{9}$	0	
3.	$-\frac{4}{5}$	0	
4.	$-\frac{4}{5}$	-1	
5.	$\frac{7}{8}$	1	
6.	$-\frac{2}{3}$	-1	
7.	0.99	1	
8.	0.01	0	
9.	-0.1	0	

Name_____ Date_____

PUMP, TANK, AND MOVIE

- A pump can pump water into or out of a tank at different rates in gallons per minute (gal./min.).

- The tank is transparent, so the level of water can be seen.

- A digital video camera records the tank level rising and falling for a long period of time.

- The movie can be played either forward or backward on the computer.

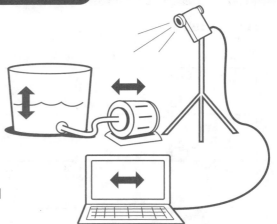

Complete the table by indicating in the last column whether the water level went up or down and whether this would represent a positive or negative number.

Pump Direction	Movie Direction	Observed Result in Water Level
1. in (+)	forward (+)	
2. in (+)	backward (−)	
3. out (−)	forward (+)	
4. out (−)	backward (−)	

Name_____ Date_____

PUMP, TANK, AND MOVIE (*continued*)

Complete the table by indicating in the last column whether
the water is rising or falling and by how much. Follow the example given in
the first row.

Pump Direction	Observed Result in Direction	Water Level
Example: in, 6 gal./min.	forward for 6 min.	rising, 36 gal., = +36
5. in, 6 gal./min.	backward for 2 min.	
6. out, 6 gal./min.	forward for 2 min.	
7. out, 6 gal./min.	backward for 3 min.	
8. in, 5 gal./min.	backward for 3 min.	
9. out, 5 gal./min.	backward for 4 min.	
10. out, 7 gal./min.	backward for 5 min.	
11. out, 7 gal./min.	forward for 5 min.	
12. in, 12 gal./min.	forward for $3\frac{1}{2}$ min.	
13. out, 12 gal./min.	forward for $3\frac{1}{2}$ min.	
14. out, 12 gal./min.	backward for $5\frac{1}{3}$ min.	
15. in, 12 gal./min.	backward for 4.5 min.	

Name_____ Date_____

APPLY SKILLS 1

Find the product for each problem.

Example:
$+7 \cdot (-8) =$ _−56_

1. $+6 \cdot (+9) =$ _____

2. $+8 \cdot (-4) =$ _____   **3.** $+8 \cdot (-11) =$ _____

4. $-2 \cdot (+16) =$ _____   **5.** $-6 \cdot (-9) =$ _____

6. $-4 \cdot (-7) =$ _____   **7.** $+3 \cdot (-7) =$ _____

8. $+11 \cdot (+5) =$ _____   **9.** $+11 \cdot (-10) =$ _____

10. $+7 \cdot (-9) =$ _____   **11.** $-5 \cdot (+5) =$ _____

12. $-6 \cdot (-4) =$ _____   **13.** $+7 \cdot (-12) =$ _____

APPLY SKILLS 1 *(continued)*

14. $-9 \cdot (-12) =$ _____

15. $+8 \cdot (+8) =$ _____

16. $-10 \cdot (+10) =$ _____

17. $+12 \cdot (-12) =$ _____

18. $+6 \cdot (-0.5) =$ _____

19. $+\frac{1}{2} \cdot \left(-\frac{1}{4}\right) =$ _____

20. $+3 \cdot (-9) =$ _____

21. $+16 \cdot (-7) =$ _____

22. $+8 \cdot (-12) =$ _____

23. $-9 \cdot (-13) =$ _____

24. $[11 \cdot (-9)] \cdot \left(-\frac{1}{3}\right) =$ _____

Name_____ Date_____

APPLY SKILLS 2

Find the quotient for each problem.

Example:
$$-16 \div (-4) = \underline{\ 4\ }$$

Example:
$$-16 \div \frac{4}{3} = \underline{\ -12\ }$$
$$\left(\frac{-16}{1}\right) \cdot \frac{3}{4}$$

1. $6 \div (3) =$ _____

2. $6 \div (-2) =$ _____

3. $-18 \div (6) =$ _____

4. $-24 \div (-3) =$ _____

5. $21 \div (7) =$ _____

6. $24 \div (-6) =$ _____

7. $-25 \div (-5) =$ _____

8. $16 \div (-4) =$ _____

9. $-32 \div (-4) =$ _____

10. $-72 \div (9) =$ _____

11. $40 \div (-8) =$ _____

12. $18 \div (9) =$ _____

APPLY SKILLS 2 *(continued)*

13. $-77 \div (11) =$ _____

14. $-42 \div (6) =$ _____

15. $-132 \div (-12) =$ _____

16. $-12 \div (-6) =$ _____

17. $-294 \div (7) =$ _____

18. $-45 \div (-9) =$ _____

19. $-17 \div (2) =$ _____

20. $-330 \div (-6) =$ _____

21. $\frac{1}{2} \div \left(-\frac{1}{2}\right) =$ _____

22. $12.5 \div (-5) =$ _____

23. $15 \div (-3) =$ _____

24. $-15 \div \left(-\frac{1}{3}\right) =$ _____

WORK SPACE

PROGRESS MONITORING

APPLY SKILLS 3

Simplify.

WORK SPACE

Example:
$$\frac{-45}{15} = \underline{-3}$$

Example:
$$-15 \cdot (-3) = \underline{45}$$

1. $-3 \cdot (-4) = \underline{}$

2. $-3 \cdot 4 = \underline{}$

3. $-5 \cdot 6 = \underline{}$

4. $-5 \cdot (-6) = \underline{}$

5. $-20 \div 4 = \underline{}$

6. $20 \div (-5) = \underline{}$

7. $30 \div (-6) = \underline{}$

8. $-30 \div (-5) = \underline{}$

9. $9 \cdot (-8) = \underline{}$

10. $-9 \cdot (-8) = \underline{}$

11. $-12 \cdot (-9) = \underline{}$

12. $12 \cdot (-11) = \underline{}$

APPLY SKILLS 3 (*continued*)

13. $-150 \div 15 =$ _____

14. $-150 \div (-10) =$ _____

15. $\frac{60}{-15} =$ _____

16. $\frac{-60}{-6} =$ _____

17. $-5 \cdot (-3 \cdot 2) =$ _____

18. $5 \cdot [-4 \cdot (-3)] =$ _____

19. $-6 \cdot [24 \div (-3)] =$ _____

20. $-5 \cdot (-35 \div 7) =$ _____

21. $24 \div [-1 \cdot (-3)] =$ _____

22. $-24 \div (-2 \cdot 4) =$ _____

APPLY SKILLS 4

Multiply.

> **Example:**
> $-8 \cdot (-3) =$ ___24___

1. $4 \cdot (-30) =$ _____

2. $-4 \cdot (-30) =$ _____

3. $-15 \cdot 12 =$ _____

4. $-15 \cdot (-12) =$ _____

5. $15 \cdot (-12) \cdot (-2) =$ _____

6. $(-4)(-2)(3) =$ _____

7. $(-7)(-5) =$ _____

8. $(-9)(17) =$ _____

9. $\left(2\frac{3}{4}\right)\left(-3\frac{4}{5}\right) =$ _____

10. $(-3.17)(-2.4) =$ _____

Solve the problems if $a = -4$.

> **Example:**
> $3a = 3(-4) =$ ___−12___

11. $2a =$ _____

12. $-3a =$ _____

13. $(4a)(-2a) =$ _____

Divide.

> **Example:**
> $\frac{-40}{-5} =$ ___8___

14. $(-120) \div (-20) =$ _____

15. $\frac{-120}{30} =$ _____

16. $48 \div (-12) =$ _____

17. $-48 \div (-8) =$ _____

18. $-480 \div 30 =$ _____

19. $\frac{-30 - 5}{-7} =$ _____

20. $(-30 + 5) \div (-5) =$ _____

APPLY SKILLS 4 (*continued*)

Solve the problems if *a* = 4.

Example:

$$\frac{-5a}{2} = \underline{\;-10\;}$$

$$\frac{-5(4)}{2} = \frac{-20}{2}$$

21. $\dfrac{6a}{-8} = $ _____

22. $\dfrac{-2a + 5a}{-12} = $ _____

23. $\dfrac{3a - 4}{8} = $ _____

Simplify.

Example:

$$(-3 \cdot 15) \div (-9) = \underline{\;5\;}$$

$$-45 \div (-9)$$

24. $(13)(-1)(-2) = $ _____

25. $\dfrac{-144}{9} = $ _____

26. $(-144) \div (-16) = $ _____

27. $(-120)\left(\dfrac{3}{4}\right) = $ _____

28. $(-12) \div \left(-\dfrac{3}{4}\right) = $ _____

FILL IN THE BLANKS

Use the integers −9 through 9 to complete the equations so that each row and column has the value indicated. Each integer can be used only once in each exercise.

1.

9	×		÷		**6**
×	▓	÷	▓	×	
	×		×		**−80**
÷	▓	×	▓	×	
	×		×		**−21**

−15	**−14**	**48**

2.

6	×		÷		**−12**
×	▓	×	▓	×	
	×		÷		**−6**
×	▓	×	▓	×	
	×		×		**35**

60	**−72**	**−84**

3.

−8	÷		×		**−24**
×	▓	×	▓	×	
	×		×		**35**
÷	▓	×	▓	÷	
	×		÷		**12**

−10	**18**	**14**

Inside Algebra

ESTIMATE, THEN CALCULATE

Estimate the square root of each number using paper and pencil only, then have one student in your group find the correct answers using a calculator.

Number	Estimate of $\sqrt{\ }$ to Nearest $\frac{1}{10}$	$\sqrt{\ }$ to Nearest $\frac{1}{10}$ by Calculator	Right	Wrong
1. 126				
2. 11				
3. 230				
4. 75				
5. 20				
6. 30				
7. 65				
8. 110				
9. 200				
10. 600				
11. 950				

PRACTICE

Name_____ Date_____

APPLY SKILLS 1

Fill in the blanks to make true statements.

> *Example:*
>
> Since (3)(3) = 9, __9__ is the __square__ of 3, and __3__ is the square root of __9__.

1. Since (4)(4) = 16, _____ is the _____ of 4, and _____ is the _____ of 16.

2. Since (6)(6) = 36, _____ is the _____ of _____, and 6 is the _____ of 36.

3. Since $(7)^2$ = 49, 49 is the _____ of _____, and 7 is the square root of _____.

4. Since $(9)^2$ = _____, _____ is the square of _____, and 9 is the square root of _____.

5. Since $\frac{1}{4} \cdot \frac{1}{4} = \frac{1}{16}$, $\frac{1}{16}$ is the square of _____, and _____ is the square root of _____.

6. Since (0.5)(0.5) = _____, _____ is the square of 0.5, and 0.5 is the square root of _____.

7. Since $\left(\frac{2}{3}\right)^2 = \frac{4}{9}$, $\frac{4}{9}$ is the _____ of $\frac{2}{3}$, and _____ is the square root of _____.

8. Since $(2.5)^2$ = _____, _____ is the square of 2.5, and 2.5 is the square root of _____.

9. Write a similar statement involving 20 and $(20)^2$.

   _____

   _____

10. Write another statement involving any number and its square.

   _____

   _____

Name_____ Date_____

APPLY SKILLS 2

Solve.

1. • • •
   • • •
   • • •

   The diagram shows that _____ is the square of _____, and _____ is the square root of _____.

2. • • • •
   • • • •
   • • • •
   • • • •

   The diagram shows that _____ is the square of _____, and _____ is the square root of _____.

3. • • • • • •
   • • • • • •
   • • • • • •
   • • • • • •
   • • • • • •
   • • • • • •

   The diagram shows that _____ is the square of _____, and _____ is the square root of _____.

4. $5 \cdot 5 = 5^2 =$ _____

5. $\sqrt{25} =$ _____

6. $(9)(9) = 9^2 =$ _____

7. $\sqrt{81} =$ _____

8. $(12)(12) = (12)^2 =$ _____

9. $\sqrt{144} =$ _____

10. $\dfrac{5}{6} \cdot \dfrac{5}{6} = \left(\dfrac{5}{6}\right)^2 =$ _____

11. $\sqrt{\dfrac{25}{36}} =$ _____

12. $\left(\dfrac{1}{7}\right)^2 =$ _____

13. $\sqrt{\dfrac{1}{49}} =$ _____

14. $(-11)(-11) =$ _____

15. $-\sqrt{121} =$ _____

16. $(-15)^2 =$ _____

17. $-\sqrt{0.49} =$ _____

18. $(1.5)^2 =$ _____

19. $\pm\sqrt{100} =$ _____

20. $\left(\dfrac{6}{7}\right)^2 =$ _____

21. $\sqrt{\dfrac{121}{144}} =$ _____

22. $(8)^2 =$ _____

23. $\sqrt{64} =$ _____

24. $\sqrt{\dfrac{64}{25}} =$ _____

Name_____ Date_____

APPLY SKILLS 3

Simplify the expressions. Estimate to the nearest $\frac{1}{100}$ when the expression is irrational. Use calculators only when you have to.

1. $3^2 =$ _____

2. $5^2 =$ _____

3. $7^2 =$ _____

4. $\sqrt{25} =$ _____

5. $\sqrt{9} =$ _____

6. $\sqrt{49} =$ _____

7. $6^2 =$ _____

8. $13^2 =$ _____

9. $15^2 =$ _____

10. $\sqrt{220} =$ _____

11. $\sqrt{30} =$ _____

12. $\sqrt{169} =$ _____

13. $-\sqrt{25} =$ _____

14. $\pm\sqrt{169} =$ _____

15. $\sqrt{\frac{25}{169}} =$ _____

16. $\sqrt{1.21} =$ _____

17. $-\sqrt{0.49} =$ _____

18. $\pm\sqrt{1.44} =$ _____

19. $\sqrt{45} =$ _____

20. $-\sqrt{3} =$ _____

21. $\sqrt{7} =$ _____

22. $\sqrt{64} =$ _____

23. $\sqrt{12} =$ _____

24. $\pm\sqrt{600} =$ _____

25. $\sqrt{100} =$ _____

26. $-\sqrt{4,900} =$ _____

27. $\sqrt{77} =$ _____

28. $\sqrt{2} =$ _____

29. $\sqrt{32} =$ _____

30. $\pm\sqrt{8} =$ _____

ORBITS

Solve for *x* in the following ellipses.

Example:
Find *x* if *y* = 0.2
$$x = \sqrt{1 - (0.2)^2}$$
$$x = \sqrt{0.96}$$
$$x \approx 0.98$$

1. Find *x* if *y* = 0.7

2. Find *x* if *y* = 0.5

3. Find *x* if *y* = 0.3

4. Find *x* if *y* = 0.9

5. Find *x* if *y* = 1

6. Find *x* if *y* = 0.33

7. Find *x* if *y* = 0

8. What would be true if *y* = 2?

PROBLEM SOLVING

This page intentionally left blank

Name_____ Date_____

OBJECTIVE 1

Graph each set of numbers on the number line.

1. {−3, 0, 5}

2. {$\frac{1}{2}$, 0.9, $1\frac{1}{3}$, −0.2}
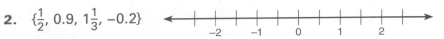

3. {integers greater than 1}

4. {−3, 2, 9}
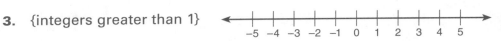

OBJECTIVE 2

Simplify.

5. 3 + (−8) = _____

6. 22 − 29 = _____

7. −9.2 + 11.6 = _____

8. 14 − (−11) = _____

OBJECTIVE 3

Place the symbol <, >, or = between each pair of numbers to make the sentence true.

9. 5 _____ −7

10. −3.6 _____ 1.1

11. −3$\frac{1}{2}$ _____ −3.5

Arrange the numbers in order from the smallest to the largest.

2. {−35, 6.35, 0, −11} _____

Algebra

Name _____ Date _____

OBJECTIVE 4

Simplify.

13. $-24 \div 3 =$ _____

14. $6 \cdot 9 =$ _____

15. $-14 \cdot (-5) =$ _____

16. $21 \div (-7) =$ _____

OBJECTIVE 5

Find the square roots. Calculators may be used. Round to the nearest $\frac{1}{100}$ when the expression is irrational.

17. $-\sqrt{36} =$ _____

18. $\sqrt{81} =$ _____

19. $\pm\sqrt{1} =$ _____

20. $\sqrt{100} =$ _____

Solving Linear Equations

In this chapter, we learn to solve basic linear equations using addition, subtraction, multiplication, division, or a combination of these operations. We use different tools to solve equations by keeping the equation balanced. Finally, we explore and solve proportions, and apply what we know to solve word problems that use linear equations and proportions.

Objective 1
Solve linear equations with addition and subtraction.

Objective 2
Solve linear equations with multiplication and division.

Objective 3
Solve linear equations using one or more operations.

Objective 4
Solve problems that can be represented as equations.

Objective 5
Solve proportions that have a missing part.

Objective 6
Use proportions to solve percent problems.

Chapter 3
VOCABULARY

acute triangle A triangle whose angles are all acute, or less than 90°

equation A statement that two quantities or mathematical expressions are equal

$x + 1 = 8$

equilateral triangle A triangle whose three sides are equal in length and three angles are equal in measure; the angles are each 60°

equivalent Equal in value

$3 = 3$
$x + 1 = x + 1$
$\frac{7}{7} = 1$

isosceles triangle A triangle with two sides of equal length, and the angles opposite the equal sides are also equal

linear equation The equation of a straight line

$y = 2x + 4$

multiplicative inverse Numbers that multiply to equal one

$3 \cdot \frac{1}{3} = 1$

obtuse triangle A triangle with one obtuse angle, or angle that is greater than 90°; the longest side is always opposite the obtuse angle

percent A ratio whose second term is 100; percent means parts per hundred

$\frac{56}{100} = 56\%$

proportion An equation that states that two ratios are equal

$\frac{2}{3} = \frac{4}{6}$

ratio A comparison of two numbers

$\frac{2}{3}$, 2:3, or 2 to 3

right triangle A triangle with one right angle, an angle that is exactly 90°

Name_____ Date_____

BANKING THE MONEY

Use the equations to play Banking the Money.

$ Values	Equations	
$1.25	**1.** $23 + t = 16$	**2.** $b - (-8) = 27$
	3. $-14 = 32 + h$	**4.** $99 = 47 + m$
$2.75	**5.** $55 - n = 51$	**6.** $-19 = 47 - t$
	7. $113 = 999 + n$	**8.** $15 = -5 + b$
$3.85	**9.** $190 - x = 216$	**10.** $-14 = 32 - (-d)$
	11. $27 - y = 99$	**12.** $\frac{3}{4} = d - 1\frac{1}{2}$
$4.80	**13.** $1.75 = m - 3.5$	**14.** $\frac{14}{15} - t = \frac{4}{3}$
	15. $1\frac{5}{7} = 2\frac{5}{21} - d$	**16.** $-1.998 = x - 3.123$
$5.35	**17.** $17 - (-2x) = 19 - (-3x)$	**18.** $y - (-14) = 2y - 9$
	19. $42 - a = -2a + 99$	**20.** $16 - (-d) = 132 + 2d$

PRACTICE

Inside Algebra

Chapter 3 • Objective 1 • PA 1   **71**

Copyright 2011 Cambium Learning Sopris West® All rights reserved.

PRACTICE

BECOME A MATH MILLIONAIRE

Use the equations to become a math millionaire.

$ Values	Equations	
$15,000	**1.** $5 = b - 2$ _____ **3.** $32 - a = 19$ _____	**2.** $a - 5 = 13$ _____ **4.** $116 + a = 97$ _____
$35,000	**5.** $3.9 + a = 5.7$ _____ **7.** $32 = -121 - y$ _____	**6.** $x - (-13) = -14$ _____ **8.** $\frac{1}{2} + m = -1\frac{1}{2}$ _____
$75,000	**9.** $18 = 89 + t$ _____ **11.** $23 - y = -81$ _____	**10.** $-x - (-7) = 5$ _____ **12.** $-1 = -t + 4.14159$ _____
$125,000	**13.** $14.9 = 3\frac{7}{10} + x$ _____ **15.** $\frac{17}{18} = \frac{35}{18} - x$ _____	**14.** $4{,}990 = 3.111 - n$ _____ **16.** $-0.5 = 3\frac{3}{4} - d$ _____
$250,000	**17.** $-\frac{3}{7} = \frac{4}{7} - y$ _____ **19.** $3\frac{5}{8} - d = 7\frac{3}{5}$ _____	**18.** $\frac{4}{11} + a = -\frac{5}{8}$ _____ **20.** $1\frac{17}{18} - h = 0.75$ _____
$500,000	**21.** $1.19 = 0.703 - x$ _____ **23.** $-7.6 = 5.3 + x + 7.34$ _____	**22.** $x + 3.07 + 2.5 = 1.8$ _____ **24.** $\frac{1}{6} - x + \frac{1}{4} = -\frac{1}{8}$ _____
$1,000,000	**25.** $x + 4 = x - 2$ _____ **27.** $x - 6 + 4 = x - 3 + 1$ _____	**26.** $3x + 4.6 = x - 2.8 + x + 6.4 + x$ _____ **28.** $x + 2.43 = 1.64 + x + 0.79$ _____

APPLY SKILLS 1

Solve each equation and check the answer.

Example:
$$x + 7 = 16$$
$$x + 7 - 7 = 16 - 7$$
$$x = 9$$
Check: $9 + 7 = 16$

1. $x - 2 = 8$

2. $3 + x = 6$

3. $x + 11 = 1$

4. $2 + x = 12$

5. $x - 3 = 14$

6. $4 + x - 10 = 14$

7. $6 + x = 14$

8. $32 + x = 12$

9. $x + 13 = -4$

APPLY SKILLS 1 (*continued*)

---

10. $4 = x - 7$

11. $7 - x = 4$

---

12. $4 + x = 2x$

13. $x - 16 = 17 + 13$

---

14. $104 + x = 212$

15. $x + 7 = 0$

---

16. $6 - x = -9$

17. $27 + x = 10$

---

18. $2 = 12 + x$

19. $x - 14 = -6$

Name_____   Date_____

APPLY SKILLS 2

Solve each equation and check the answer.

Example: $3.2 = 1.4 + x$
$3.2 - 1.4 = 1.4 + x - 1.4$
$1.8 = x$
Check: $3.2 = 1.4 + 1.8$
$3.2 = 3.2$

1. $a = -19 - 17$

2. $a + 19 = -17$

3. $a + 17 = -19$

4. $x = 28 + (-47)$

5. $47 = 28 + x$

6. $-28 = -47 - x$

7. $-15 + d = -22$

8. $4.8 = 13.9 + m$

9. $-7 = -19 + (-k)$

APPLY SKILLS 2 (*continued*)

10. $\frac{1}{6} + 2m = \frac{2}{3}$

11. $t + (-9) = 18$

12. $g - 37 = 49$

13. $-142 = m + 217$

14. $s - 13.5 = -9.1$

15. $u - \left(-\frac{7}{8}\right) = \frac{15}{16}$

16. $\$4.18 = t - \$17.97$

17. $0.6 = y - 0.7$

18. $4{,}987 + d = -7{,}289$

19. $x - \left(-\frac{27}{18}\right) = \frac{5}{9}$

REAL-LIFE PROBLEMS—PART 1

**Write an equation to represent each problem.
Solve the equation and check your solution.**

1. Alicia has a job in her neighborhood pharmacy. Her earnings last week, less deductions of $1.50, were equal to $30. How much did she earn last week?

   _____

   _____

2. The pharmacy where Alicia works has a great cosmetics department. Alicia wants to buy a complete array of skin products. Her last two weeks' pay totaled $58.00. After buying the skin products, she will have $14.85 left. How much did the skin products cost?

   _____

   _____

3. Alicia earns $6.45 each hour she works. She needs to work 4 hours to earn enough money to buy her little brother the skateboard he wants. She will have $1.80 remaining after buying the skateboard. How much does it cost?

   _____

   _____

4. Alicia will receive a discount of $2.50 on the skateboard purchase because she is an employee. How much would the board cost a nonemployee?

   _____

   _____

PROBLEM SOLVING

Name _____ Date _____

REAL-LIFE PROBLEMS—PART 2

**Write an equation to represent each problem.
Solve the equation and check your solution.**

1. Carlos works in a sporting goods store on weekends. His earnings last Saturday, less $2.00 for deductions, were $35.00. How much did he earn on Saturday?

   _____

   _____

2. This sporting goods store has an excellent skateboard department. Carlos wants to buy new wheels for his board. His last paycheck was for $38.00. He has $12 remaining after buying one set of wheels. How much did one set of wheels cost him?

   _____

   _____

3. The owner of the sporting goods store pays Carlos $6.40 for each hour he works. He needs to work 5 hours to earn enough money to buy his sister the in-line skates she wants for her birthday. Carlos will have $3.20 remaining after he buys the skates. How much will the skates cost Carlos?

   _____

   _____

4. Carlos received an employee discount of $3.15 when he bought the skates. How much would the skates have cost someone who did not receive an employee discount?

   _____

   _____

Name_____ Date_____

MULTIPLICATIVE INVERSE

Write the multiplicative inverse, or reciprocal, of each of the numbers below.

1. 27 _____

2. −13 _____

3. $\frac{1}{7}$ _____

4. $-\frac{1}{5}$ _____

5. $\frac{4}{5}$ _____

6. $-\frac{15}{16}$ _____

7. $\frac{3}{4}$ _____

8. $-\frac{3}{7}$ _____

9. $\frac{5}{8}$ _____

10. −1 _____

Write the simplest equivalent expression for each of the products below.

11. $\frac{1}{2}(2x)$ _____

12. $3\left(\frac{1}{3}\right)x$ _____

13. $\frac{1}{7}(7y)$ _____

14. $8\left(\frac{1}{8}x\right)$ _____

15. $\frac{2}{3}\left(\frac{3}{2}x\right)$ _____

16. $-5\left(-\frac{1}{5}y\right)$ _____

17. $-\frac{3}{2}\left(-\frac{2}{3}y\right)$ _____

18. $\frac{1}{-9}(-9x)$ _____

19. What can be said about any number and its reciprocal?

_____

_____

20. How would you describe the multiplicative inverse of a number?

_____

_____

By what number would you multiply each expression to get 1x or x as the final expression?

21. $2x$ _____

22. $-5x$ _____

23. $17x$ _____

24. $-8x$ _____

25. $\frac{1}{3}x$ _____

26. $-\frac{3}{4}x$ _____

27. $\frac{14}{15}x$ _____

28. $\frac{2x}{3}$ _____

Name_____ Date_____

GUIDED MAZE

APPLY SKILLS 1

Solve each equation and check the answer.

Example:

$$17x = -34$$
$$\left(\frac{1}{17}\right)17x = -34\left(\frac{1}{17}\right)$$
$$x = -2$$

Check: **17(−2) = −34**

1. $4x = 12$

2. $-3y = 18$

3. $75 = 5x$

4. $-146 = 2y$

5. $3n = -210$

6. $7x = \frac{3}{4}$

7. $7.5x = 1.5$

8. $0.8y = 3.20$

9. $-8.8 = 2.2x$

10. $5x = 480\left(\frac{1}{2}\right)$

11. $18x = 36$

APPLY SKILLS 1 *(continued)*

12. $6x = -120$

13. $-9x = -72$

14. $-76 = 4x$

15. $16y = -8$

16. $18x = 45$

17. $3.2x = 0.32$

18. $0.04x = (0.3)(0.4)$

19. $0x = 120$

20. $-2 = 6x$

APPLY SKILLS 2

Solve each equation and check the answer.

Example:
$$\frac{1}{2}x = 10$$
$$(2)\frac{1}{2}x = 10(2)$$
$$x = 20$$
Check: $\frac{1}{2}(20) = 10$

1. $\frac{1}{3}x = -5$

2. $\frac{x}{3} = -5$

3. $-\frac{1}{7}x = 4$

4. $-\frac{x}{7} = 4$

5. $\frac{y}{-7} = 2$

6. $\frac{y}{4} = \frac{5}{6}$

7. $\frac{6m}{5} = -6$

8. $\frac{1}{5}(6n) = -6$

9. $\frac{x}{4} = 22$

10. $-40 = \frac{8}{5}b$

11. $\frac{x}{4} = 54$

PROGRESS MONITORING

APPLY SKILLS 2 *(continued)*

12. $\frac{1}{2x} = -5$

13. $6x = -18$

14. $4y = -28$

15. $\frac{3x}{4} = 9$

16. $\frac{1}{8}(3x) = 6$

17. $x \div 7 = 106$

18. $-\frac{1}{2}x = -14$

19. $x \cdot \frac{3}{4} = -24$

20. $3x + 8 = 29$

SOLVING AND WRITING EQUATIONS

Solve each equation for *x*.

1. $6x = 30$ $x = $ _____

Write five equations whose solution is the same as that for $6x = 30$.

_____

_____

_____

_____

_____

2. $4x = 6$ $x = $ _____

Write five equations whose solution is the same as that for $4x = 6$.

_____

_____

_____

_____

_____

Determine whether the solution to each equation is an integer.

3. $\frac{1}{2}x = 4$ _____

4. $4x = 2$ _____

5. $7x = 20$ _____

6. $-3x = 42$ _____

7. $30x = 100$ _____

8. $25x = 100$ _____

PROBLEM SOLVING

PROBLEM SOLVING

PHONE CALLS

Find the solution to each problem.

1. A telephone company has a long-distance calling card that charges 7¢ per minute for any call anytime. Write an equation for the cost (*c*) of a call that lasts (*m*) minutes.

   _____

2. For the charges in Problem 1, how much will a 10-minute phone call cost? (Solve for *c* when *m* = 10 minutes.)

   _____

3. How long can you talk if you want to spend only $3.50? (Solve for *m* when the total cost is $3.50.)

   _____

4. How long could you talk for $5.00? Write your equation and solve for *m*.

   _____

5. Write the equation for the cost of phone calls if the charge is 10¢ per minute.

   _____

6. How long could you talk at 10¢ per minute if you wanted to spend only $5.00? Write the equation and solve for *m*.

   _____

7. Write the equation for a plan where the cost of a phone call is 14¢ per minute.

   _____

APPLY SKILLS 1

Solve each equation and check the answer.

Example: *Check:*

$2x + 4 = 9$ $2\left(\dfrac{5}{2}\right) + 4 = 9$

$\quad 2x = 5$ $2\left(\dfrac{1}{2}\right)(5) + 4 = 9$

$\qquad x = \dfrac{5}{2}$ or $2\dfrac{1}{2}$ $5 + 4 = 9$

1. $9x - 8x = 14$

2. $21y + (-13) - 20y = 8$

3. $21y - 20y + (-13) = 8$

4. $21y - 20y = 8 + 13$

5. $21y - 20y = 21$

6. $13t + (-12)t = 3.14$

7. $13t + (-12t) = 12t + (-12t) + 3.14$

8. $13t = 12t + 3.14$

PROGRESS MONITORING

APPLY SKILLS 1 (continued)

9. $-32 = 17a - 16a$

10. $4y = 28$

11. $4y - 2y = 8$

12. $2x + 3 = 17$

13. $11 = 2y + 1$

14. $4x + 2 = 0$

15. $2 - 3x = 8$

16. $-19 = 3x + (-7)$

17. $9 - 2x = 3$

18. $73 = 8x + 9$

APPLY SKILLS 2

Solve the equations in each row. Check your answers. Once you see a relationship between columns, state what the relationship is. You can shortcut the activity by solving only the equations in the right-hand column.

	Column 1	Column 2	Column 3	Solutions
1.	$5n - 9 = 71$	$5n = 71 + 9$	$5n = 80$	_____
2.	$4d + 9 = -3$	$4d = -3 - 9$	$4d = -12$	_____
3.	$3y - 4 = 14$	$3y = 14 + 4$	$3y = 18$	_____
4.	$2x - 1 = 11$	$2x = 12$	$\frac{1}{2}(2x) = \frac{1}{2}(12)$	_____
5.	$3p + 8 = -16$	$3p = -24$	$\frac{1}{3}(3p) = \frac{1}{3}(-24)$	_____
6.	$-2x + 5 = 19$	$-2x = 14$	$\left(-\frac{1}{2}\right)(-2x) = \left(-\frac{1}{2}\right)(14)$	_____
7.	$5n = 80$	$\frac{1}{5}(5n) = \frac{1}{5}(80)$		_____
8.	$\frac{x}{2} = 15$	$2\left(\frac{x}{2}\right) = 2(15)$		_____
9.	$\frac{1}{7}y = -3$	$7\left(\frac{1}{7}y\right) = (7)(-3)$		_____
10.	$\frac{a}{8} = \frac{3}{4}$	$8\left(\frac{a}{8}\right) = 8\left(\frac{3}{4}\right)$		_____
11.	$\frac{2 + m}{7} = -3$	$7\left(\frac{2 + m}{7}\right) = (7)(-3)$	$2 + m = -21$	_____
12.	$-\frac{2}{3}(2y + 4) = 8$	$-\frac{3}{2}\left(-\frac{2}{3}\right)(2y + 4) = \left(-\frac{3}{2}\right)8$	$2y + 4 = -12$	_____
13.	$7 = \frac{15 + 9x}{6}$	$(6)(7) = 6\left(\frac{15 + 9x}{6}\right)$	$42 = 15 + 9x$	_____

APPLY SKILLS 3

Solve each equation and check the answer.

Example:

$$7x - 3 = 4x + 15$$
$$7x - 4x - 3 = 4x - 4x + 15$$
$$3x - 3 + 3 = 15 + 3$$
$$3x = 18$$
$$x = 6$$

Check:

$$7(6) - 3 = 4(6) + 15$$
$$42 - 3 = 24 + 15$$
$$39 = 39$$

1. $2x - 9 = 3 - x$

2. $4x + 5 = 2x + 7$

3. $4x + 12 = x + 3$

4. $2(x - 5) = 12$

5. $24 = 4(y - 3)$

6. $\frac{1}{2}(28) = 2(3 + 2n)$

7. $7x + 4 = 9x + 24 - 2x$

8. $3y + 9 = 4y + 15$

APPLY SKILLS 3 (*continued*)

9. $4x + 1 = 7x - 17$

10. $-6x + 9 = -4x - 3$

11. $-3y - 8 = -5y + 12$

12. $t - 7 = 3\frac{1}{2} + 2t$

13. $2x - 20 = 20$

14. $3x + 5 = -7$

15. $4x + 8 = 3x$

16. $7x = -2x + 18$

17. $-3x + 24 = 2x - 1$

18. $5(m - 5) = 45$

APPLY SKILLS 4

Solve each equation and check the answer.

Example:

$$\frac{1}{2}(x + 3) = x + 2$$

$$2\left(\frac{1}{2}\right)(x + 3) = 2(x + 2)$$

$$x + 3 = 2x + 4$$

$$x + 3 - 4 = 2x + 4 - 4$$

$$x - 1 - x = 2x - x \qquad -1 = x$$

1. $\frac{1}{4}x + \frac{3}{4}x = 0 - x$

2. $0.7x + 0.3x = 2x - 4$

3. $x + 2 = \frac{x}{2} - 2$

4. $4(x + 2) = 3x$

5. $4x + 8 = 3x$

6. $2x = 3x + 2$

7. $-7x = 2x + 18$

8. $4x + 5 = 2x + 1$

9. $17x + 17 = -17$

APPLY SKILLS 4 *(continued)*

10. $\dfrac{x+4}{3} = 8$

11. $y + 6y = 22 - 4y$

12. $1.3 + 9.4x - 9.03x = 3.52$

13. $\dfrac{1}{2}x + 14 = 30$

14. $6x - 7 = 2x + 9$

15. $2y + 2 = \dfrac{3y}{2}$

16. $0.5x - 3 = 2.25 + 1.5x$

17. $\dfrac{1}{4}(4x + 12) = x + 3$

18. $6x + 19 - 2x = x + 16$

19. $\dfrac{1}{5}(4x + 3) = 7$

FIND THE NUMBER

Write an equation to represent each stated problem. Solve the equation and check your solution.

1. A number decreased by twelve is twice the opposite of ten. Find the number.

   _____

2. The sum of two numbers is three times negative seven. If one of the numbers is negative twenty-four, what is the other number?

   _____

3. Two times the number forty-one added to twice another number is thirty-four. Find the other number.

   _____

4. Negative six times a number is negative forty-eight. What is that number?

   _____

5. Three-fourths of a number added to fourteen is twenty-three. Find that number.

   _____

6. What is a number that when multiplied by three and decreased by twice itself equals fifty?

   _____

7. If two and one-fourth of a number is the sum of negative four added to the opposite of one-half, what is the number?

   _____

8. Four times a number divided by three is five more than that number divided by two. Find the value of that number.

   _____

9. One-half added to three times a number is equal to one-half of the sum of seven added to eight times the number. What is that number?

   _____

PROBLEMS INVOLVING GEOMETRY

There are many types of triangles, but every triangle has angles that sum to 180°. The different types are pictured below.

 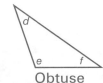

Isosceles   Obtuse   Right   Acute   Equilateral

Write the equations and solve for the variables in the sentences below. Be sure to check your answers.

WORK SPACE

1. If two angles of a triangle add to 93°, what is the measure of the third angle?

    _____

2. A triangle has one angle that is twice the measure of the second angle. If the third angle is 90°, what are the measures of the other two angles?

    _____

3. An isosceles triangle has two angles that measure 15° each. What is the measure of the third angle?

    _____

4. An obtuse triangle has one angle that measures 110°. If the other two angles are the same in measure, how many degrees are there in each of those angles?

    _____

5. An equilateral triangle has three equal sides and three equal angles. What is the measure of each of the three angles?

    _____

6. Draw any quadrilateral (four-sided figure) on your paper. Can you divide it into triangles? How many?

    _____

7. What do you think is the total measurement of the angles of any quadrilateral?

    _____

Name_____ Date_____

WRITING AND SOLVING NUMBER THEORY SENTENCES

Convert the sentences into equations, then solve. Check your answers for accuracy.

1. Find two consecutive integers whose sum is 31.

   _____

2. Find three consecutive even integers whose sum is 24.

   _____

3. What three consecutive odd integers add up to −27?

   _____

4. Find three consecutive integers whose sum is 27.

   _____

5. Can you identify three consecutive even integers whose sum is 219?

   _____

6. Find four consecutive odd integers whose sum is −8.

   _____

7. Explain why the three consecutive odd integers $(2x + 1)$, $(2x + 3)$, and $(2x + 5)$ cannot have a sum of 100.

   _____

8. Write an expression for the sum of three consecutive even integers if $3n - 1$ is the smallest integer of the three.

   _____

Name _____   Date _____

APPLY SKILLS 1

Write equations for each of the sentences, then answer the questions by solving the equations. Check your work.

1. The sum of twice a number and 32 is 78. What is the number?

   _____

2. Two times a number added to 32 is 78. What is the number?

   _____

3. Taking three times a given number, dividing it by two, and adding that result to eight gives the same result as multiplying the number by four and then subtracting the result from 32. What is the number?

   _____

4. The decimal 1.4 subtracted from a number is zero. What is the number?

   _____

5. An amount of money less $\frac{3}{4}$ of a dollar leaves $4\frac{1}{4}$. What was the original amount of money?

   _____

6. Find a number that is 96 greater than its opposite.

   _____

7. Find a number whose product with 9 is the same as its sum with 56.

   _____

8. Find a number that is 68 greater than three times its opposite.

   _____

APPLY SKILLS 1 (*continued*)

9. Four times a number increased by 25 is 13 less than 6 times the number. Find the number.

   _____

10. If twice an integer is the same as one-third of six times that integer, what is the integer?

    _____

11. What are three consecutive integers whose sum is 39?

    _____

    _____

12. Find four consecutive even integers whose sum is −92.

    _____

    _____

    _____

13. Two odd integers differ by 4 and their sum is 226. What are the integers?

    _____

    _____

    _____

14. Five consecutive even integers have a sum of 0. Write an equation you would use to find these integers. Solve the equation and write the five integers.

    _____

    _____

    _____

APPLY SKILLS 2

Write equations for each of the geometry sentences, then answer the questions by solving the equations. Check your work.

1. A triangle has three angles labeled *A*, *B*, and *C*. If ∠A measures 15° and ∠B measures 90°, what is the measure of ∠C?

   _____

   _____

2. An isosceles triangle has two angles that measure 50°. What is the measure of the third angle?

   _____

   _____

3. A right triangle has one angle that measures 52°. What are the measures of the other two angles?

   _____

   _____

4. An equilateral triangle has three sides that are equal in length and three angles that are equal in measure. What is the measure of each angle of an equilateral triangle?

   _____

   _____

5. One angle of a triangle is three times the measure of another. If the third angle measures 80°, what are the measures of the other two angles?

   _____

   _____

6. An obtuse triangle is also isosceles. If the obtuse angle measures 120°, what is the measure of the other two angles?

   _____

   _____

Name_____ Date_____

APPLY SKILLS 2 (*continued*)

Given the quadrilateral shown here, find the solution to the problems if ∠B = 60° and ∠E = 85°.

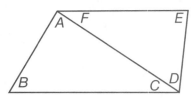

7. If ∠C measures 25°, what is the measure of ∠A?

   _____

   _____

8. Find the measure of ∠D if ∠F measures 17°.

   _____

   _____

9. If ∠A + ∠F = 115°, what is the sum of the measure of ∠C + ∠D?

   _____

   _____

10. If ∠A + ∠F = 120° and ∠C = 40°, what is the measure of ∠D?

   _____

   _____

WORK SPACE

Name_____ Date_____

WRITING EQUIVALENT EQUATIONS AND FINDING THEIR SOLUTIONS

Answer each question using complete sentences.

1. Explain, in your own words, the steps you would take to solve the problem $\frac{2x+4}{3} = 12$.

   _____

   _____

   _____

2. Write two equivalent equations for $\frac{2}{3}x + \frac{4}{3} = 12$ that lead to the solution of the equation.

   _____

   _____

   _____

3. Write two word sentences that are equivalent to, "The difference of a number and 14 is 38." Use the word "subtracted" in one sentence and the word "decreased" in the other.

   _____

   _____

   _____

4. Explain how to solve $2p + 10 = 42$ if you have to undo the multiplication first.

   _____

   _____

   _____

5. Explain why undoing the multiplication first is inconvenient for solving the equation $7x - 4 = 24$.

   _____

   _____

   _____

PROBLEM SOLVING

PROBLEM SOLVING

WRITING EQUIVALENT EQUATIONS AND FINDING THEIR SOLUTIONS *(continued)*

6. If 14 times a number added to 127 is the same as the difference between 13 times that number and 899, what is that number?

_____

7. A number is decreased by 35, then that quantity is multiplied by 6, then the result is added to 87, and finally that result is divided by 3. The value of that expression is 49. Find that number.

_____

8. You are eight years younger than your cousin Quinten. In four years you will be $\frac{2}{3}$ as old as he will be then. What are your ages now?

_____

9. A city block is half as wide as it is long. If the distance around the block is 840 yards, what are the dimensions of the city block?

_____

10. Your ongoing share of income for designing the Web page for a new company is $50 per week plus $0.05 per transaction. How many transactions per week must the site conduct for you to earn an average of $15 per day from this Web page, assuming a 5-day work week?

_____

WORK SPACE

APPLY SKILLS 1

The comparison of two numbers by division, $\frac{a}{b}$, is a ratio.

The equation formed by two equivalent ratios, $\frac{a}{b} = \frac{c}{d}$, is a proportion.

The cross product, $ad = bc$, can be shown as being equivalent by using the multiplication principle of equality. That is, if two ratios are equal, $\frac{a}{b} = \frac{c}{d}$, then $(bd)\frac{a}{b} = (bd)\frac{c}{d}$, and $ad = bc$, where ad and bc are cross products.

Using the cross product, show which of the pairs of ratios are proportions.

Example:
$\frac{1}{4}, \frac{2}{8}$
$1 \cdot 8 = 2 \cdot 4$
$8 = 8$, yes

1. $\frac{1}{2}, \frac{2}{4}$ _____

2. $\frac{4}{7}, \frac{7}{14}$ _____

3. $\frac{3}{8}, \frac{18}{48}$ _____

4. 7:13, 21:39 _____

5. $\frac{2.5}{6}, \frac{5}{11}$ _____

6. 3.7:37, 1:10 _____

Name_____ Date_____

APPLY SKILLS 1 (*continued*)

Solve the proportions.

Example:
$$\frac{2}{5} = \frac{x}{20}$$
$$5x = 40$$
$$x = 8$$

7. $\frac{x}{5} = \frac{15}{25}$

8. $\frac{4}{7} = \frac{12}{x}$

9. $\frac{9}{4t} = \frac{3}{8}$

10. $\frac{8}{5t} = \frac{2}{5}$

11. $\frac{3}{x} = \frac{15}{60}$

12. $\frac{x}{100} = \frac{49}{7}$

13. $\frac{7}{8} = \frac{x}{40}$

14. $\frac{11}{x} = \frac{132}{24}$

15. $\frac{x}{5} = \frac{14}{20}$

Name_____   Date_____

APPLY SKILLS 2

Solve the proportions.

1. $\dfrac{x}{9} = \dfrac{2}{3}$

2. $\dfrac{20}{100} = \dfrac{4}{x}$

3. $\dfrac{2}{x} = \dfrac{1}{15}$

4. $\dfrac{5}{x} = \dfrac{1}{5}$

5. $\dfrac{6}{21} = \dfrac{x}{7}$

6. $\dfrac{1}{12} = \dfrac{10}{x}$

7. $\dfrac{4}{x} = \dfrac{2}{9}$

8. $\dfrac{x}{18} = \dfrac{5}{6}$

9. $\dfrac{x}{24} = \dfrac{2}{3}$

10. $\dfrac{15}{100} = \dfrac{3}{x}$

APPLY SKILLS 2 (*continued*)

11. $\frac{x}{8} = \frac{2}{20}$

12. $\frac{25}{100} = \frac{x}{32}$

13. $\frac{9}{2} = \frac{3x}{4}$

14. $\frac{8}{x} = \frac{1}{15}$

15. $\frac{x}{6} = \frac{7}{3}$

16. $\frac{3 + 2m}{3 - 2m} = \frac{-3}{1}$

17. $\frac{m}{8} = 2$

18. $\frac{2.5}{4} = \frac{10}{x}$

19. $\frac{x + 2}{4} = \frac{20}{8}$

20. $\frac{1}{x} = \frac{21}{44 - x}$

Inside Algebra

APPLY SKILLS 3

Solve the proportions.

1. $\dfrac{x}{12} = \dfrac{3}{4}$

2. $\dfrac{15}{90} = \dfrac{5}{x}$

3. $\dfrac{4}{x} = \dfrac{16}{32}$

4. $\dfrac{6}{x} = \dfrac{16}{24}$

5. $\dfrac{4}{11} = \dfrac{x}{44}$

6. $\dfrac{1}{5} = \dfrac{8}{x}$

7. $\dfrac{3}{x} = \dfrac{9}{21}$

8. $\dfrac{x}{21} = \dfrac{2}{14}$

9. $\dfrac{x}{18} = \dfrac{1}{6}$

10. $\dfrac{25}{100} = \dfrac{7}{x}$

PROGRESS MONITORING

BODY PROPORTIONS

The height of the average human body, if divided into 16 units of measure, is approximately proportioned in these ratios:

Head	2:16
Neck to shoulder	1:16
Body	6:16
Thigh	3:16
Calf	3:16
Ankle and foot	1:16
Shoulder to waist	2:16
Arm	5:16
Shoulder to elbow	2:16
Elbow to wrist	2:16
Hand	1:16

1. Working in pairs, determine how close these ratios are to the actual proportions in your bodies. Measure your height and compute the proportions. For example, if your height is 64 inches, then your neck height would be calculated as $\frac{1}{16} = \frac{x}{64}$, or $x = 4$ inches.

2. After the computations are completed, determine how closely your measurements conform to the proportions.

PERCENT AS PROPORTION

Complete the tables. Remember that $n\% = \frac{n}{100}$ and n represents the decimal n-hundredths.

n	1	3	5	10	17	25
$\frac{n}{100}$						
$n\%$						
n as a decimal number						

n	43	72	98	100	125	250
$\frac{n}{100}$						
$n\%$						
n as a decimal number						

CONCEPT DEVELOPMENT

Name _____ Date _____

APPLY SKILLS 1

Find the solutions to the problems.

1. What percent of a dollar is one nickel? _____

2. What decimal number is equivalent to 5 cents? _____

3. If *n* is 0.47, what is 0.47 as a percent? _____

4. The fraction $\frac{60}{100}$ represents what percent? _____
    What decimal number? _____

5. *N* is 78% of 100. What is the value of *N*? _____

6. What decimal number is equivalent to 78%? _____

7. The top 35 feet of a 100-foot high flagpole is repainted. What percent of
    the pole is repainted? If $\frac{35}{100}$ of the flagpole is repainted, what decimal number
    is represented? What percent of the pole is yet to be painted? What decimal
    number represents that percent? How many feet of the pole are yet to
    be painted?

    _____

    _____

    _____

8. What percent of one dollar is 100 cents? What decimal number represents
    100% of one dollar?

    _____

9. The Statue of Liberty is approximately 300 feet high, including the base upon
    which the statue stands. If the base is 150 feet high, what percent of the total
    height is the statue itself?

    _____

APPLY SKILLS 2

Complete the sentences.

Example:
13% of 200 is ____.

$$\frac{percent}{100} = \frac{part}{whole}$$

$$\frac{13}{100} = \frac{x}{200}$$

$100x = 2,600$

$x = 26$

1. 35% of 28 is _____.

2. 32% of $3.00 is _____.

3. 3% of 480 is _____.

4. 40% of $25.00 is _____.

5. 75% of 900 is _____.

6. 120% of 50 is _____.

7. 50 less 20% of 50 is _____.

8. 80% of 50 is _____.

9. 40 less 20% of 50 is _____.

APPLY SKILLS 2 *(continued)*

Write the corresponding proportions for the problems, and solve for *n*.

Example:

6 is 15% of *n*

$\frac{6}{n} = \frac{15}{100}$

$15n = 600$

$n = 40$

10. *a*% of *b* = *n*

11. 15 is 20% of *n*.

12. 21 is 6% of *n*.

13. $4.50 is 75% of $*n*.

14. $75 is 300% of $*n*.

Answer the questions.

Example:

What % of 20 is 15?

$\frac{x}{100} = \frac{15}{20}$

$20x = 1,500$

75%

15. What percent of 36 is 9?

16. What percent of $45 is $7.50?

17. What percent of 250 is 50?

18. What percent of 50 is 250?

19. How would you write "*n*% of *y* is *z*" as a proportion?

Name_____   Date_____

APPLY SKILLS 3

Use proportions to solve the problems.

Example:

35% of 246 is what number?

$$\frac{35}{100} = \frac{x}{246}$$

or

$0.35 \cdot 246 = x$

$\qquad x = 86.1$

Example:

90% of what number is 72?

$$\frac{90}{100} = \frac{72}{x}$$

$90x = 7{,}200$

$\quad x = 80$

---

1. 25% of 80 is what number?

_____

2. 72% of 5 is what number?

_____

---

3. 35% of 28 is _____.

4. 115% of 130 is _____.

---

5. 3% of what number is 18.6?

_____

6. 125% of what number is 45?

_____

---

7. 1% of what number is 8.1? _____

8. 90% of what number is 48.6?

_____

Inside Algebra   **Chapter 3 • Objective 6 • PM 3**   **113**

Name_____ Date_____

APPLY SKILLS 3 (*continued*)

Use proportions to solve the problems.

> *Example:*
>   What percent of 96 is 72?
> $\frac{x}{100} = \frac{72}{96}$
> $96x = 7{,}200$ *or* $y = \frac{72}{96}$
> $x = 75\%$ $y = 0.75 = 75\%$

---

9. What percent of 7.5 is 45?

  _____

10. What percent of 150 is 6?

  _____

11. _____% of 70 is 28.

12. _____% of 70 is 42.

13. Before the senior class can take a field trip, 36 persons must sign up. At this time 30 have signed up. What percent of the senior class's goal has been achieved?

  _____

14. How much will Eduardo save if the shirt he wants to buy for $21.50 is 12% off?

  _____

15. The girls' basketball team has won eight games. This is 40% of the games they have played. How many games has the team played?

  _____

16. How much sulfur is in 50 pounds of a 27% sulfur mixture?

  _____

WORK SPACE

EVERYDAY PROBLEMS

Find the solutions to the problems.

1. In a sale, a disk player that usually costs $120 is advertised for 30% off. How much is the sale price?

   _____

   _____

2. A racing bicycle that regularly sells for $1,500 is advertised for $1,200. What is the percent of discount?

   _____

   _____

3. A shirt that regularly sells for $22 is on sale for $18. A special sale is advertised at 40% off the regular price or 25% off the sale price. Which is the better deal?

   _____

   _____

4. Last year 15,600 people attended a particular rock concert. This year, the attendance was down 6%. About how many people attended the concert this year?

   _____

   _____

5. Members of a ski club are given 20% off their lift ticket price. What is the regular price of a lift ticket if a member is given an eight dollar discount?

   _____

   _____

PROBLEM SOLVING

PROBLEM SOLVING

EVERYDAY PROBLEMS *(continued)*

WORK SPACE

6. The list price for a pair of in-line skates is $60, but they are on sale for $48. What is the percent of discount?

_____

_____

7. If you earn $6.50/hour at the Star Drive-in and are given a raise to $7.02, what is the percent of increase in wages that you were awarded?

_____

_____

8. The basic monthly payment for Pablo's car is $425. With interest, that payment is $476. What is the interest rate?

_____

_____

9. You paid $138 for a new driver to use with your golf clubs. I bought the same driver for $118.70. What percent more did you pay for your driver than I paid for mine?

_____

_____

10. In Problem 9, what percent of your $138 price could you have saved by buying your driver where I bought mine?

_____

_____

Name_____ Date_____

OBJECTIVE 1

Solve the equations.

1. $x = 6 - 18$

2. $-4 + x = 11$

3. $9 = x + 25$

4. $x + 0.2 = 3.5$

OBJECTIVE 2

Solve the equations.

5. If three x's are 18, what would one x be?

6. $5x = 20$

7. $\frac{x}{4} = -3$

8. $\frac{2}{3} \cdot x = -6$

OBJECTIVE 3

Solve the equations.

9. $2x + 3 = 13$

10. $\frac{x}{4} - 16 = -11$

11. $3x - 4 = x + 2$

12. $\frac{2}{3}x - 4 = 12$

Name_____ Date_____

OBJECTIVE 4

Find the solution to each problem.

13. At a school dance, $\frac{1}{3}$ of the boys were wearing white shirts. If 26 boys were wearing white shirts, how many boys were at the dance?

_____

14. The sum of three consecutive integers is −54. What are the integers?

_____

OBJECTIVE 5

Solve the proportions.

15. $\frac{3}{x} = \frac{12}{20}$

16. $\frac{2x}{-5} = \frac{16}{5}$

17. $\frac{x}{100} = \frac{9}{4}$

18. $\frac{15}{100} = \frac{6}{x}$

OBJECTIVE 6

Find the solution to each problem.

19. _____% of 120 is 24.

20. 70% of 50 is _____.

21. 30% of _____ is 21.

22. A store is advertising that bikes are on sale for 25% off the regular price. What is the sale price for a $160 bike?

Graphing Relations and Functions

In this chapter, we begin to graph ordered pairs, relations, and linear equations that use two variables. We learn about algebraic relations, and how to use tables, graphs, and sets to identify and write the domain, range, and inverse of a relation. We also learn what makes a relation a function and use function notation.

Objective 1
Graph ordered pairs and relations.

Objective 2
Identify the domain, range, and the inverse of a relation.

Objective 3
Determine the range for a given domain of a relation.

Objective 4
Graph linear equations.

Objective 5
Determine whether a relation is a function, and find a value for a given function.

Chapter 4
VOCABULARY

coordinate plane The plane determined by a horizontal number line, called the x-axis, and a vertical number line, called the y-axis, intersecting at a point called the origin

dependent variable A variable whose value is dependent upon the value of another variable

If you are traveling by car on a long stretch of highway with no gas stations, the distance you are able to travel is the dependent variable because it depends on the amount of gas you previously put in the car.

domain The possible values for x in a relation

$y = 2x + 5$	
x	y
−1	3
0	5
3	11

function A relation in which every element in the domain is paired with exactly one element in the range

$f(x) = x + 3$

independent variable A variable whose value does not depend upon the value of another variable

The length of your hair after a haircut depends on the length that you request to be cut from your hair, for example, 1 inch. The independent variable is the length cut from your hair.

inverse relation The set of ordered pairs obtained from switching the x- and y-values

The inverse relation for {(5, 8), (6, 9), (7, 10), (8, 11), (9, 12)} is {(8, 5), (9, 6), (10, 7), (11, 8), (12, 9)}.

ordered pair Two numbers that name the coordinates of a point on a graph, with the horizontal coordinate listed first and the vertical coordinate listed second

(x, y) or $(5, 8)$

parallel Lines that do not intersect; they are always the same distance apart

perpendicular Lines that intersect at right angles

quadrant One of four regions on a coordinate plane formed by the intersection of the x-axis and the y-axis

range The possible values for y in a relation

$y = 2x + 5$	
x	y
−1	3
0	5
3	11

relation A set of ordered pairs

{(5, 8), (6, 9), (7, 10), (8, 11), (9, 12)}

x-coordinate The horizontal distance from the point of origin of a graph; in an ordered pair, this value is always written first

y-coordinate The vertical distance from the point of origin of a graph; in an ordered pair, this value is always written second

Name_____ Date_____

WHO WON?

The tables show the ordered pairs selected by Team X and Team O for each game. Plot the points to determine who won each game (four in a row), and on what turn.

Game 1

Turn	1	2	3	4	5	6	7	8	9
X	(2, 3)	(3, 2)	(1, 4)	(0, 4)	(1, 5)	(1, 6)	(1, 3)	(0, 3)	(3, 3)
O	(2, 2)	(4, 1)	(0, 5)	(−1, 4)	(−2, 3)	(−3, 2)	(1, 2)	(0, 2)	(−1, 2)

1. Which team won? _____

2. On what turn? _____

3. List the ordered pairs that created the straight line. _____

_____

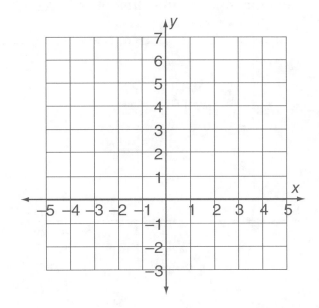

Name_____ **Date**_____

WHO WON? *(continued)*

Game 2

Turn	1	2	3	4	5	6
X	(−2, −2)	(−1, −2)	(−3, −2)	(−2, 0)	(−3, −1)	(1, −1)
O	(−1, −1)	(0, −2)	(−4, −2)	(−2, −1)	(0, −1)	(0, 0)

Turn	7	8	9	10	11	12
X	(0, 1)	(0, −3)	(0, −4)	(−1, −3)	(−1, 1)	(−3, 0)
O	(1, −3)	(2, −4)	(1, 1)	(2, 2)	(2, 1)	(2, 3)

1. Which team won? _____

2. On what turn? _____

3. List the ordered pairs that created the straight line. _____

_____

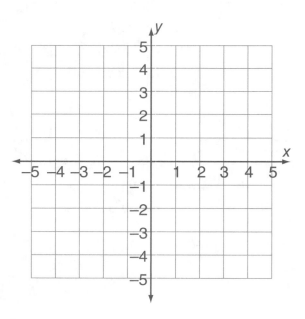

IT FITS

Find the number that solves each equation. Use that number to replace the letter in the ordered pairs for the plots at the bottom of the page.

1. $\frac{2}{3} = \frac{A}{7.5}$

2. $\frac{B}{8} = \frac{1}{2}$

3. $\frac{10}{15} = \frac{2}{C}$

4. $\frac{D}{33} = \frac{1}{3}$

5. $\frac{E}{56} = \frac{1}{7}$

6. $\frac{2}{18} = \frac{F}{90}$

7. $\frac{2}{G} = \frac{6}{27}$

8. $\frac{H}{13} = \frac{3}{39}$

9. $\frac{25}{35} = \frac{5}{J}$

10. $\frac{-1}{K} = \frac{15}{30}$

11. $\frac{M}{15} = \frac{4}{10}$

A = _____

B = _____

C = _____

D = _____

E = _____

F = _____

G = _____

H = _____

J = _____

K = _____

M = _____

Plot the points and connect each point in order. Make all five plots on the same coordinate plane.

1st Plot:	2nd Plot:	3rd Plot:	4th Plot:	5th Plot:
(−6, K)	(−2, A)	(−8.5, −6)	(−5, −4)	(−4, H)
(−5, −4)	(2, C)	(−11, −10)	(−2, −7)	(−6, H)
(0, C)	(C, C)	(−10, −11)	(0, −5)	(−9, −2)
(2, 2)	(B, B)	(−8, −9)	(−1, −4)	(−9, −4)
(C, 2)	(C, M)	(−7, −10)	(−2, −5)	(−8, −7)
(A, B)	(B, J)	(−8, −11)	(−3, −4)	(0, −14)
(B, M)	(B, G)	(−6, −13)	(−3, −2)	(7, −7)
(A, J)	(C, F)	(−4, −10.5)	(−3.5, −2)	(G, −4)
(A, G)	(H, F)	STOP	STOP	(G, −2)
(C, D)	(0, G)	Pick up pencil	Pick up pencil	(A, H)
(H, D)	(−2, G)			(1, H)
(0, F)	(−3, E)			(0, −1)
(K, F)	(−3, J)			(−1.5, H)
(−4, G)	(−2, A)			STOP
(−4, J)	STOP			
(−3, A)	Pick up pencil			
(−2, B)				
(−6, −2)				
STOP				
Pick up pencil				

12. What picture did you get? _____

APPLY SKILLS 1

Solve the problems involving coordinate graphs.

Example:

A: (_0_ , _0_)
B: (_4_ , _0_)
C: (_−4_ , _−4_)

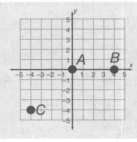

1. Name the ordered pairs for the labeled points.

   A: (_____, _____)

   B: (_____, _____)

   C: (_____, _____)

   D: (_____, _____)

   E: (_____, _____)

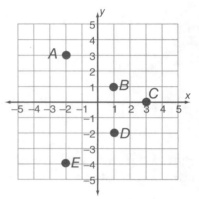

2. Plot the points listed below and label each point with its letter.

   A is (2, −3)

   B is (5, 0)

   C is (−3, −2)

   D is (−3, 4)

   E is (0, −1)

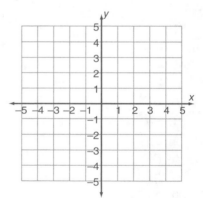

3. Name a point in Quadrant I. _____

   What is its coordinate? (_____, _____)

4. Name a point in Quadrant IV. _____

   What is its coordinate? (_____, _____)

5. Name a point in Quadrant II. _____

   What is its coordinate? (_____, _____)

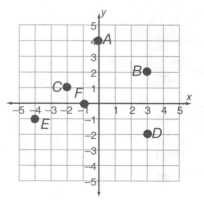

APPLY SKILLS 2

Plot the four ordered pairs on the graphs below them. Name the quadrilateral formed by connecting the four points. You may need to look up the definitions of quadrilateral, parallelogram, rectangle, trapezoid, and square.

Example:

(2, 2), (−2, 2), (−2, −2), (2, −2)

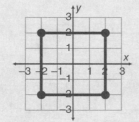

Name the quadrilateral:
square

1. (2, 3), (2, −1), (−3, 1), (−3, −3)

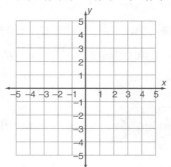

Name the quadrilateral:

_____

2. (−3, −1), (−4, 2), (1, 2), (2, −1)

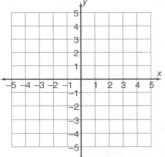

Name the quadrilateral:

_____

3. (3, −1), (0, −4), (−3, −1), (0, 2)

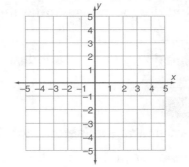

Name the quadrilateral:

_____

4. (0, 2), (2, −2), (−3, −2), (−2, 2)

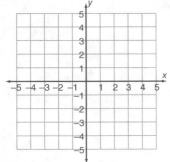

Name the quadrilateral:

_____

5. (2, 0), (0, −2), (−3, 1), (−1, 3)

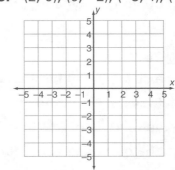

Name the quadrilateral:

_____

Name_____ Date_____

QUADRANT GRAPHING

Answer the problems about coordinate graphs.

Part A

1. Draw a coordinate plane on a piece of graph paper.
2. Draw a straight line through Quadrants I and IV only.
3. Label four points on the line with the letters *A*, *B*, *C*, and *D*.
4. Give the relation of this line. _____
5. What do you notice about the *x*-coordinates?

   _____

6. What do you notice about the *y*-coordinates?

   _____

Part B

1. Draw a straight line through Quadrants III and II only.
2. Label four points on the line with the letters *W*, *X*, *Y*, and *Z*.
3. Give the relation of this line. _____
4. What do you notice about the *x*-coordinates?

   _____

5. What do you notice about the *y*-coordinates?

   _____

Part C

1. Draw a straight line through Quadrants III, II, and I.
2. Label four points on the line with the letters *H*, *I*, *J*, and *K*.
3. Give the relation of this line. _____
4. What do you notice about the *x*-coordinates?

   _____

5. What do you notice about the *y*-coordinates?

   _____

Part D

1. Draw a straight line through Quadrants IV, III, and II.
2. Label four points on the line with the letters *P*, *Q*, *R*, and *S*.
3. Give the relation of this line. _____
4. What do you notice about the *x*-coordinates?

   _____

5. What do you notice about the *y*-coordinates?

RELATION MATCHING

Match each number with the correct letter, and write it on the line.

1. domain _____

2. inverse _____

3. quadrants _____

4. Quadrant III _____

5. the second number of an ordered pair that corresponds to the numbers on the *y*-axis _____

6.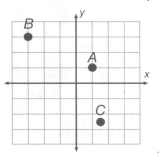
    _____

7. the plane that contains the *x*- and *y*-axes _____

8. relation _____

9. range _____

10. the section of the coordinate plane that would have this ordered pair: (3, −5) _____

11. the common endpoint of two rays (corner) _____

12. *x*-axis _____

13. Quadrant I _____

14. upper left quadrant of a coordinate plane _____

15. (*x*, *y*) _____

16. the point formed by the intersection of the *x*-axis and the *y*-axis _____

a. shows how the numbers in two sets of data are related

b. ordered pair

c. the section of the coordinate plane that has ordered pairs where both the *x*- and *y*-coordinates are negative

d. Quadrant II

e. origin

f. the switching of coordinates in each ordered pair of a relation

g. coordinate plane

h. graph

i. *y*-coordinate

j. the set of all second coordinates from the ordered pairs

k. Quadrant IV

l. the horizontal number line on the coordinate plane

m.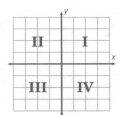

n. vertex

o. the set of all first coordinates from the ordered pairs in a relation

p. only positive values for both the *x*- and *y*-coordinates

APPLY SKILLS 1

A video store charges $5.00 to rent a video for a weekend. The store gives a $5.00 discount if four or more videos are rented.

1. Make a table that shows this relation between the number of videos and the total cost for up to eight videos.

Number of Videos	Cost ($)
1	
2	
3	
4	
5	
6	
7	
8	

2. List the ordered pairs so that the number of videos is the domain.

_____

3. Give the range of this relation. _____

4. What is the inverse of this relation?

_____

5. Graph the ordered pairs with the number of videos as the *x*-axis.

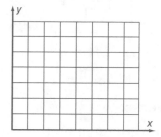

6. Write three questions that you could ask a classmate about information obtained from this relation.

_____

_____

_____

Name_____ Date_____

APPLY SKILLS 2

The table below shows dollars earned for 1 to 5 hours of work.

Hours	Dollars Earned
1	5.25
2	10.50
3	15.75
4	21.00
5	26.25

1. The domain is represented by what? _____

   Give the domain: _____

2. Give the range: _____

3. What would the inverse relation be?

   _____

4. Write a math question that uses this relationship between the domain and the range.

   _____

   _____

   _____

Name_____ Date_____

APPLY SKILLS 2 (continued)

5. Describe what you would have to do to figure out how much a person would earn if he or she worked $4\frac{1}{2}$ hours.

_____

_____

_____

6. Graph the relation.

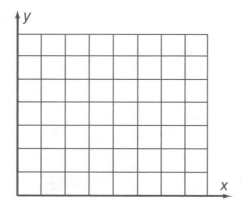

7. List the domain and range of the following relation: {(1, $4), (2, $7), (3, $10), (4, $13)}

_____

8. Write the inverse of the relation in Problem 7.

_____

9. Write a math problem that uses this relationship between the domain and the range.

_____

_____

BUDGET MOVIE TICKETS

Answer the questions by referring to the chart below.

1. What is the domain of the relation?

   _____

   _____

   _____

2. What is the range of the relation?

   _____

   _____

   _____

3. When graphing the relation, which data should be used on the *x*-axis?

   _____

Year	Movie Ticket Price
1996	$4.40
1997	$4.60
1998	$4.70
1999	$5.10
2000	$5.40
2001	$5.65
2002	$5.80
2003	$6.05
2004	$6.20
2005	$6.40
2006	$6.55
2007	$6.90
2008	$7.20
2009	$7.40

Graph the relation, then use your graph to answer the questions below.

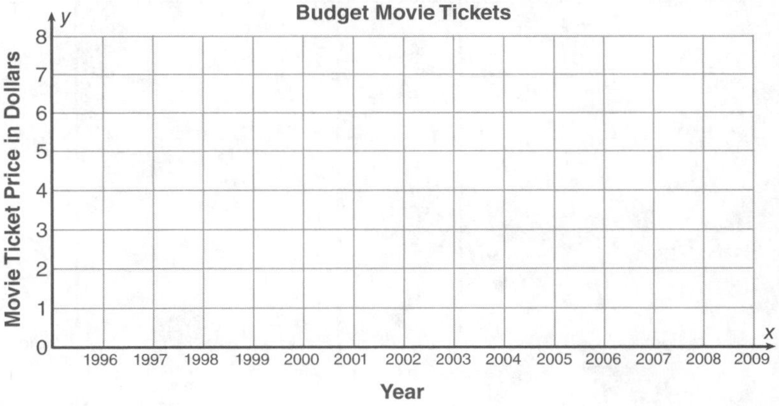

4. Between which years did the price of tickets rise the least?

   _____

Budget Movie Tickets

Movie Ticket Price in Dollars (y-axis): 0 1 2 3 4 5 6 7 8

Year (x-axis): 1996 1997 1998 1999 2000 2001 2002 2003 2004 2005 2006 2007 2008 2009

5. Between which years did the price of tickets rise the most? _____

6. What is the highest and lowest range? _____

7. What adjustments would you need to make if you graphed the inverse?

   _____

   _____

8. How much did the price of a ticket increase between 1999 and 2009?

   _____

MAKING TABLES

Fill in each table.

1. Substitute for *x* and find *y*.
    $2x + y = 6$

x	y
−4	
−3	
−2	
−1	
0	
1	
2	

2. Substitute for *x* and solve the equation for *y*, then list the values for *y* and write the ordered pairs (*x, y*).

x	2x + y = 6	y	(x, y)
−4			
−3			
−2			
−1			
0			
1			
2			

Name _____ Date _____

APPLY SKILLS 1

Find the values for y if $y = \frac{1}{2}x + 2$.

Example:

$$y = \frac{1}{2}x + 2$$

If $x = -8$, then $y = \frac{1}{2}(-8) + 2$

$$y = -4 + 2$$
$$y = -2$$

1. If $x = 2$, then $y =$ _____.

2. If $x = 0$, then $y =$ _____.

3. If $x = 6$, then $y =$ _____.

4. If $x = -2$, then $y =$ _____.

5. The value we use for x is called the domain. The domain for this equation is _____.

6. Complete the table below for the equation $y = 2x - 4$.
   The domain is $\{-2, 0, 2, 4, 6\}$.

x	$y = 2x - 4$	y	(x, y)
Example:			
−2	$y = 2(-2) - 4$	−8	(−2, −8)
0			
2			
4			
6			

7. Complete the table below for the equation $x + y = 8$.
   The domain is $\{-2, -1, 0, 2, 4\}$.

x	$x + y = 8$	y	(x, y)
Example:			
0	$0 + y = 8$	8	(0, 8)
−2			
−1			
2			
4			

APPLY SKILLS 2

Solve the problems involving relations.

1. If the domain is {−5, −3, 0, 3, 5} for the relation $y = 5 − x$, find the ordered pairs that satisfy the relation.

   {(_____, _____), (_____, _____), (_____, _____),

   (_____, _____), (_____, _____)}

2. Complete the table below for the domain of {−2, −1, 0, 1, 2}.

x	$2x − y = 4$	y	(x, y)
−2			
−1			
0			
1			
2			

3. Find five ordered pairs that satisfy the relation $y = 2x + 1$.

   {(_____, _____), (_____, _____), (_____, _____),

   (_____, _____), (_____, _____)}

4. What is the domain in Problem 3? _____

5. What is the range in Problem 3? _____

6. Find the ordered pairs below that satisfy the relation $y − x = 4$. Use the domain of {−3, −1, 0, 2, 4}.

   {(−3, _____), (−1, _____), (0, _____), (2, _____), (4, _____)}

APPLY SKILLS 3

Match the equation with the group of ordered pairs that represent solutions to the equation. The ordered pairs are in (x, y) form. Not all sets of ordered pairs are used.

1. $x + y = 9$ _____

2. $y = 2x - 3$ _____

3. $x - y = 2$ _____

4. $y = -x$ _____

5. $2x + y = 5$ _____

6. $2x + 2y = 2$ _____

7. $6x - 2y = 6$ _____

8. $y = -2x$ _____

9. $x = 5$ _____

10. $x + 2y = 8$ _____

a. {(1, 0), (0, 1), (0, 0)}

b. {(4, 5), (3, 0), (5, 4)}

c. {(5, 0), (5, 4), (5, −5)}

d. {(1, 0), (0, 1), (−1, 2)}

e. {(0, 5), (4, 5), (−5, 5)}

f. {(3, 3), (1, 1), (−1, −1)}

g. {(4, 5), (−1, −5), (1, −1)}

h. {(5, 3), (0, −2), (3, 1)}

i. {(1, 0), (2, 3), (0, −3)}

j. {(2, 3), (0, 4), (4, 2)}

k. {(2, 1), (−3, 11), (4, −3)}

l. {(3, −3), (−3, 3), (−3, 0)}

m. {(0, 0), (−2, 4), (1, −2)}

n. {(2, 1), (−3, −1), (4, 3)}

o. {(4, 5), (8, 1), (2, 7)}

p. {(3, −3), (4, −4), (0, 0)}

q. {(0, 0), (4, −2), (1, −2)}

MAKING LINE GRAPHS

To graph a linear equation, find three or four ordered pairs that satisfy the equation. Plot these points. If you are not sure of the graph, find more ordered pairs to complete the graph.

Complete the table to find the ordered pairs, then draw the graph.

1. $y = 2x + 1$

x	$y = 2x + 1$	y	(x, y)
−1	$y = 2(-1) + 1$	−1	(−1, −1)
−2			
0			
2			

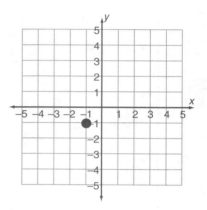

Make a table and sketch the graph of the equations.

2. $y = x + 3$

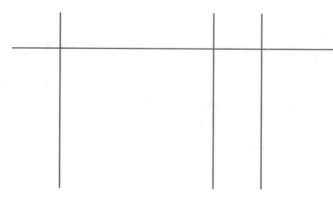

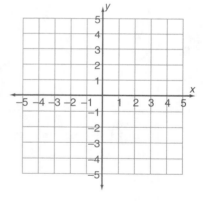

Inside Algebra

MAKING LINE GRAPHS (*continued*)

3. $y = 2x$

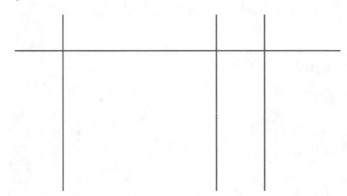

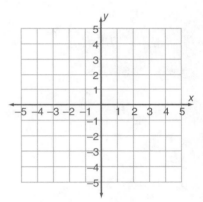

4. $2y - x = 4$

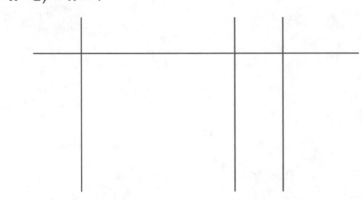

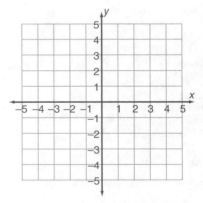

5. $x - y = 4$

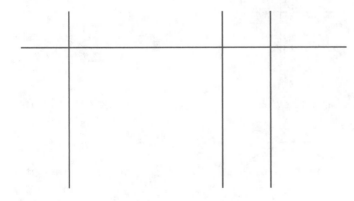

Name_____ Date_____

GRAPHING LINES

Use a graphing calculator to graph each equation and find where the line crosses the *x*-axis and *y*-axis, as shown in the two examples. Sketch the graph in the space provided.

Example:

$y = x + 3$

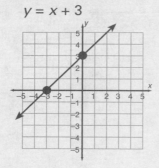

Crosses *y*-axis at

___(0, 3)___

Crosses *x*-axis at

___(−3, 0)___

Example:

$y = x - 5$

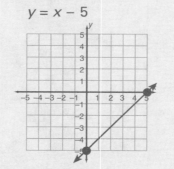

Crosses *y*-axis at

___(0, −5)___

Crosses *x*-axis at

___(5, 0)___

1. $y = 2x - 5$

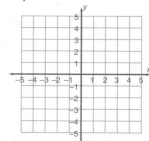

Crosses *y*-axis at

_____

Crosses *x*-axis at

_____

2. $y = 3x - 2$

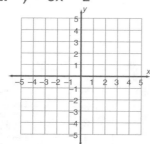

Crosses *y*-axis at

_____

Crosses *x*-axis at

_____

3. $y = 2x + 0$

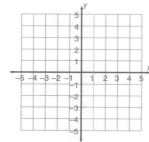

Crosses *y*-axis at

_____

Crosses *x*-axis at

_____

4. $y = 2x$

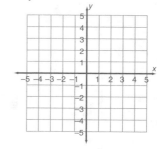

Crosses *y*-axis at

_____

Crosses *x*-axis at

_____

Name_____ Date_____

GRAPHING LINES   (*continued*)

5. $y = -2x$

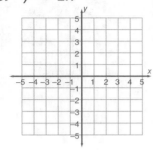

Crosses *y*-axis at

_____

Crosses *x*-axis at

_____

6. $y = \frac{1}{2}x + 0$

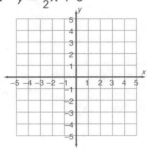

Crosses *y*-axis at

_____

Crosses *x*-axis at

_____

7. $y = -6x$

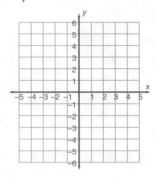

Crosses *y*-axis at

_____

Crosses *x*-axis at

_____

8. $y = -3x + 7$

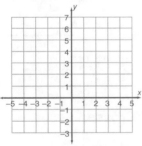

Crosses *y*-axis at

_____

Crosses *x*-axis at

_____

9. $y = -3x$

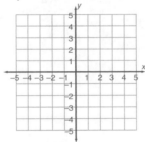

Crosses *y*-axis at

_____

Crosses *x*-axis at

_____

10. $x + y = 0$

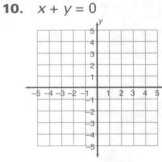

Crosses *y*-axis at

_____

Crosses *x*-axis at

_____

GRAPHING LINES (*continued*)

11. $5x + y = 2$

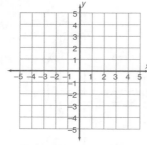

Crosses *y*-axis at

_____

Crosses *x*-axis at

_____

12. $2x + y = 2$

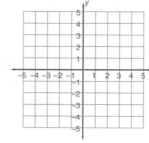

Crosses *y*-axis at

_____

Crosses *x*-axis at

_____

13. $-1x = 3 + y$

Crosses *y*-axis at

_____

Crosses *x*-axis at

_____

14. $7x - y = 10$

Crosses *y*-axis at

_____

Crosses *x*-axis at

_____

15. $7x + 4y - 2 = 10$

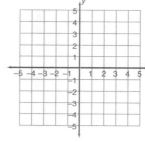

Crosses *y*-axis at

_____

Crosses *x*-axis at

_____

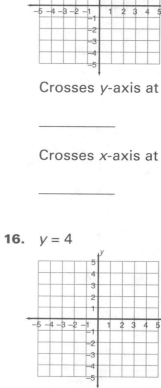

16. $y = 4$

Crosses *y*-axis at

_____

Crosses *x*-axis at

_____

Name_____ **Date**_____

GRAPHING LINES (*continued*)

17. $y = -2$

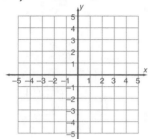

Crosses *y*-axis at

_____

Crosses *x*-axis at

_____

18. $x = 3$

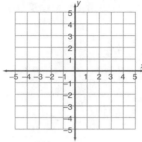

Crosses *y*-axis at

_____

Crosses *x*-axis at

_____

19. $x = -3$

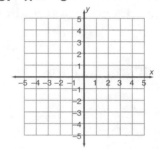

Crosses *y*-axis at

_____

Crosses *x*-axis at

_____

20. $y = 0$

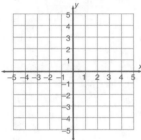

Crosses *y*-axis at

_____

Crosses *x*-axis at

_____

21. $x = 0$

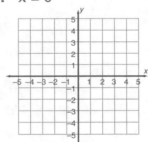

Crosses *y*-axis at

_____

Crosses *x*-axis at

_____

CONCEPT DEVELOPMENT

x-AXIS AND *y*-AXIS

Find the three solutions to each equation, given the domain or range for each. Graph the equation and tell where the line goes through the *x*-axis and the *y*-axis.

1. $y = x - 4$

(0, _____)

(_____, 0)

(5, _____)

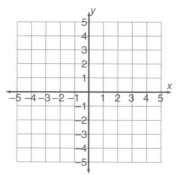

2. $2x - y = 4$

(0, _____)

(_____, 0)

(3, _____)

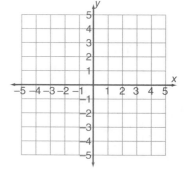

3. $y = 2x + 3$

(0, _____)

(_____, 0)

(_____, 5)

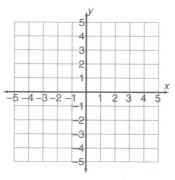

4. $3y = 2x$

(0, _____)

(_____, 0)

(3, _____)

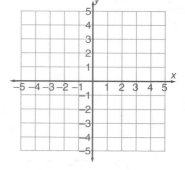

5. $y = 3$

(_____, 3)

(_____, 3)

(_____, 3)

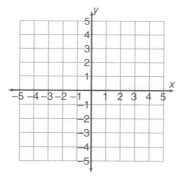

6. $x = 2$

(2, _____)

(2, _____)

(2, _____)

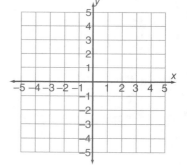

x-AXIS AND *y*-AXIS   (*continued*)

7. At the point where the graph goes through the *y*-axis, the domain is always

   _____.

8. At the point where the graph goes through the *x*-axis, the range is always

   _____.

9. Explain how you would graph any linear equation and how many points you would use.

   _____

   _____

   _____

Name_____ Date_____

APPLY SKILLS 1

Find three ordered pairs for each equation, and graph the line.

> *Example:*
>
> $y - 2x = 4$
>
> $y = 4 + 2x$
>
> $(2, 8), (0, 4), (-1, 2)$

1. $y = 2x - 1$

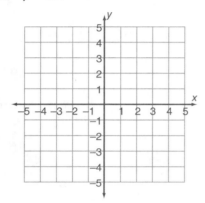

_____

2. $y = 2 - x$

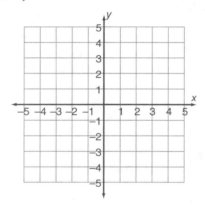

_____

3. $y = x$

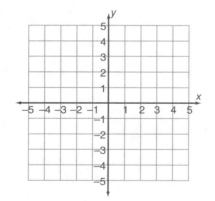

_____

4. $2x + y = 3$

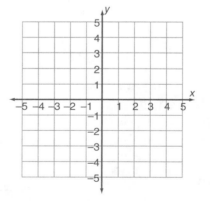

_____

APPLY SKILLS 1 (*continued*)

5. $y = 4$

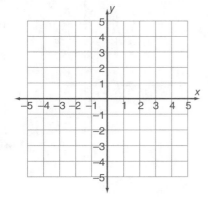

_____

6. $y = 4x$

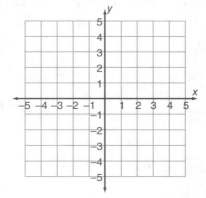

_____

7. $y - 5x = 2$

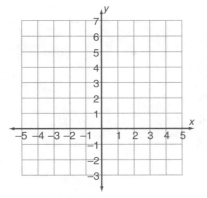

_____

8. $2x + 2y = 8$

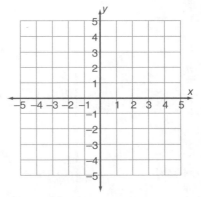

_____

APPLY SKILLS 2

1. Find the ordered pair solutions for $y = 2x - 1$ when the domain is {1, 2, 3, 4}. Graph these ordered pairs.

   {(_____, _____), (_____, _____),

   (_____, _____), (_____, _____)}

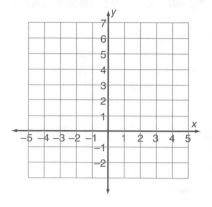

2. Complete the table and graph the equation $x - y = 4$.

x	$x - y = 4$	y	(x, y)
−2			
0			
1			
2			

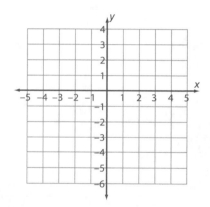

3. Choose any three values of x and find the range for the linear equation $2x + y = -3$. Graph these ordered pairs and the equation $2x + y = -3$.

   {(_____, _____), (_____, _____),

   (_____, _____)}

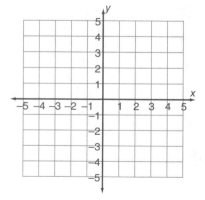

Inside Algebra

Name_____   Date_____

APPLY SKILLS 2 (continued)

4. If the domain is {−1, 0, 1, 2}, graph the relation
    y = −2x + 4.

x	y

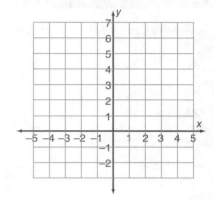

5. Complete the table and graph the equation
    x + y = −2.

x	x + y = −2	y	(x, y)
	x + 2 = −2	2	
		0	
−1			
0	0 + y = −2		

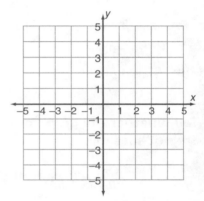

APPLY SKILLS 3

Tell whether each equation is a linear equation. Explain your answer.

1. $3x + 7y = 10$ _____

2. $\frac{1}{2}x = y + 5$ _____

3. $y = x^2$ _____

4. $y = x^2 + 4$ _____

5. $x^2 + 2x = y$ _____

6. $xy = 12$ _____

Tell whether the graph of each equation will be a straight line. Graph any that you are not sure of.

7. $y = 2x + 1$ _____

8. $2x = 3y$ _____

9. $x + 4 = 0$ _____

10. $4x + 3y = 6$ _____

11. $y = x^2$ _____

12. $y = x^2 + 2x$ _____

13. All equations that graph a straight line are called _____ equations.

Name_____ Date_____

APPLY SKILLS 3 (*continued*)

Solve for *y* in terms of *x*.

14. $2x + y = 4$

15. $3x = 5y$

16. $2x - 8 = -y$

17. $\frac{1}{3}y = 2x$

18. $2x - y = 7$

19. $\frac{2}{3}y = 12x$

Graph the equations from Problems 8, 14, and 16.

20. $2x = 3y$

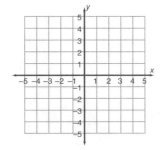

21. $2x + y = 4$

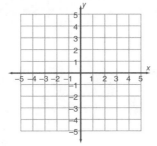

22. $2x - 8 = -y$

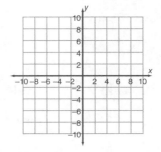

NAME YOUR EQUATION

Look at each graph, write down some ordered pairs that are on the graph, and guess at what the equation will be. Write these equations on your paper.

Test your guess by using a graphing calculator, or find three ordered pairs for your equation, graph them, and see if the two graphs are the same straight line.

Example:

x	y	Rule
−2	0	
−1	1	$y = x + 2$
1	3	

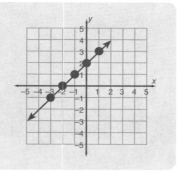

1.

x	y	Rule

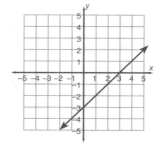

2.

x	y	Rule

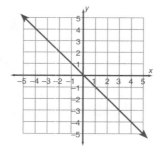

3.

x	y	Rule

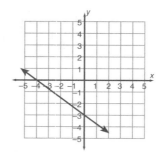

STRAIGHT OR CURVED?

Determine whether the situations will graph a straight line after setting up a table and a solution set of at least four ordered pairs. Sketch the graphs on graph paper. If the graph is a straight line, write an equation.

1. The area of a room is length times width ($l \cdot w$). If the area is 40 square meters, make a table of four possibilities for the length and width, and graph the solutions.

   _____

2. Costs for a cold drink at the corner store are as follows:

   12 oz. drink costs $2.50
   18 oz. drink costs $3.50
   32 oz. drink costs $4.50
   64 oz. drink costs $5.50

   (When you graph these, be sure you make a scale for the ounces.)

   _____

3. CDs are on sale at your favorite music store for $15, and with your coupon you get $5 off the total purchase. Make a table for buying one to four CDs.

   _____

PROBLEM SOLVING

STRAIGHT OR CURVED? (*continued*)

4. You have 40 cents in your pocket, and the coins are all nickels and dimes. Make a table of all possible combinations and graph it.

   _____

5. When I traveled to Alaska, I learned that the part of the iceberg that we see above water is only one-eighth the size of the whole iceberg. That means the iceberg is one-eighth above the surface of the ocean and seven-eighths below the surface of the ocean. Find out how much is below the ocean if the domain is 5,000 tons, 6,000 tons, and 7,000 tons above the ocean. Extend the graph so that we can read what is below for a 10,000-ton ice tip.

   _____

STRAIGHT OR CURVED? (*continued*)

Determine whether the situations will graph a straight line after setting up a table and a solution set of at least four ordered pairs. Sketch the graphs on graph paper. If the graph is a straight line, write an equation.

6. An advertisement for Internet access reads: "Internet access for $3.00 plus $0.20 per minute." Set up your table to find the cost in dollars for different numbers of minutes of access time, for example, 1 minute, 5 minutes, 10 minutes, etc.

   _____

7. Every state has a certain way to figure out the cost of a speeding ticket on the highway. One state uses the formula: Ticket price = 10(speed of car − 55) + $40.

   Figure the ticket price for a car going 60, 65, and 75 mph in that state. Set up a table and graph the results. Can you read the graph and figure out the ticket cost if you were going 90 mph or any other speed?

   _____

8. The area of a circle is $A = \pi r^2$. Find the area if the radius, r, is 2 feet, 4 feet, 6 feet, and 8 feet. Is the graph a straight line?

   _____

Name _____ Date _____

FUNCTION GRAPHS

Determine whether the relation shown is a function. Answer yes or no.

1.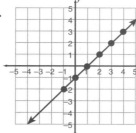

Is this a function?

_____

2.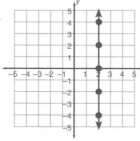

Is this a function?

_____

3.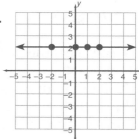

Is this a function?

_____

4.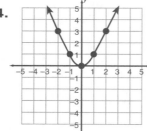

Is this a function?

_____

5.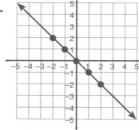

Is this a function?

_____

6.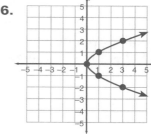

Is this a function?

_____

7.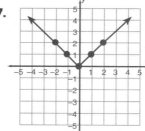

Is this a function?

_____

8.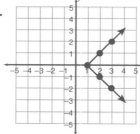

Is this a function?

_____

9.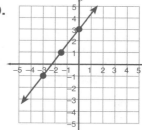

Is this a function?

_____

APPLY SKILLS 1

Determine whether the relation shown is a function.

1. {(2, −3), (3, 6), (5, −8), (1, 2)} _____

2. {(1, 5), (1, −2), (1, 0), (1, 3)} _____

3. {(1, 4), (−2, 4), (3, 4), (0, 4)} _____

4.

x	y
−3	3
−2	4
2	4
0	2
4	4	_____

5.

x	y
−4	3
3	2
−4	1
−3	0
−4	0	_____

6.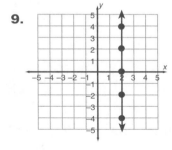

_____

7.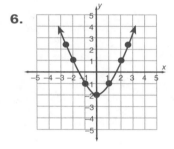

_____

8.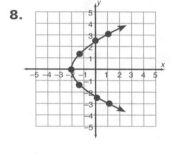

_____

9.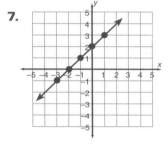

_____

10.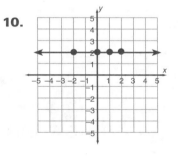

_____

APPLY SKILLS 2

Solve each set of problems.

> **Example:**
> If $f(x) = 5x + 0$, find each value for $f(6)$, $f(-3)$.
> $f(6) = 5(6) + 0 = 30$
> $f(-3) = 5(-3) + 0 = -15$

If $f(x) = 3x - 2$, find each value.

1. $f(6) =$ _____   **2.** $f(-2) =$ _____

3. $f(2) =$ _____

If $f(x) = x^2 - 1$, find each value.

4. $f(3) =$ _____   **5.** $f(-3) =$ _____

6. $f(0) =$ _____

If $f(x) = 3x + 2$, find each value.

7. $f(-4) =$ _____   **8.** $f(-2) =$ _____

9. $f(w) =$ _____

If $f(x) = x^2 - 2x$, find each value.

10. $f(-4) =$ _____   **11.** $f(4) =$ _____

12. $f(1.5) =$ _____

Find three values for each relation and determine if it is a function.

13. $f(x) = \sqrt{x}$ _____

14. $f(x) = \pm |x|$ _____

Name_____ Date_____

WINDCHILL TEMPERATURE

Windchill represents the cooling effect of wind combined with actual temperature.

In the relation, the y variable (range) represents the windchill temperature and the x variable (domain) represents the actual temperature.

- The windchill function for a 10 mph wind speed is: $f(x) = 1.2x - 21$.
- The windchill function for a 40 mph wind speed is: $f(x) = 1.6x - 52.5$.

Using your graphing calculator, find the windchill values (to the nearest whole number) for the temperatures {30, 20, 5, 0, –10, –20}.

Complete the chart below, then graph the two functions.

Windchill Temperature						
Temperature (Actual) / Wind Speed	30	20	5	0	–10	–20
10						
40						

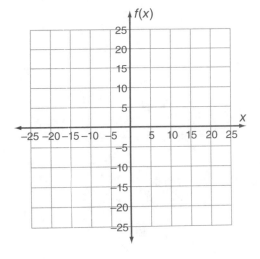
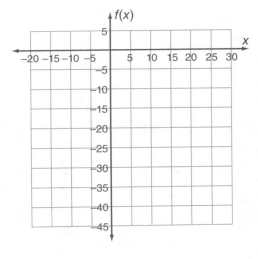

...de Algebra

This page intentionally left blank

OBJECTIVE 1

Use the graph to complete the problems.

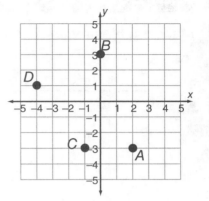

1. Name the ordered pair for point *A*. (_____, _____)

2. Name the ordered pair for point *B*. (_____, _____)

3. Name a point in Quadrant II. _____

4. Graph the ordered pair. *E* (4, 4)

5. Graph the ordered pair. *F* (0, −4)

6. Graph the ordered pair. *G* (−1, −2)

OBJECTIVE 2

Complete the statements about relations.

In Problems 7–9, the relation is {(1, 0), (2, 1), (0, −1), (−1, −2)}.

7. The domain of the relation is _____

8. The range of the relation is _____

9. The inverse of the relation is _____

OBJECTIVE 3

Solve each problem based on the given information about the domain and relation.

10. $2x + y = 6$

x	$2x + y = 6$	y	(x, y)
−4			
−3			
0			
7			

11. Find the ordered pairs that satisfy the relation $x = y - 2$ when the domain is {4, 2, 0, −2}.

    _____

OBJECTIVE 4

Make a table of values and construct the graph for each equation.

12. $x - 2y = 4$

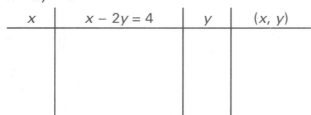

x	$x - 2y = 4$	y	(x, y)

13. Graph of $x - 2y = 4$

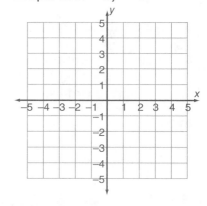

14. $x = y - 3$

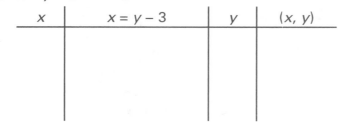

x	$x = y - 3$	y	(x, y)

15. Graph of $x = y - 3$

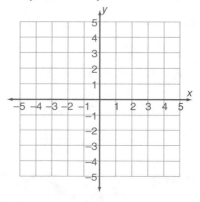

OBJECTIVE 5

Evaluate.

16. Given $f(x) = 2x^2 - 3x + 4$, find $f(-3)$.

Determine whether each is a function relation.

17. $\{(2, 4), (3, -2), (0, -2), (5, 2)\}$ _____

18.

x	y
2	5
3	6
3	7
4	8

_____

19.

x	y
0	11
1	14
-2	7
4	-3

_____

Analyzing Linear Equations

In this chapter, we learn about linear equations. We learn to find the slope of a line, and we also use the slope to decide if two or more lines are parallel or perpendicular. We discover three different ways to write an equation and also how to change from one form to another.

Objective 1
Determine the slope given a line on a graph or two points on the line.

Objective 2
Write the equation of a line in standard form given two points on the line.

Objective 3
Draw a best-fit line, and find the equation of the best-fit line for a scatter plot.

Objective 4
Write linear equations in slope-intercept form to find the slope, x-intercept, and y-intercept, and sketch the graph.

Objective 5
Use the slope of lines to determine if two lines are parallel or perpendicular.

Chapter 5
VOCABULARY

best-fit line The line on a graph that will best connect the data or points

point-slope form A linear equation in the form $y - y_1 = m(x - x_1)$

For the points (3, 7) and (0, −2), the point-slope form is $y - 7 = 3(x - 3)$

rise The vertical distance traveled

run The horizontal distance traveled

scatter plot A number of coordinate pairs plotted on a graph; used to investigate a possible relationship between two variables

slope The steepness of a line

Slope: $\frac{2}{3}$

slope-intercept form A linear equation in the form $y = mx + b$

$y = 4x + 1$

standard form A linear equation in the form $ax + by = c$

$2x - y = -4$

x-intercept The point where the line crosses the x-axis

x-intercept: (2, 0)

y-intercept The point where the line crosses the y-axis

y-intercept: (0, 1)

GRAPHS AND RELATED NUMBERS

Find the relationship between the number in the parentheses and the line.

1.

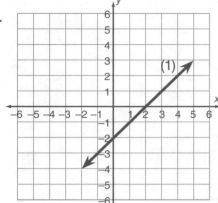

2.

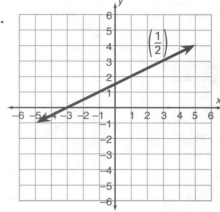

3.

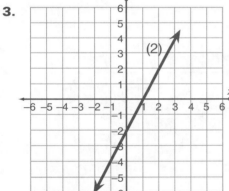

4.

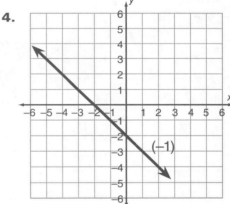

5.

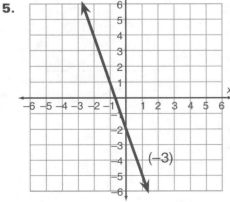

6.

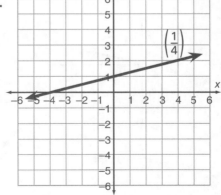

GRAPHS

1.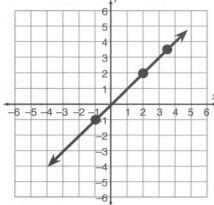

2.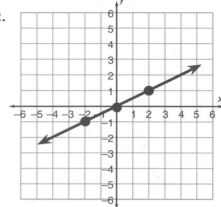

3.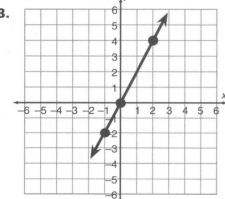

4.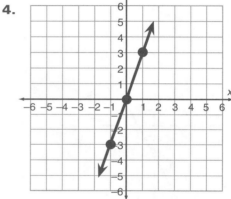

5.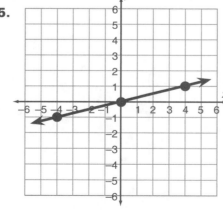

6.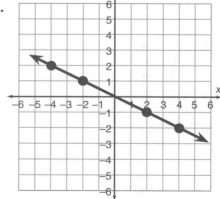

CONCEPT DEVELOPMENT

Name_____   Date_____

APPLY SKILLS 1

Name the slope for each graph.

1.

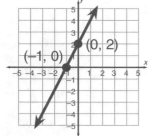

Slope _____

2.

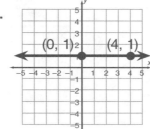

Slope _____

3.

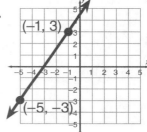

Slope _____

4.

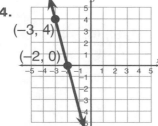

Slope _____

5.

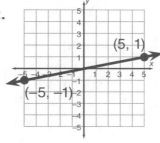

Slope _____

6.

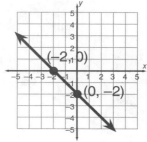

Slope _____

7.

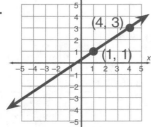

Slope _____

8.

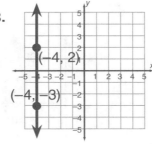

Slope _____

9.

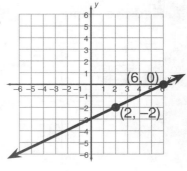

Slope _____

Name_____ Date_____

APPLY SKILLS 2

Find the slope for each line.

1.

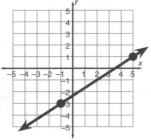

Slope _____

2.

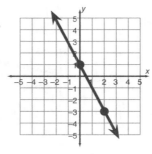

Slope _____

3.

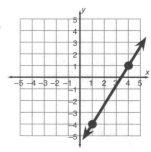

Slope _____

Find the slope using $m = \dfrac{(y_2 - y_1)}{(x_2 - x_1)}$.

4. $(2, 6), (-2, 4)$

5. $(-7, -2), (3, 3)$

6. $(1, 8), (4, -4)$

Find the slope.

7.

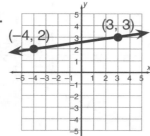

Slope _____

8.

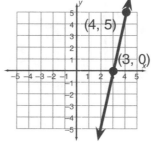

Slope _____

9.

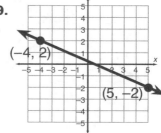

Slope _____

Inside Algebra

APPLY SKILLS 3

Name the slope for each graph.

1. Draw the graph of $y + 3 = x$

   What is the slope?

   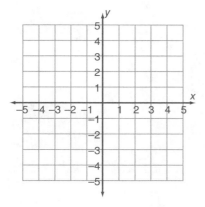

   Slope _____

2. Draw the graph of $2x + y = 0$

   What is the slope?

   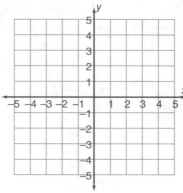

   Slope _____

3. Draw the graph of $2y = 2x + 8$

   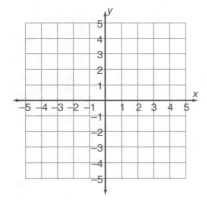

   Slope _____

4. What is the slope of a line that contains (2, 5) and (3, 1)? Sketch the graph.

   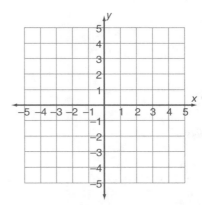

   Slope _____

Name_____ Date_____

WHAT IS THE EQUATION?

Find the equation of the line. You may use a table, "guess and check," or find an algebra method.

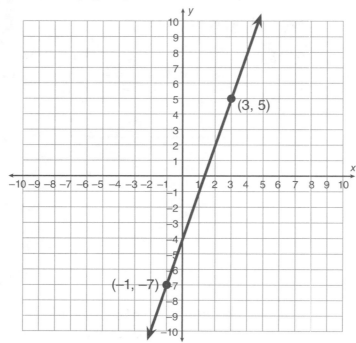

APPLY SKILLS 1

Solve.

Example:

Find the slope of the line.

$$m = \frac{(y_2 - y_1)}{(x_2 - x_1)} = \frac{[0 - (-2)]}{(3 - 0)} = \frac{2}{3}$$

Write the point-slope equation of the line using the slope and point (0, −2).

$$y - y_1 = m(x - x_1)$$

$$y - (-2) = \frac{2}{3}(x - 0)$$

$$y + 2 = \frac{2}{3}x$$

Write the equation in standard form, (ax + by = c).

$$2x - 3y = 6$$

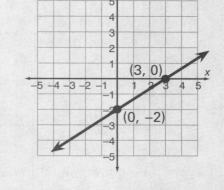

1. Find the slope of the line.

   _____

2. Write the point-slope equation of the line
   $y - y_1 = m(x - x_1)$.

   _____

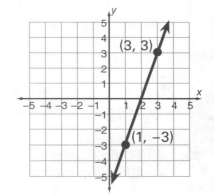

3. Write the equation in standard form, $ax + by = c$.

   _____

4. Given the slope of a line is −2 and it contains the point (4, 1), write the point-slope equation, $y - y_1 = m(x - x_1)$.

   _____

5. Write the equation in standard form, $ax + by = c$.

   _____

APPLY SKILLS 1 (*continued*)

**Find the equation of a line containing the points (–2, –4) and (1, 5).
Use the given steps.**

6. Find the slope of the line, $m = \frac{(y_2 - y_1)}{(x_2 - x_1)}$.

   _____

7. Write the equation in point-slope form, $y - y_1 = m(x - x_1)$.

   _____

8. Write the equation in standard form, $ax + by = c$.

   _____

9. Write the equation of the line containing the points (3, –1), (2, 2) in point-slope form and standard form.

   _____

   _____

10. Write the equation of the line with slope 1 and containing the point (–1, –1) in point-slope form and standard form.

    _____

    _____

Name_____ Date_____

APPLY SKILLS 2

Write the equation in point-slope form, $(y - y_1) = m(x - x_1)$, for the line containing the point and slope given.

1. (3, 4), slope of −1

_____

2. (−3, 1), slope of 2

_____

3. (0, 0), slope of 6

_____

4. (3, 3), slope of $\frac{1}{2}$

_____

5. (−5, −1), slope of −4

_____

6. (6, −3), slope of $-1\frac{1}{2}$

_____

These equations are written in point-slope form. Rewrite them in standard form, ($ax + by = c$).

7. $(y - 3) = 2(x + 2)$

8. $(y + 2) = -1(x - 5)$

9. $y - 6 = -3(x + 3)$

10. $(y + 2) = -\frac{1}{2}(x + 6)$

Inside Algebra

Chapter 5 • Objective 2 • PM 2

171

Name_____ Date_____

APPLY SKILLS 2 (*continued*)

Write the equation in standard form for the line containing the point and slope given.

11. $(2, 4)$, $m = 4$

12. $(-1, 4)$, $m = -2$

13. $(-2, -4)$, $m = \frac{1}{4}$

14. $\left(\frac{1}{2}, 3\right)$, $m = 8$

Name_____ Date_____

APPLY SKILLS 3

Find the equation of each line given in the graphs below. Write the equation in standard form.

1.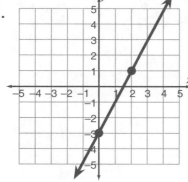

_____

2.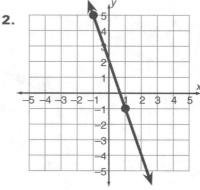

_____

Find the equation of a line containing the two points. Write the equation in standard form.

3. (4, 1), (3, 3)

4. (−1, 2), (−4, −4)

5. (1, 7), (−4, 2)

6. (−2, 3), (2, 5)

Find the equation of a line with the point and slope given below. Write the equation in standard form.

7. (4, 6), $m = \frac{1}{2}$

8. (−1, −5), $m = -2$

PROGRESS MONITORING

AIRPLANE MILES

WORK SPACE

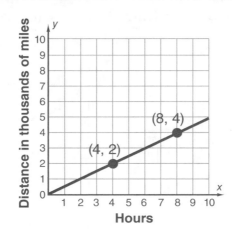

1. The graph above represents the miles flown by an airplane one day. The plane flew for a total of 10 hours that day. Find the slope of the line. Explain what the slope represents for this graph.

_____

_____

2. Find the equation of the line. Explain what the equation represents.

_____

_____

_____

_____

3. At the rate represented by the equation in Problem 2, how many miles will the plane fly in 24 hours of flying? In 100 hours of flying?

_____

_____

AVERAGE GIRLS' HEIGHT

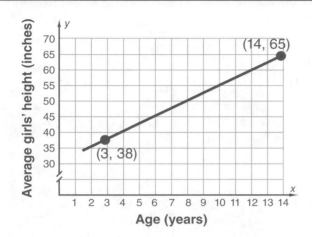

1. The graph above represents the average girls' height from ages 2 years through 14 years. Find the slope of the line and explain what the slope represents. (Round off or approximate.)

   _____

   _____

2. Find the equation of the line for this graph. What do you think the equation represents?

   _____

   _____

3. What is the average height for a 10-year-old girl? Using the equation in Problem 2, what would you predict for the height for a 30-year-old female? Is this the height of a 30-year-old female? Explain.

   _____

   _____

   _____

   _____

   _____

   _____

PROBLEM SOLVING

Name_____ **Date**_____

PHONE RATES

Graph the points and draw the best-fit line.

Company A		Company B		Company C	
Time (min.)	Charge (cents)	Time (min.)	Charge (cents)	Time (min.)	Charge (cents)
1	7	1	15	1	10
2	12	2	20	3	29
3	17	5	38	5	45
4	23	8	55	7	57
5	30	10	63	10	74
10	72	14	77	13	92
15	101	18	99	16	110
20	133	20	110	18	122
				20	136

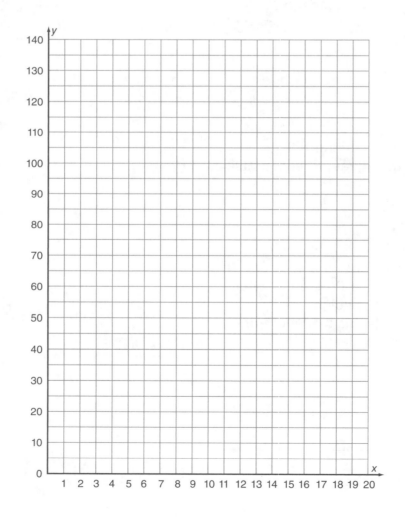

ELECTRONIC CALCULATOR

Cost of a Basic 4-Function Calculator

1. Draw the best-fit line.

2. Find the equation of the best-fit line.

   _____

3. Predict the cost 12 years and 18 years after the invention.

   _____

   _____

APPLY SKILLS 1

Draw the best-fit lines for each graph.

1.

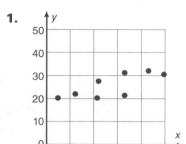

2.

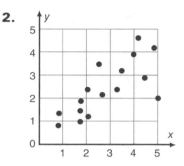

Find the equation of the best-fit line for each graph. (Find the slope, then find the equation.)

3.

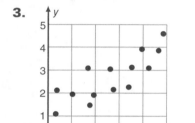

_____

4.

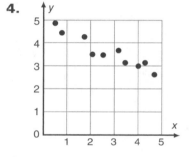

_____

Name _____ Date _____

APPLY SKILLS 2

Which line—A, B, or C—is the best-fit line for the points graphed?

1.

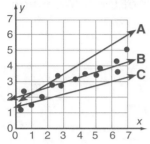

_____

2.

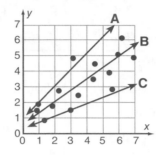

_____

Draw the best-fit line and find the equation.

3.

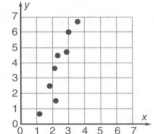

_____

4.

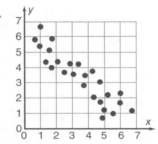

_____

5.

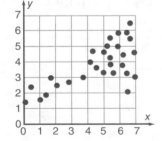

_____

6.

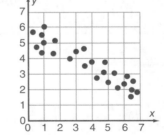

_____

Name_____   Date_____

APPLY SKILLS 3

1. The information below represents the high scores earned on a video arcade game and the number of games played. Make a graph of the information.

Name	Game	High Score
Juan	8 games	2,000
Tim	2 games	600
Sally	10 games	2,500
Fran	6 games	1,400
Bill	7 games	1,700
Jordan	4 games	1,100
Andy	3 games	800

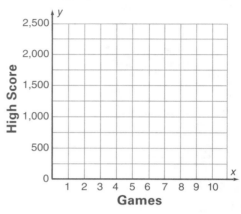

2. Draw the best-fit line for these data. What is the equation of the best-fit line?

   _____

3. Explain what the equation represents.

   _____

   _____

4. What would you predict for a high score if a person played 20 games?

   _____

   _____

Name_____   Date_____

APPLY SKILLS 1

Name the *y*-intercept and *x*-intercept (when *x* = 0 and when *y* = 0) in the graphs below. The *y*-intercept is the *y* value where the graph intersects the *y*-axis. The *x*-intercept is the *x* value where the graph intersects the *x*-axis.

Example:

$y = -\frac{1}{3}x + 1$

Let $x = 0 \rightarrow y = 1$
(0, 1)

Let $y = 0 \rightarrow x = 3$
(3, 0)

x-intercept = __3__
y-intercept = __1__

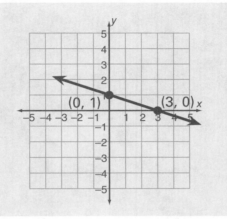

1.

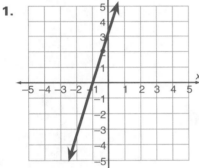

y-intercept = _____
x-intercept = _____

2.

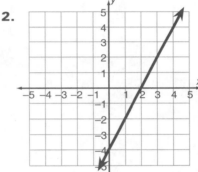

y-intercept = _____
x-intercept = _____

APPLY SKILLS 1 (*continued*)

Find the *y*-intercept and *x*-intercept for the equations.

3. $y = x + 6$

4. $y = -2x + 8$

5. $y = \frac{1}{2}x + 5$

6. $x + y = -2$

7. $x + 2y = 10$

8. $y - 2x = 6$

Name_____   Date_____

APPLY SKILLS 2

Sketch the graphs using the given information.

1. x-intercept is 3
    y-intercept is −2

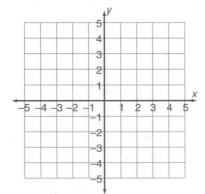

2. slope is 2
    y-intercept is 1

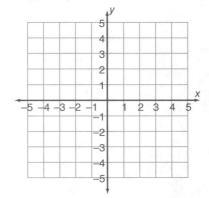

3. slope is $\frac{1}{2}$
    x-intercept is −2

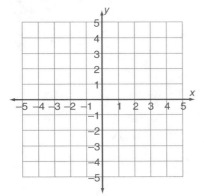

4. x-intercept is 3
    y-intercept is 3

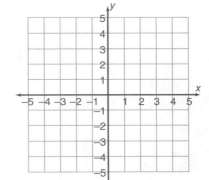

5. slope is −1
    y-intercept is 2

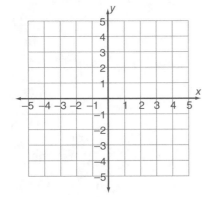

6. slope is 2
    y-intercept is 0

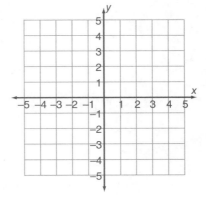

APPLY SKILLS 3

Write the linear equations in slope-intercept form ($y = mx + b$). Name the slope and y-intercept (when $x = 0$).

1. $x + y = 6$

2. $y + 3 = x$

3. $4x + 4y = 20$

4. $x - y = 7$

5. $x = y + 1$

6. $x + 2y + 3 = 0$

7. $2x + 3y = 9$

8. $\frac{1}{2}y = x - 4$

9. $0.3x + y = 5$

Name_____ Date_____

(*continued*)

Write the equations in slope-intercept form and sketch the graph.

10. $2x - y = 2$

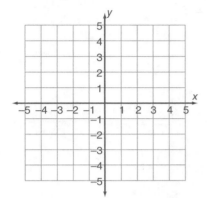

_____

11. $2y + 4x - 6 = 0$

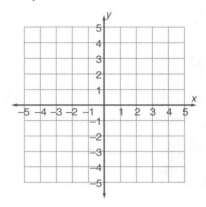

_____

12. $3y - 3 = 6x$

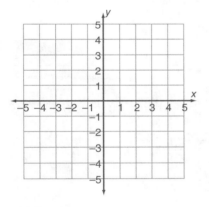

_____

13. $x + 0.5y = -1$

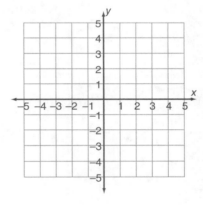

_____

APPLY SKILLS 4

Rewrite each linear equation in slope-intercept form. Name the slope and *y*-intercept and sketch the graph.

1. $x = 2y + 4$

2. $x + y = 3$

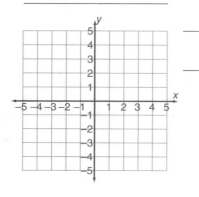

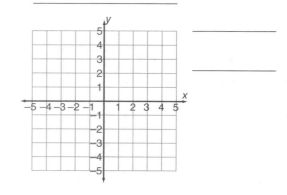

3. $4x + 4y = 20$

4. $4y - 2x = 4$

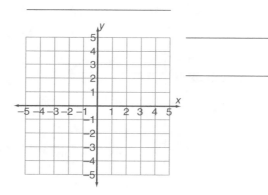

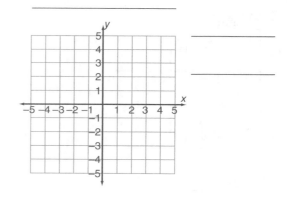

5. $x + \frac{1}{2}y + 2 = 0$

6. $5x = 5y + 10$

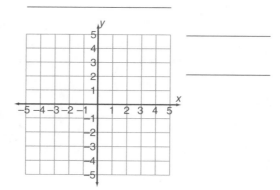

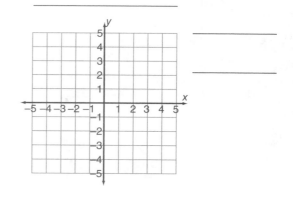

Name_____ Date_____

LONG-DISTANCE AND CHECKING

The long-distance phone rates for Company D are computed by using the formula $R = 0.07t + 0.26$, where R is the rate and t is the time in minutes. (*Hint:* Rewrite equations as cents instead of dollars.)

1. What is the slope of this line?

   _____

2. What does the slope represent?

   _____

   _____

3. What is the R-intercept for this line? _____

4. What does the R-intercept represent?

   _____

   _____

5. What is the rate for a 20-minute phone call?

   _____

6. What is the rate for a 30-minute phone call?

   _____

7. Sketch the graph of the equation.

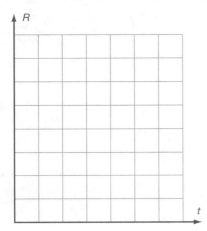

Name _____ Date _____

LONG-DISTANCE AND CHECKING (*continued*)

The service charge for a checking account at Bank K is figured by the following formula: $S = 0.1c + 2.00$, where S is the service charge and c is the number of checks written.

8. What is the slope of this line?

_____

9. What does the slope represent?

_____

10. What is the S-intercept for this line? _____

11. What does the S-intercept represent?

_____

_____

12. What is the service charge if you write 6 checks?

_____

13. What is the service charge if you write 15 checks?

_____

14. Sketch the graph of the equation.

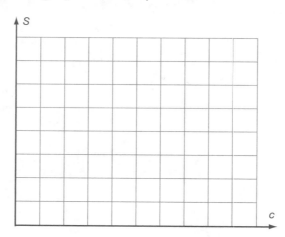

NAME THE EQUATION

Follow your teacher's instructions to fill in the table.

Equation	Parallel Equation	Perpendicular Equation
1. $y = x + 3$		
2. $y = 2x - 1$		
3. $y = 2x + 4$		
4.		$y = \frac{1}{3}x + 1$
5.		$x + 1 = y$
6. $x + y = 6$		
7.	$y - 2x = 3$	
8.		$2y + x = 5$
9. $\frac{1}{2}y + x = 3$		
10.	$y + 6 = 2x + 1$	
11. $2x + y = x - 1$		
12.		$y + 3 = \frac{1}{2}x - 1$
13.	$2x + 2y = 6$	

PRACTICE

Name_____ Date_____

APPLY SKILLS 1

1. Write the equations for the lines on the graph that are parallel.

   _____

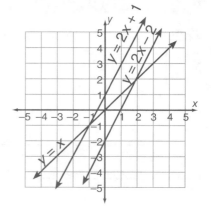

2. Can you tell by looking at the equations if the graph of the two lines will be parallel?

   _____

   _____

In each problem below, circle the two equations whose graphs will be parallel. Sketch the graphs if necessary.

3. $y = x + 4$	$y = x - 10$	$y = 4 - x$
4. $y = 3x + 6$	$y = 2x - 8$	$y = 2x - 6$
5. $y = -x + 1$	$y = x + 1$	$y = -x + 3$
6. $x + y = 2$	$y = 3 - x$	$y = x + 2$
7. $2x - y = 4$	$y = 4 + x$	$y = 2x + 4$
8. $7x = y$	$y = 7x + 2$	$y = 2x - 7$

Name an equation whose graph will be parallel to the graph of the equation given.

9. $y = 2x - 1$

   _____

10. $y = 4x + 1$

   _____

11. $x + y = 1$

   _____

12. $y = 3 - x$

   _____

13. $4 - y = x$

   _____

14. $y = 9x + 0$

   _____

APPLY SKILLS 2

1. Write the equations for the lines on the graph that are perpendicular.

   _____

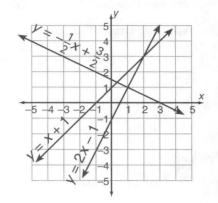

2. What relationship do you see between the slopes of lines that are perpendicular?

   _____

   _____

In each problem below, circle the two equations whose graphs will be perpendicular. Sketch the graphs if necessary.

3. $y = 3x + 1$	$y = x + 3$	$y = -\frac{1}{3}x + 2$
4. $y = x + 4$	$y = -x + 1$	$y = 2x - 3$
5. $y = 2x + 1$	$y = \frac{1}{2}x - 1$	$y = -\frac{1}{2}x + 2$
6. $y + 2x = 4$	$y - 2x = -4$	$y = \frac{1}{2}x + 1$
7. $3 - 2y = x$	$y = -2x + 4$	$2x - y = 5$
8. $y + x = \frac{1}{7}$	$y = 7x - 3$	$y + \frac{1}{7}x = 1$

Name an equation whose graph will be perpendicular to the graph of the equation given.

9. $y = \frac{1}{2}x + 3$

_____

10. $y = x + 1$

_____

11. $y = \frac{1}{4}x - 4$

_____

12. $2x - y = 4$

_____

13. $x - 2y = 8$

_____

14. $5y + x = 10$

_____

APPLY SKILLS 3

Answer the questions about each pair of equations.

1. Sketch the graphs of these two equations:

   $y = 2x - 1$

   $y = 2x + 3$

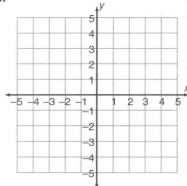

2. What can be said about the graphs of the equations in Problem 1?

   _____

3. Sketch the graphs of these two equations:

   $y = 3x - 1$

   $y = -\frac{1}{3}x + 1$

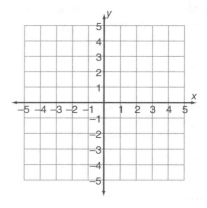

4. What can be said about the graphs of the equations in Problem 3?

   _____

Tell whether each pair of equations below is parallel or perpendicular.

5. $y = x + 1$ $y = -x + 2$ _____

6. $y = \frac{1}{2}x - 1$ $y = -2x + 3$ _____

7. $y = 5x + 4$ $y = 5x + \frac{1}{5}$ _____

8. $x + 2y = 4$ $2x - y = 4$ _____

9. Sketch the graphs of these two equations:

   $y = 2x - 3$

   $9 + 3y = 6x$

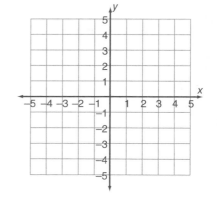

10. What can be said about the graphs of the equations in Problem 9?

    _____

SLOPE-INTERCEPT

Solve.

1. Write the equation of the line that passes through the point (1, 2) and is parallel to the graph of $x + y = 8$. Write the equation in slope-intercept form.

   _____

2. Write an equation in slope-intercept form of the line that passes through the point (2, 0) and is perpendicular to the graph of $2x + y = 3$.

   _____

3. Write an equation in slope-intercept form of the line that passes through the point (2, 2) and is parallel to the graph of $3 + y = x$.

   _____

4. Write the equation of two lines that are perpendicular and each contain the point (2, 4).

   _____

   _____

PROBLEM SOLVING

Name_____ Date_____

TWO SHIPS

Use the graph to answer the questions.

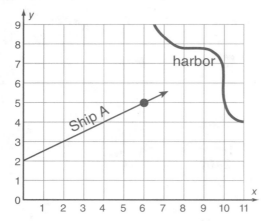

1. Two ships are traveling to the same destination. To be safe, the ships are given parallel routes so they will not collide if one goes faster than the other. Ship A has the route shown in the graph. What is the equation for a good route for Ship B?

    _____

2. If two ships are going to cross each other's path, the best way is to cross at a 90° angle so the time is minimized when they could collide. If Ship C is going to intersect Ship A's path at (6, 5), what is the equation of the route Ship C should follow through the point (6, 5)?

    _____

Name_____ **Date**_____

OBJECTIVE 1

Solve the problems involving slope.

1. Based on the graph, what is the slope of the line?

   _____

2. Find the slope of a line that contains the points (0, −2), (3, 1).

   _____

3. Find the slope of a line that contains the points (0, −2), (2, −8).

   _____

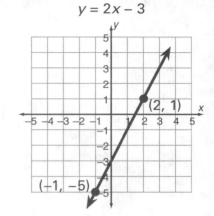

$y = 2x - 3$

(2, 1)

(−1, −5)

OBJECTIVE 2

Find the equation of each line from the given information. Write the equation in standard form. Show your work.

4. Write in standard form the equation of a line that has a slope of 3 and contains the point (0, 4).

   _____

5. Write in standard form the equation of a line that contains the two points (0, 3) and (4, 5).

   _____

6. Given the graph to the right, what is the equation of the line in standard form?

   _____

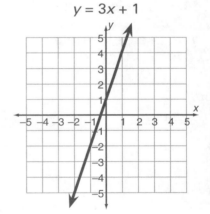

$y = 3x + 1$

Name _____ Date _____

OBJECTIVE 3

Draw the best-fit line, if it exists, and name the equation of the best-fit line. Write the equation in slope-intercept form.

7.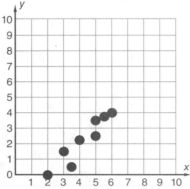

_____

8.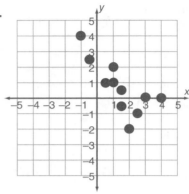

_____

OBJECTIVE 4

Answer the questions about the equation.

9. Write the equation $y - 4 = 2x$ in slope-intercept form. _____

10. What is the slope? _____

11. Sketch the graph.

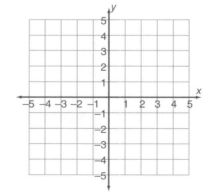

OBJECTIVE 5

Indicate if the graphs of the two equations in each problem would be parallel, perpendicular, or neither.

12. $2x + y = 3$

$2x + y = 7$

_____

13. $x = y + 4$

$y - x + 1 = 0$

_____

14. $x + 2y = 6$

$2x = y - 1$

_____

Solving Linear Inequalities

In this chapter, we explore inequalities in one and two variables. We also solve and graph inequalities, compound inequalities, and inequalities involving absolute value. At the end of the chapter, we learn to graph inequalities that use two variables and recognize that the graph represents the solution.

Objective 1
Solve and graph the solution set of inequalities with addition and subtraction.

Objective 2
Solve and graph the solution set of inequalities with multiplication and division.

Objective 3
Solve and graph the solution set of inequalities using more than one operation.

Objective 4
Solve and graph the solution set of compound inequalities and inequalities involving absolute value.

Objective 5
Graph inequalities in the coordinate plane.

Chapter 6
VOCABULARY

and All conditions must be true for the statement to be true

$x \geq -1$ and $x \leq 3$

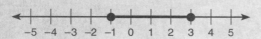

coefficient A number or quantity placed before a variable, which indicates multiplication of that variable

In 8*x*, the coefficient of *x* is 8.

compound inequality Two inequalities connected by *and* or *or*

$x > 0$ and $x \leq 7$

$x < 3$ or $x > 13$

inequality A mathematical sentence that compares two expressions using one of the following symbols:

> Greater than
< Less than
≥ Greater than or equal to
≤ Less than or equal to

$x < 3$; $x \leq 7$

or If either or both conditions are true, the whole statement is true

$x \leq -5$ or $x > -2$

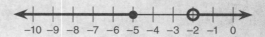

strict inequality An inequality that compares two expressions using only greater than (>) or less than (<)

$x > -2$; $x < 3$

Name _____   Date _____

INTRODUCTION TO INEQUALITIES

Circle the numbers in the replacement set that make each inequality true.

1. $t < 7$

{4, 7, 6, 8, 0, −6, 11}

2. $h > 4$

{6, 2, 4, −7, −1, 4.5}

3. $a \leq -4$

{−1, 3, −7, −4, 0, 6}

4. $n \geq -5$

{−10, 7, −1, −5, −6, −4}

5. $k + 5 < 9$

{−1, 3, 4, 5, −2, 4.5, 3.5}

6. $y - 7 > 3$

{−4, 2, 9, 10, 11, 10.01}

7. $u - 5 \geq -1$

{4, 3, 5, −2, 4.1, 3.9}

8. $x + 3 \leq -6$

{−3, −9, −10, −8, −11, −9.6, −8.4}

9. Write four more numbers that would make the inequality in Problem 1 true.

_____

10. What is the largest number in the list of circled answers in Problem 2? _____
If you can, write a number that is larger than that number that will make
Problem 2 true. _____

11. What is the largest number in the list of circled answers in Problem 3? _____
If you can, write a number that is larger than that number that will make
Problem 3 true. _____

12. What is the smallest number in the list of circled answers in Problem 5? _____
If you can, write a number that is smaller than that number that will make
Problem 5 true. _____

13. What is the smallest number in the list of circled answers in Problem 7? _____
If you can, write a number that is smaller than that number that will make
Problem 7 true. _____

CONCEPT DEVELOPMENT

Name_____   Date_____

APPLY SKILLS 1

Construct the linear graph for each inequality.

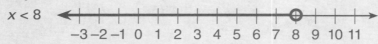

Example:

$x < 8$ ←——————————————————⊕——→
‑3 ‑2 ‑1 0 1 2 3 4 5 6 7 8 9 10 11

1. $x > 2$ ←—————————————————————→
        ‑7 ‑6 ‑5 ‑4 ‑3 ‑2 ‑1 0 1 2 3 4 5 6 7

2. $x \geq -4$ ←—————————————————————→
        ‑7 ‑6 ‑5 ‑4 ‑3 ‑2 ‑1 0 1 2 3 4 5 6 7

3. $x < 3$ ←—————————————————————→
        ‑7 ‑6 ‑5 ‑4 ‑3 ‑2 ‑1 0 1 2 3 4 5 6 7

4. $x \leq -1$ ←—————————————————————→
        ‑7 ‑6 ‑5 ‑4 ‑3 ‑2 ‑1 0 1 2 3 4 5 6 7

5. $x < -2$ ←—————————————————————→
        ‑7 ‑6 ‑5 ‑4 ‑3 ‑2 ‑1 0 1 2 3 4 5 6 7

6. $x < 10$ ←—————————————————————→
        ‑3 ‑2 ‑1 0 1 2 3 4 5 6 7 8 9 10 11

7. $x > 5$ ←—————————————————————→
        ‑7 ‑6 ‑5 ‑4 ‑3 ‑2 ‑1 0 1 2 3 4 5 6 7

8. $x \geq -2$ ←—————————————————————→
        ‑7 ‑6 ‑5 ‑4 ‑3 ‑2 ‑1 0 1 2 3 4 5 6 7

9. $x > -3$ ←—————————————————————→
        ‑7 ‑6 ‑5 ‑4 ‑3 ‑2 ‑1 0 1 2 3 4 5 6 7

10. $x \geq 4$ ←—————————————————————→
        ‑7 ‑6 ‑5 ‑4 ‑3 ‑2 ‑1 0 1 2 3 4 5 6 7

APPLY SKILLS 2

Solve each inequality and graph the solution on the number line.

Example:

$x + 4 < 2$ ___$x < -2$___
$x + 4 - 4 < 2 - 4$

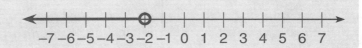

1. $x + 3 < 9$ _____

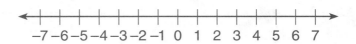

2. $w - 7 > -4$ _____

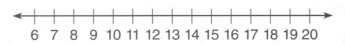

3. $a - 12 \leq 6$ _____

4. $y + 14 \geq 23$ _____

5. $b + 6 \geq -2$ _____

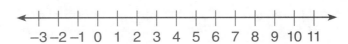

6. $h - 10 \leq 4$ _____

APPLY SKILLS 2 (*continued*)

7. $5 < t - 6$ _____

8. $-9 \geq c - 7$ _____

9. $x - 34 < 27$ _____

10. $y + 37 \geq 18$ _____

11. $64 + k > -26$ _____

12. $d - 34 \geq 0$ _____

INEQUALITIES QUESTIONS

Read the sentences and respond.

1. Write an inequality if the graph of the solution
    set has a filled-in dot at 3 and an arrow to the right. _____

2. Write an inequality if the graph of the solution
    set has an open dot at 6 and an arrow to the left. _____

3. Write an inequality if the graph of the solution
    set has an open dot at −5 and an arrow to the right. _____

4. Write an inequality if the graph of the solution
    set has a filled-in dot at −8 and an arrow to the left. _____

5. Write an inequality with addition in it that has a solution of $n > 4$.

    _____

6. Write an inequality with subtraction in it that has a solution of $n \leq -3$.

    _____

7. Last year, a youth baseball player hit 32 home runs in a single season. This
    year, the same player hit 15 home runs in the first half of the season. Write
    an inequality that shows how many home runs the player needs to hit in the
    second half of the season to break his record from last season.

    _____

8. Another player hit 12 home runs in the first half of the season. Write an
    inequality that shows how many home runs he needs to hit to break the
    record of 32 home runs in a season.

    _____

9. Write an inequality for the graph below. _____

    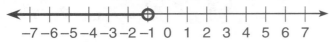

10. Write another inequality that would have the same graph as in Problem 9.

    _____

11. Write an inequality for the graph below. _____

    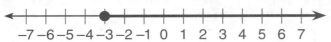

Name_____ Date_____

MAPPING PRODUCTS ON THE NUMBER LINE

Multiply the numbers by the value given, and graph the multiplied numbers on the second number line. Write the distance between each set of numbers. For the second number line, determine the relationship between the two numbers using the > or < symbols.

1. 3 < 7

 Distance from 3 to 7 is _____

Multiply each by 2.   3 • 2 _____ 7 • 2

 Distance from _____ to _____
is _____

2. 4 > 2

 Distance from 4 to 2 is _____

Multiply each by 3.   4 • 3 _____ 2 • 3

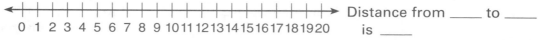 Distance from _____ to _____
is _____

3. 2 < 6

 Distance from 2 to 6 is _____

Multiply each by –2.   2 • –2 _____ 6 • –2

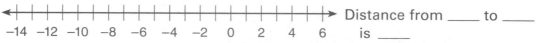 Distance from _____ to _____
is _____

4. 1 > –3

 Distance from 1 to –3 is _____

Multiply each by –3.   1 • –3 _____ –3 • –3

 Distance from _____ to _____
is _____

INEQUALITIES WITH MULTIPLICATION

Circle the numbers that make each inequality true, then read the sentences and respond. (An example of a mathematical sentence is "$a < 3$.")

1. $4a < 28$

   $a \in \{-6, -4, 0, 4, 6.8, 7, 8, 11\}$

   List four more numbers that would make this inequality true. _____

   Describe in words all the numbers that would make this inequality true.

   _____

   Write a mathematical sentence for these numbers. _____

2. $3h > -12$

   $h \in \{-7, -5, -4, -3, -1, 0, 4, 6\}$

   List four more numbers that would make this inequality true. _____

   Describe in words all the numbers that would make this inequality true.

   _____

   Write a mathematical sentence for these numbers. _____

3. $\frac{b}{2} \leq -2$

   $b \in \{-8, -6, -4, -2, 0, 2, 4\}$

   List four more numbers that would make this inequality true. _____

   Describe in words all the numbers that would make this inequality true.

   _____

   Write a mathematical sentence for these numbers. _____

4. $4n \geq -20$

   $n \in \{-8, -6, -5, -4, -2, 0, 2, 4\}$

   List four more numbers that would make this inequality true. _____

   Describe in words all the numbers that would make this inequality true.

   _____

   Write a mathematical sentence for these numbers. _____

Name_____ Date_____

INEQUALITIES WITH MULTIPLICATION

(continued)

5. $-5g < 20$

$g \in \{-8, -6, -4, -2, -1, 0, 2, 4\}$

List four more numbers that would make this inequality true. _____

Describe in words all the numbers that would make this inequality true.

_____

Write a mathematical sentence for these numbers. _____

6. $-4y > 12$

$y \in \{-9, -7, -5, -3, -1, 3, 5\}$

List four more numbers that would make this inequality true. _____

Describe in words all the numbers that would make this inequality true.

_____

Write a mathematical sentence for these numbers. _____

7. $-8z \geq -32$

$z \in \{-2, 0, 2, 4, 6, 8, 9\}$

List four more numbers that would make this inequality true. _____

Describe in words all the numbers that would make this inequality true.

_____

Write a mathematical sentence for these numbers. _____

8. $-4x \leq -36$

$x \in \{-3, -1, 3, 5, 7, 9, 11, 13\}$

List four more numbers that would make this inequality true. _____

Describe in words all the numbers that would make this inequality true.

_____

Write a mathematical sentence for these numbers. _____

Name _____ **Date** _____

APPLY SKILLS 1

Solve and graph the solution for each inequality.

Example:

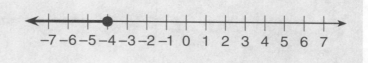

$$\frac{x}{2} \le -2 \quad \underline{x \le -4}$$

$$\frac{x}{2} \cdot 2 \le -2 \cdot 2$$

1. $3x < 18$ _____

2. $-4y \ge 8$ _____

3. $-\frac{z}{3} \le -5$ _____

4. $\frac{a}{7} > 3$ _____

5. $6b > -36$ _____

6. $-5c \ge -15$ _____

7. $\frac{d}{8} > -1$ _____

8. $\frac{f}{12} \le -2$ _____

9. $x - 12 < -15$ _____

10. $y + 15 \ge 9$ _____

APPLY SKILLS 2

Solve and graph the solution for each inequality.

Example:

$4x < 32$ ___$x < 8$___

$\frac{4x}{4} < \frac{32}{4}$

1. $7x < 56$ _____

2. $-4y \geq 28$ _____

3. $-\frac{z}{6} \leq -8$ _____

4. $\frac{a}{8} > -4$ _____

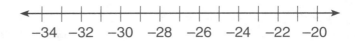

5. $9b > -36$ _____

6. $-5c \geq -75$ _____

7. $-\frac{d}{7} > -9$ _____

8. $\frac{f}{12} \leq -2$ _____

9. $x - 27 < -18$ _____

10. $y + 19 \geq 36$ _____

INEQUALITIES AND EQUATIONS

Solve the equation, then solve the inequalities and answer the questions.

1. $4x + 7 = 19$

2. $4x + 7 < 19$

3. $4x + 7 \geq 19$

4. Are the steps different in solving the equation and the inequalities? _____
Explain:

_____

_____

5. $3x - 11 = -20$

6. $3x - 11 > -20$

7. $3x - 11 \leq -20$

8. Are the steps in solving the equation and the inequalities still the same? _____
Explain:

_____

_____

9. Did the negative sign in front of the 20 cause the steps to be any different in the equation and the inequalities? _____

10. $-5x + 12 = 27$

11. $-5x + 12 < 27$

12. $-5x + 12 \geq 27$

13. Are the steps in solving the equation and the inequalities still the same? _____
Explain:

_____

_____

14. Did the negative sign in front of the 5 cause the steps to be any different in the equation and the inequalities? _____

15. What is true when you multiply or divide an inequality by a negative number?

_____

CONCEPT DEVELOPMENT

Name_____ Date_____

APPLY SKILLS 1

Solve each inequality and graph the solution set on the number line.

Example:

$2x + 3 > 9$ ___$x > 3$___
$2x + 3 - 3 > 9 - 3$
$2x > 6$
$\dfrac{2x}{2} > \dfrac{6}{2}$

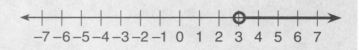

1. $5x < 20$ _____

2. $-3x > 15$ _____

3. $x + 14 \geq 20$ _____

4. $x - 6 \leq 7$ _____

5. $-\dfrac{1}{2}x > 4$ _____

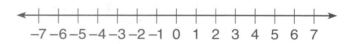

6. $\dfrac{x}{3} \leq -6$ _____

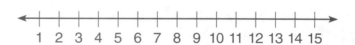

Name_____ **Date**_____

APPLY SKILLS 1 (*continued*)

7. $2x + 6 > 16$ _____

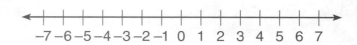

$$-7 -6 -5 -4 -3 -2 -1 \quad 0 \quad 1 \quad 2 \quad 3 \quad 4 \quad 5 \quad 6 \quad 7$$

8. $-x + 7 < 3$ _____

$$-7 -6 -5 -4 -3 -2 -1 \quad 0 \quad 1 \quad 2 \quad 3 \quad 4 \quad 5 \quad 6 \quad 7$$

9. $\frac{3}{2}x - 1 > 8$ _____

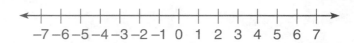

$$-7 -6 -5 -4 -3 -2 -1 \quad 0 \quad 1 \quad 2 \quad 3 \quad 4 \quad 5 \quad 6 \quad 7$$

10. $-4x + 6 \leq -2$ _____

$$-7 -6 -5 -4 -3 -2 -1 \quad 0 \quad 1 \quad 2 \quad 3 \quad 4 \quad 5 \quad 6 \quad 7$$

11. $3x - 4 \geq 8$ _____

$$-7 -6 -5 -4 -3 -2 -1 \quad 0 \quad 1 \quad 2 \quad 3 \quad 4 \quad 5 \quad 6 \quad 7$$

12. $2x - 9 < -13$ _____

$$-7 -6 -5 -4 -3 -2 -1 \quad 0 \quad 1 \quad 2 \quad 3 \quad 4 \quad 5 \quad 6 \quad 7$$

Name_____ Date_____

APPLY SKILLS 2

Solve and graph the solution for each inequality.

Example:

$2x - 1 > 5 - x$ _____$x > 2$_____

$2x - 1 + x > 5 - x + x$

$3x - 1 > 5$

$3x - 1 + 1 > 5 + 1$

$3x > 6$

$\frac{3x}{3} > \frac{6}{3}$

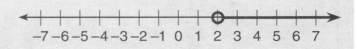

1. $5x - 12 \geq 13$ _____

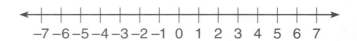

2. $-8y + 13 < -11$ _____

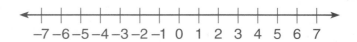

3. $9z + 25 \leq 7$ _____

4. $16 < 3x + 1$ _____

5. $25 \leq -4y - 7$ _____

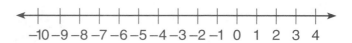

6. $19 > 13 - 3z$ _____

7. $2x - 2 \leq x + 7$ _____

Name_____ **Date**_____

APPLY SKILLS 2 (*continued*)

8. $3y - 5 > 2y - 9$ _____

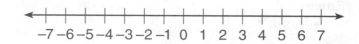

9. $z + 15 < 3z + 11$ _____

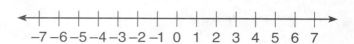

10. $15 - 3x \geq 2x + 5$ _____

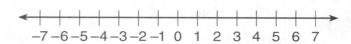

11. $6z + 20 > 4z + 10$ _____

12. $\frac{2z}{5} > 4$ _____

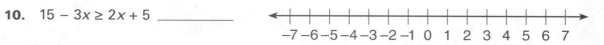

13. $\frac{x}{2} - 3 \leq 5$ _____

14. $-\frac{z}{5} - 4 < z + 2$ _____

APPLY SKILLS 3

Solve and graph the solution for each inequality.

Example:

$5x - 7 < 3x + 5$ __$x < 6$__

$5x - 7 - 3x < 3x + 5 - 3x$

$2x - 7 < 5$

$2x - 7 + 7 < 5 + 7$

$2x < 12$

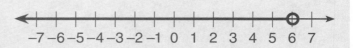

1. $3x + 12 \geq 33$ _____

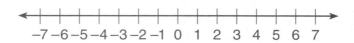

2. $5y - 13 < 7$ _____

3. $9 - 3z \leq 21$ _____

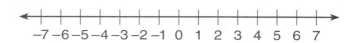

4. $26 < -3x + 14$ _____

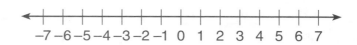

5. $25 \leq 4 - 7y$ _____

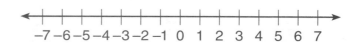

6. $19 > 2z + 5$ _____

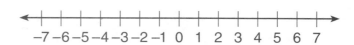

7. $6y + 22 > 8y$ _____

Inside Algebra

Name _____ **Date** _____

APPLY SKILLS 3 (*continued*)

8. $2z + 4 > z + 3$ _____

9. $5 - 3x \geq 2x + 25$ _____

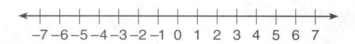

10. $19 - y \leq 2y + 25$ _____

```
←—+——+——+——+——+——+——+——+——+——+——+——+——+——+——+→
  −7 −6 −5 −4 −3 −2 −1  0  1  2  3  4  5  6  7
```

11. $-\dfrac{3z}{4} > 2$ _____

```
←—+——+——+——+——+——+——+——+——+——+——+——+——+——+——+→
  −7 −6 −5 −4 −3 −2 −1  0  1  2  3  4  5  6  7
```

12. $\dfrac{2x}{3} - 4 \leq 0$ _____

```
←—+——+——+——+——+——+——+——+——+——+——+——+——+——+——+→
  −7 −6 −5 −4 −3 −2 −1  0  1  2  3  4  5  6  7
```

13. $\dfrac{y}{2} + 7 > 5 + y$ _____

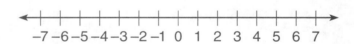

14. $-\dfrac{z}{3} - 2 < -3$ _____

```
←—+——+——+——+——+——+——+——+——+——+——+——+——+——+——+→
  −7 −6 −5 −4 −3 −2 −1  0  1  2  3  4  5  6  7
```

Name_____   Date_____

WRITING AND SOLVING INEQUALITIES

1. Write an inequality that has the solution $x < 3$. The inequality problem must have a solution that involves multiplication (by something other than 1 or −1) and addition or subtraction of a constant.

   _____

2. Write an inequality that has the solution $x > -2$. The inequality problem must have a solution that involves multiplication and a reversal of the inequality sign. It must also involve addition or subtraction of a constant.

   _____

3. Write an inequality that matches the graph.

   The inequality problem must have a solution that involves multiplication and a reversal of the inequality sign. It must also involve addition or subtraction of a constant.

   _____

4. Write an inequality that matches the graph.

   The inequality problem must have a solution that involves multiplication. It must also involve addition or subtraction of a constant.

   _____

5. Write an inequality that has the solution $x \leq 4$. The inequality problem must have a solution that involves division. It must also involve addition or subtraction of a constant.

   _____

Name_____ Date_____

WRITING AND SOLVING INEQUALITIES

(continued)

6. Write an inequality that has the solution $x \geq -3$. The inequality problem must have a solution that involves division and a reversal of the inequality sign. It must also involve addition or subtraction of a constant.

_____

7. Write an inequality that matches the graph.

The inequality problem must have a solution that involves division. It must also involve addition or subtraction of a constant.

_____

8. Write an inequality that matches the graph.

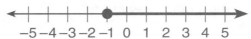

The inequality problem must have a solution that involves division and a reversal of the inequality sign. It must also involve addition or subtraction of a constant.

_____

9. Write an inequality that has the solution $x < 3$. The inequality problem must have a variable term and a constant term on both sides of the inequality sign.

_____

10. Write an inequality that matches the graph.

The inequality problem must have a variable term and a constant term on both sides of the inequality sign.

_____

INEQUALITY WORD PROBLEMS

Juanita wants to buy a house. To qualify for a loan, she must earn at least $30,000 per year. She makes $4,000 a year in her part-time job at a specialty shop. In her regular job as a computer technician, she works 8 hours per day, 5 days a week. She works or gets paid vacation for all 52 weeks per year.

WORK SPACE

1. How much must Juanita earn per year to qualify for the loan? _____

2. How much does she earn in her part-time job? _____

3. How much must she earn from her regular job in one year to qualify for the mortgage? _____

4. Must Juanita's salary be exactly that amount or could she make more? _____

5. Counting 52 weeks in a year, how much would Juanita need to earn per week at her regular job? _____

6. If Juanita works 8 hours per day and 5 days a week, how many hours does Juanita work in a week? _____

7. Write an inequality, using *w* for Juanita's hourly wage, that shows how much Juanita must be paid per hour to qualify for the loan.

   _____

8. Solve the inequality. _____

Bob is renting a car for the first time. Classic Rentals will rent him a car for $20 per day plus $0.12 a mile. He has a three-day trip planned and cannot spend more than $180 total for the rental car.

9. Write an inequality for how many miles he could drive in the three days.

   _____

10. Without counting mileage, how much will Bob spend on the car in three days? _____

11. How much money does Bob have to spend for the car rental? _____

INEQUALITY WORD PROBLEMS *(continued)*

12. Must Bob spend exactly $180 or could it be less? _____

13. How much money does that leave him for mileage? _____

14. What would be the mileage charge for 100 miles? _____

15. Write an inequality, using *m* for the number of miles Bob drives on his trip, that shows how many miles Bob can drive within his budget.
_____

16. Solve the inequality. _____

Paulo and Maria are going out to dinner. They have exactly $50, the tax rate is 5%, and they plan to tip the waiter 15% of the cost of the dinner.

17. How much do Paulo and Maria have to spend on dinner including tax and tip? _____

18. What is the total percent for tax and tip?
_____

19. If they spent $45 on dinner, how much would tax and tip cost? _____

20. Could they spend $45 just for dinner and have enough for tax and tip? _____

21. Do they need to spend exactly $50? Can they spend more? Less? _____
_____
_____

22. Write an inequality, using *d* for the price of the food, that shows how much they can spend on dinner. _____

23. Solve the inequality. _____

Name_____ Date_____

ABSOLUTE VALUE AND DISTANCE—PART 1, EQUALITY

Recall that $|x| = 5$ means x represents the numbers that are a distance of 5 from 0. An absolute value problem such as $|x - 4| = 5$ means that $x - 4$ represents the numbers that are a distance of 5 from 0, or simply that the distance from x to 4 is 5. On the number line, we can represent the problem as:

As an algebraic equation, we can write $|x - 4| = 5$ as the compound equation

$$x - 4 = 5 \quad \text{or} \quad x - 4 = -5$$

By adding 4 to both sides of these equations, we have

$$x - 4 + 4 = 5 + 4 \quad \text{or} \quad x - 4 + 4 = -5 + 4$$

Therefore, our solution is $\qquad x = 9 \quad \text{or} \quad x = -1$

Complete each problem, and graph the distance on the number line.

1. $|x - 1| = 4$

   The distance between x and 1 is _____.
   On the number line, the problem can be represented by $x =$ _____ or
   $x =$ _____.

   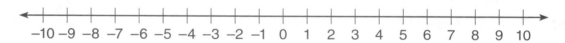

2. $|x - 7| = 2$

   The distance between x and _____ is 2.
   On the number line, the problem can be represented by $x =$ _____ or
   $x =$ _____.

   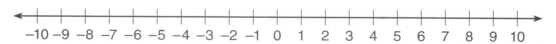

3. $|x - 8| = 1$

   The distance between x and _____ is _____.
   On the number line, the problem can be represented by $x =$ _____ or
   $x =$ _____.

Name_____ Date_____

ABSOLUTE VALUE AND DISTANCE—PART 1, EQUALITY *(continued)*

Recall now that since $|x| = 6$ means x represents the numbers that are a distance of 6 from 0, then $|x + 3| = 6$, which can be thought of as $|x - (-3)| = 6$, means that the distance between x and -3 is 6. On the number line, we can represent $|x + 3| = 6$ as:

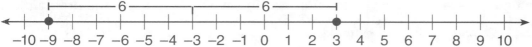

As an algebraic equation, we can write $|x + 3| = 6$ as the compound equation

$$x + 3 = 6 \quad \text{or} \quad x + 3 = -6$$

By subtracting 3 from both sides of these equations, we have

$$x + 3 - 3 = 6 - 3 \quad \text{or} \quad x + 3 - 3 = -6 - 3$$

Therefore, our solution is $\quad x = 3 \quad$ or $\quad x = -9$

Complete each problem, and graph the distance on the number line.

4. $|x + 2| = 5$

The distance between x and -2 is _____.
On the number line, the problem can be represented by $x =$ _____ or
$x =$ _____.

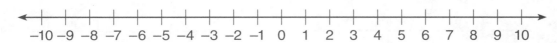

5. $|x + 4| = 6$

The distance between x and _____ is 6.
On the number line, the problem can be represented by $x =$ _____ or
$x =$ _____.

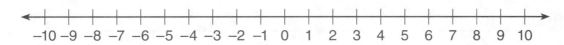

6. $|x + 7| = 5$

The distance between x and _____ is _____.
On the number line, the problem can be represented by $x =$ _____ or
$x =$ _____.

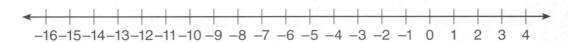

Name_____ Date_____

ABSOLUTE VALUE AND DISTANCE—PART 2, LESS THAN

Recall that $|x| < 5$ means x represents the numbers that are less than a distance of 5 from 0. An absolute value problem such as $|x - 4| < 5$ means that $x - 4$ represents the numbers that are less than a distance of 5 from 0, or simply that the distance between x and 4 is less than 5. On the number line, we can represent the problem as:

As an algebraic inequality, we can write $|x - 4| < 5$ as the compound inequality

$$x - 4 < 5 \quad \text{and} \quad x - 4 > -5$$

By adding 4 to both sides of these inequalities, we have

$$x - 4 + 4 < 5 + 4 \quad \text{and} \quad x - 4 + 4 > -5 + 4$$

Therefore, our solution is $\qquad x < 9 \quad$ and $\quad x > -1$

Complete each problem, and graph the distance on the number line.

1. $|x - 1| < 4$

   The distance between x and 1 is less than _____.
   On the number line, the problem can be represented by $x <$ _____ and $x >$ _____.

   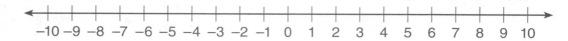

2. $|x - 7| < 2$

   The distance between x and _____ is less than 2.
   On the number line, the problem can be represented by $x <$ _____ and $x >$ _____.

   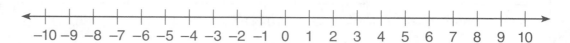

3. $|x - 8| < 1$

   The distance between x and _____ is less than _____.
   On the number line, the problem can be represented by $x <$ _____ and $x >$ _____.

   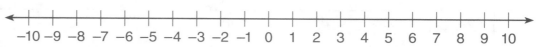

Inside Algebra

ABSOLUTE VALUE AND DISTANCE—PART 2, LESS THAN (*continued*)

Recall now that since $|x| < 6$ means x represents the numbers that are less than a distance of 6 from 0, then $|x + 3| < 6$, which can be thought of as $|x - (-3)| < 6$, means that the distance between x and -3 is less than 6. On the number line, we can represent $|x + 3| < 6$ as:

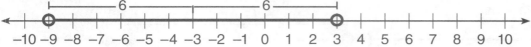

As an algebraic inequality, we can write $|x + 3| < 6$ as the compound inequality

$$x + 3 < 6 \quad \text{and} \quad x + 3 > -6$$

By subtracting 3 from both sides of these inequalities, we have

$$x + 3 - 3 < 6 - 3 \quad \text{and} \quad x + 3 - 3 > -6 - 3$$

Therefore, our solution is $\quad x < 3 \quad \text{and} \quad x > -9$

Complete each problem, and graph the distance on the number line.

4. $|x + 2| < 5$

The distance between x and -2 is less than _____.
On the number line, the problem can be represented by $x < $ _____ and
$x > $ _____.

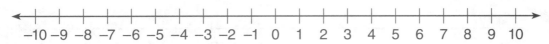

5. $|x + 4| < 6$

The distance between x and _____ is less than 6.
On the number line, the problem can be represented by $x < $ _____ and
$x > $ _____.

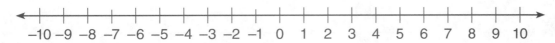

6. $|x + 7| < 5$

The distance between x and _____ is less than _____.
On the number line, the problem can be represented by $x < $ _____ and
$x > $ _____.

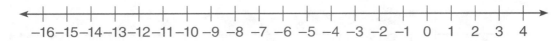

CONCEPT DEVELOPMENT

ABSOLUTE VALUE AND DISTANCE— PART 3, GREATER THAN

Recall that $|x| > 5$ means x represents the numbers that are more than a distance of 5 from 0. An absolute value problem such as $|x - 4| > 5$ means that $x - 4$ represents the numbers that are more than a distance of 5 from 0, or simply that the distance between x and 4 is more than 5. On the number line, we can represent the problem as:

As an algebraic inequality, we can write $|x - 4| > 5$ as the compound inequality

$$x - 4 > 5 \quad \text{or} \quad x - 4 < -5$$

By adding 4 to both sides of these inequalities, we have

$$x - 4 + 4 > 5 + 4 \quad \text{or} \quad x - 4 + 4 < -5 + 4$$

Therefore, our solution is $\quad\quad\quad x > 9 \quad \text{or} \quad x < -1$

Complete each problem, and graph the distance on the number line.

1. $|x - 1| > 4$

The distance between x and 1 is more than _____.
On the number line, the problem can be represented by $x >$ _____ or $x <$ _____.

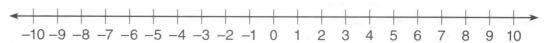

2. $|x - 7| > 2$

The distance between x and _____ is more than 2.
On the number line, the problem can be represented by $x >$ _____ or $x <$ _____.

3. $|x - 8| > 1$

The distance between x and _____ is more than _____.
On the number line, the problem can be represented by $x >$ _____ or $x <$ _____.

ABSOLUTE VALUE AND DISTANCE— PART 3, GREATER THAN *(continued)*

Recall now that since $|x| > 6$ means x represents the numbers that are more than a distance of 6 from 0, then $|x + 3| > 6$, which can be thought of as $|x - (-3)| > 6$, means that the distance between x and -3 is more than 6. On the number line, we can represent $|x + 3| > 6$ as:

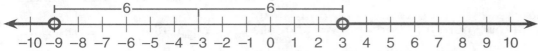

As an algebraic inequality, we can write $|x + 3| > 6$ as the compound inequality

$$x + 3 > 6 \quad \text{or} \quad x + 3 < -6$$

By subtracting 3 from both sides of these inequalities, we have

$$x + 3 - 3 > 6 - 3 \quad \text{or} \quad x + 3 - 3 < -6 - 3$$

Therefore, our solution is $\quad x > 3 \quad \text{or} \quad x < -9$

Complete each problem, and graph the distance on the number line.

4. $|x + 2| > 5$

    The distance between x and -2 is more than _____.
    On the number line, the problem can be represented by $x >$ _____ or
    $x <$ _____.

5. $|x + 4| > 6$

    The distance between x and _____ is more than 6.
    On the number line, the problem can be represented by $x >$ _____ or
    $x <$ _____.

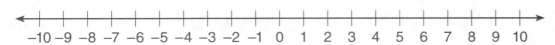

6. $|x + 7| > 5$

    The distance between x and _____ is more than _____.
    On the number line, the problem can be represented by $x >$ _____ or
    $x <$ _____.

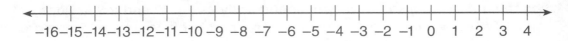

Name _____ Date _____

APPLY SKILLS 1

Read each problem carefully and write the answer.

1. A number is less than 7 or greater than 15. Could the number be 11? _____
   17? _____ 6.8? _____ 14.99? _____

2. Name four more numbers that would make Problem 1 true. _____

3. Name four more numbers that would make Problem 1 false. _____

4. Plot, on the number line, all the points that make Problem 1 true.

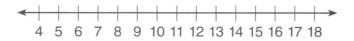

5. If a number is less than 10 and greater than 4, could it be 7? _____ 15? _____
   10? _____ 5.6? _____ 2? _____

6. Name four more numbers that would make Problem 5 true. _____

7. Name four more numbers that would make Problem 5 false. _____

8. Plot, on the number line, all the points that make Problem 5 true.

9. Problem 1 could also be written algebraically as $n < 7$ or $n > 15$.
   Does $n < 7$ or $n > 15$ mean the same thing as a number is less than 7
   or greater than 15? _____

10. If $n < 3$ or $n > 9$, which of the following would make the compound inequality
    true? Circle the correct answers.

    $\{-3, 1, 2.7, 3, 5, 8, 9, 9.2, 12, 15\}$

11. Name four more numbers that would make Problem 10 true. _____

12. Name four more numbers that would make Problem 10 false. _____

13. Plot, on the number line, all the points that make Problem 10 true.

14. Problem 5 could also be written algebraically as $y < 10$ and $y > 4$. Does
    $y < 10$ and $y > 4$ mean the same thing as a number is less than 10 and greater
    than 4? _____

APPLY SKILLS 1 *(continued)*

15. If $x < -5$ and $x > -1$, which of the following would make the compound inequality true? Circle the correct answers.

$$\{-10, -7, -5, -4, -3, -1.5, -1.1, -0.7, 0, 2, 5\}$$

16. Name four more numbers that would make Problem 15 true. _____

17. Name four more numbers that would make Problem 15 false. _____

18. Plot, on the number line, all the points that make Problem 15 true.

19. If a number is between 10 and 20, could it be 4? _____ 8? _____ 10? _____ 12? _____ 16? _____ 20? _____ 24? _____

20. Name four more numbers that would make Problem 19 true. _____

21. Name four more numbers that would make Problem 19 false. _____

22. Plot, on the number line, all the points that make Problem 19 true.

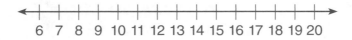

APPLY SKILLS 2

Solve and graph the given inequality.

1. $3x - 4 < 17$ _____

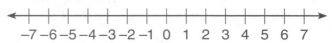

2. $5 - 2x < 1$ _____

3. $2x + 7 \leq 13$ _____

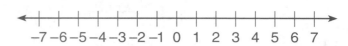

4. $5x - 19 \geq 16$ _____

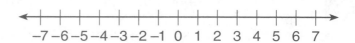

5. Now consider the compound inequality $3x - 4 < 17$ and $5 - 2x < 1$.

    The inequality on the left side of the "and" is the same as in Problem 1, and the inequality on the right side of the "and" is the same as in Problem 2. The solutions to Problems 1 and 2 gave easier forms of the solution to the compound inequality. The solution to the compund inequality in Problem 5 is the answers in Problems 1 and 2 linked with an "and."

    Write and graph the solution to Problem 5. _____

Name_____ **Date**_____

APPLY SKILLS 2 (*continued*)

6. Now consider the compound inequality $2x + 7 \leq 13$ or $5x - 19 \geq 16$.

   The inequality on the left side of the "or" is the same as in Problem 3, and the inequality on the right side of the "or" is the same as in Problem 4. The solutions to Problems 3 and 4 gave easier forms of the solution to the compound inequality. The solution to the compound inequality in Problem 6 is the answers in Problems 3 and 4 linked with an "or."

   Write and graph the solution to Problem 6. _____

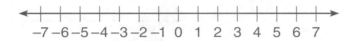

Solve and graph the compound inequalities.

7. $x + 5 < 8$ or $-3x < -18$ _____

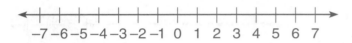

8. $4x - 3 < 17$ and $2x + 9 > 13$ _____

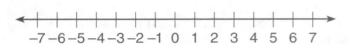

9. $7 - 2x \leq 1$ and $5x - 26 \leq 14$ _____

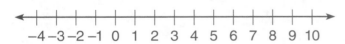

10. $2x + 3 < x - 2$ or $5x - 6 \geq 2x + 3$ _____

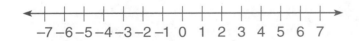

APPLY SKILLS 3

In Problems 1 through 6, draw a line from the compound inequality to the matching graph.

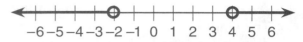

1. $x < 4$ and $x > -2$

2. $x > 4$ or $x < -2$

3. $x \le 4$ and $x \ge -2$

4. $x > 4$ or $x \le -2$

5. $x > 4$ and $x > -2$

6. $x \le 4$ or $x \le -2$

In Problems 7 through 12, draw a line from the graph of each compound inequality to the matching inequality.

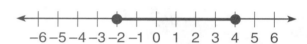

7. $y < 2$ and $y < -3$

8. $y \le -3$ or $y \ge 2$

9. $y \ge -3$ and $y \ge 2$

10. $y < 2$ or $y < -3$

11. $-3 < y \le 2$

12. $y < -3$ or $y \ge 2$

APPLY SKILLS 3 (*continued*)

Graph each inequality on the number line provided.

13. $x < 9$ and $x \geq 3$

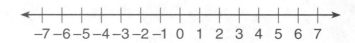

14. $y < 2$ or $y \geq 7$

15. $x > -3$ or $x > -5$

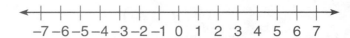

16. $y \leq -4$ and $y \leq -6$

17. $x < 8$ or $x > 4$

18. $y \leq 0$ and $y \geq 4$

Name_____ Date_____

APPLY SKILLS 4

Solve each inequality and graph the solution set on the number line.

Example:

$2x - 7 < 1$ and $3x + 5 > -1$ ___$x < 4$___ and ___$x > -2$___

$2x - 7 + 7 < 1 + 7$ $3x + 5 - 5 > -1 - 5$

    $2x < 8$ and $3x > -6$

    $\dfrac{2x}{2} < \dfrac{8}{2}$ $\dfrac{3x}{3} > -\dfrac{6}{3}$

1. $2x - 5 < 1$ and $3x > -9$ _____

2. $4x - 9 > 7$ or $5 - 2x > 7$ _____

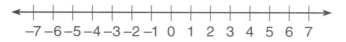

3. $5x \le 10$ and $x + 6 \ge 4$ _____

4. $3x + 4 \le 16$ or $5x - 9 \ge 16$ _____

Name_____ Date_____

5. $-3x \leq 9$ and $4x + 7 < 3$ _____

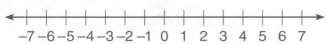

6. $2x - 7 < 5x + 2$ or $12 - 2x \geq 22$ _____

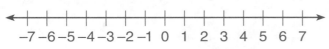

7. $\frac{x}{3} \leq 2$ and $5x - 9 \geq 11$ _____

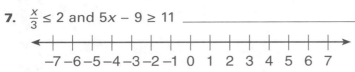

8. $3x - 4 < x + 2$ or $-\frac{x}{2} + 5 > 4$ _____

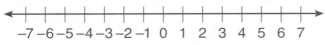

9. $3x - 7 > 8 - 2x$ and $14 - x > 3x + 14$ _____

APPLY SKILLS 5

Solve each absolute value problem and graph the solution set on the number line.

Example:

$|x + 2| < 5$ ___ $x < 3$ ___ and ___ $x > -7$ ___

$$x + 2 < 5$$
$$x + 2 - 2 < 5 - 2$$

and

$$x + 2 > -5$$
$$x + 2 - 2 > -5 - 2$$

1. $|x - 5| \leq 3$ _____

2. $|x - 3| = 2$ _____

3. $|x - 4| > 1$ _____

4. $|x + 1| = 4$ _____

5. $|x + 2| \geq 2$ _____

APPLY SKILLS 5 (*continued*)

6. $|x + 3| < 1$ _____

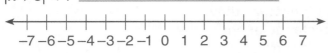

7. $|2x - 5| = 3$ _____

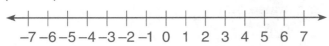

8. $|2x + 6| < 6$ _____

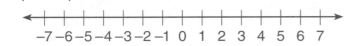

9. $|3x - 9| \geq 6$ _____

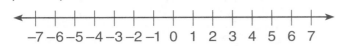

10. $|2x - 3| \leq 4$ _____

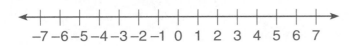

Name_____ Date_____

INVESTIGATIONS WITH INEQUALITIES

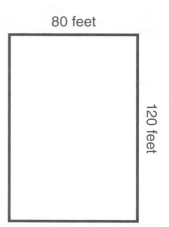

80 feet

120 feet

The Baxters have just bought a lot on which they plan to build a house. The lot is rectangular and 80 feet across. It is 120 feet deep from front to back. The front faces the street.

1. The local building codes restrict the smallest building dimension to 24 feet. They also state that one cannot build closer than 10 feet to the side lot line. Write an inequality that represents the width of the house that will face the street.

_____

2. The building codes also state that the house cannot be closer than 25 feet from the street and must be at least 15 feet from the back lot line. Write an inequality that shows the possible depths of the house from front to back.

_____

3. The Baxters want a two-stall garage that will measure 20 feet by 25 feet. The cost of the garage is $20 per square foot. How much will the garage cost?

_____

4. The Baxters have asked that the total cost of the house and garage be about $150,000, but they are willing to deviate from this price by $14,000. Write an inequality that shows how much they can spend on the house if they do not build the garage.

_____

5. Write an inequality that shows how much they can spend on the house if they do build the garage.

_____

6. Write the inequality for Problem 4 using absolute values.

_____

WORK SPACE

Name_____ **Date**_____

POINTS ON AND NOT ON A LINE

Complete the problems given the inequality $y < 2x + 1$.

1. Tell which of the following points satisfy the
   inequality (state "yes" or "no").

   (2, 6) _____   (2, 5) _____   (2, 3) _____

   (1, 3) _____   (1, 1) _____   (1, 5) _____

   (0, 0) _____   (0, 4) _____   (0, 1) _____

   (−1, −1) _____   (−1, −3) _____   (−1, 1) _____

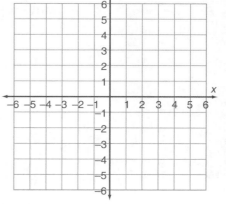

2. Graph the line $y = 2x + 1$.

3. Plot the 12 points from Problem 1 on the graph.
   Label the ordered pairs and indicate whether they satisfy the inequality
   $y < 2x + 1$ with a "Y" for "yes" and an "N" for "no" according to Problem 1.

4. What do you observe about all the points that satisfy the inequality?

   _____

5. List four more ordered pairs that satisfy the inequality $y < 2x + 1$.

   _____

6. Where are the points that satisfy $y = 2x + 1$?

   _____

7. Where are the points that satisfy $y > 2x + 1$?

   _____

8. What points would be included if we changed $y < 2x + 1$ to $y \leq 2x + 1$?

   _____

POINTS ON AND NOT ON A LINE (*continued*)

Complete the problems given the inequality $x - y < 3$.

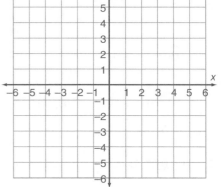

9. Tell which of the following points satisfy the inequality (state "yes" or "no").

(2, −4) _____   (2, −1) _____   (2, 3) _____

(1, 3) _____   (1, −2) _____   (1, −4) _____

(0, −3) _____   (0, −4) _____   (0, 1) _____

(−1, −4) _____   (−1, −3) _____   (−1, −5) _____

10. Graph the line $x - y = 3$.

11. Plot the 12 points from Problem 9 on the graph.
Label the ordered pairs and indicate whether they satisfy the inequality
$x - y < 3$ with a "Y" for "yes" and an "N" for "no" according to Problem 9.

12. What do you observe about all the points that satisfy the inequality?

_____

13. List four more ordered pairs that satisfy the inequality $x - y < 3$.

_____

14. Where are the points that satisfy $x - y = 3$?

_____

15. Where are the points that satisfy $x - y > 3$?

_____

16. What points would be included if we changed $x - y < 3$ to $x - y \leq 3$?

_____

Name _____ **Date** _____

APPLY SKILLS 1

Graph the equation $y = x - 1$.

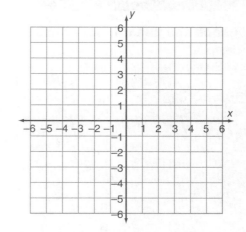

1. Plot the point $(-1, 2)$.

2. Plot the point $(3, -1)$.

3. For the inequality $y \leq x - 1$, which point makes it true, $(-1, 2)$ or $(3, -1)$?

4. Shade the part of the graph where $y \leq x - 1$ is true.

Graph the equation $y = 3 - x$.

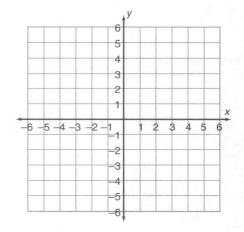

5. Plot the point $(-1, 1)$.

6. Plot the point $(3, 3)$.

7. For the inequality $y \geq 3 - x$, which point makes it true, $(-1, 1)$ or $(3, 3)$?

8. Shade the part of the graph where $y \geq 3 - x$ is true.

Graph the equation $x + y = 0$.

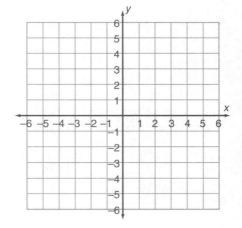

9. Plot the point $(2, 2)$.

10. Plot the point $(-2, -2)$.

11. For the inequality $x + y \geq 0$, which point makes it true, $(2, 2)$ or $(-2, -2)$?

12. Shade the part of the graph where $x + y \geq 0$ is true.

APPLY SKILLS 2

Graph the linear inequalities.

Example:

$y < x + 2$

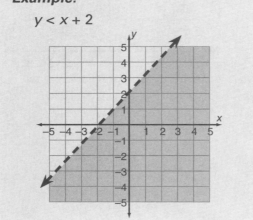

1. $y \geq 2x - 1$

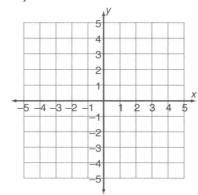

2. $y \leq 4$

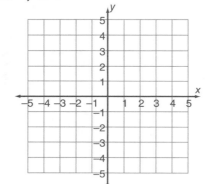

3. $x > -3$

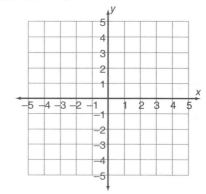

4. $y > 2x + 6$

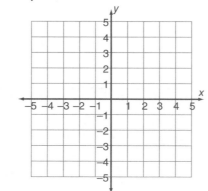

5. $y \leq 4 - x$

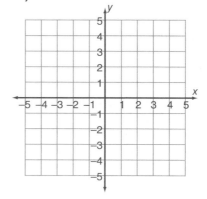

Name_____   **Date**_____

APPLY SKILLS 2 (*continued*)

6. $x - y \leq 4$

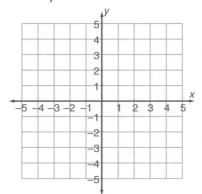

7. $x + y > 2$

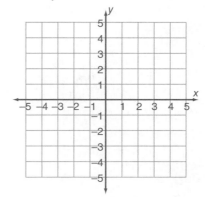

8. $3x + y < -2$

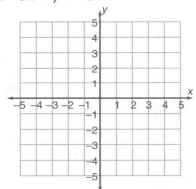

9. $4x - y \geq 3$

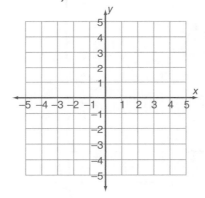

10. $3x \leq 9$

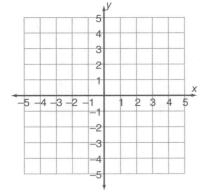

11. $2y > -4$

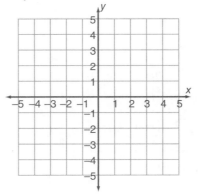

Name _____   Date _____

APPLY SKILLS 3

Graph the linear inequalities.

Example:

$y - x < 2$

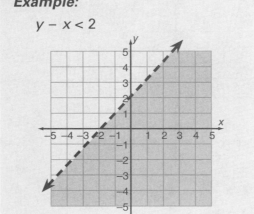

1. $2x - y \geq 1$

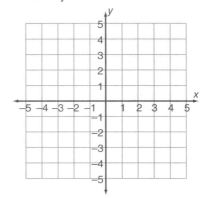

2. $y \leq -2$

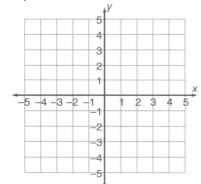

3. $x > 1$

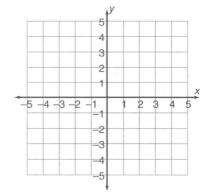

4. $3x - y > 4$

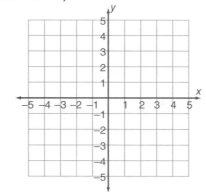

5. $2x + y \leq 3$

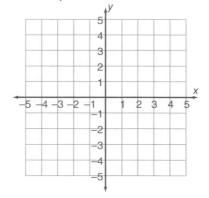

APPLY SKILLS 3 *(continued)*

6. $x - 5y \leq 15$

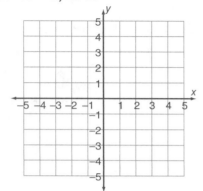

7. $x + 4y > 8$

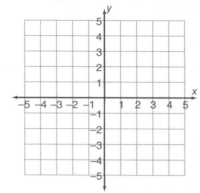

8. $5x + 2y < -2$

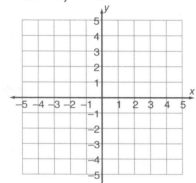

9. $4x - 3y \geq 6$

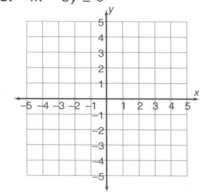

10. $-3y < x + 6$

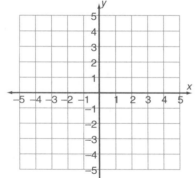

11. $3y > -6$

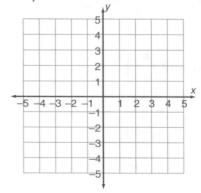

Name_____ Date_____

GRAPHING SITUATIONS

Write the inequality for each problem and graph the result, choosing an appropriate scale. Answer the question about each graph.

1. The ski club is going on a ski trip to Gold Mountain Resort. The lift tickets for students under the age of 17 cost $30; for people age 17 and older, the cost is $40. The ski club has at most $900 to spend on lift tickets. Write an inequality for the possible cost of the lift tickets in which x represents the number of lift tickets for those under age 17 and y represents the number of lift tickets for those age 17 and older.

   _____

2. What might the graph mean?

   _____

   _____

   _____

   _____

   _____

   _____

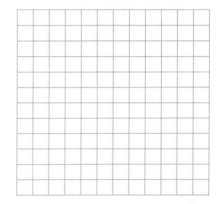

3. The jazz band wants to attend a concert. Tickets cost $40 for general admission and $60 for reserved seating. The jazz band can spend at most $1,000 on the concert. Write an inequality for the possible cost of the tickets in which x represents the number of general admission tickets and y the number of reserved seat tickets.

   _____

4. What might the graph mean?

   _____

   _____

   _____

   _____

   _____

   _____

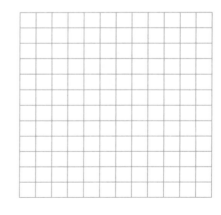

Name_____ Date_____

COMPOUND THE COMPOUND

Graph each system of inequalities.

1. $x > y + 2$ and $x + y \geq 3$ and $5x > y - 5$

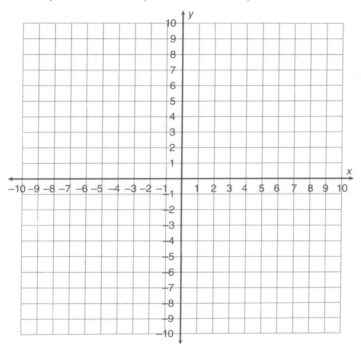

2. $x + 2y \leq 6$ or $y \geq x + 4$ and $y \leq \frac{1}{4}x + 8$

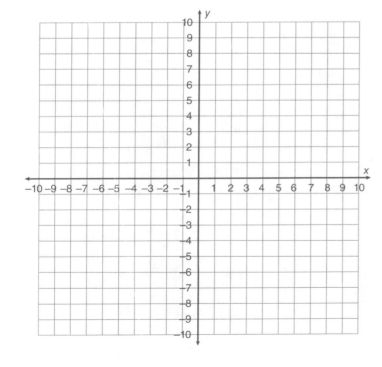

This page intentionally left blank

OBJECTIVE 1

Solve and graph the solution set for each inequality.

1. $x + 6 > 5$ _____

$$\xleftarrow{\quad}\overset{\displaystyle +\,+\,+\,+\,+\,+\,+\,+\,+\,+\,+\,+\,+\,+\,+}{\underset{-7\;-6\;-5\;-4\;-3\;-2\;-1\;\;0\;\;1\;\;2\;\;3\;\;4\;\;5\;\;6\;\;7}{}}\xrightarrow{\quad}$$

2. $3 + y \le 6$ _____

$$\xleftarrow{\quad}\overset{\displaystyle +\,+\,+\,+\,+\,+\,+\,+\,+\,+\,+\,+\,+\,+\,+}{\underset{-7\;-6\;-5\;-4\;-3\;-2\;-1\;\;0\;\;1\;\;2\;\;3\;\;4\;\;5\;\;6\;\;7}{}}\xrightarrow{\quad}$$

3. $x - 2 < -4$ _____

$$\xleftarrow{\quad}\overset{\displaystyle +\,+\,+\,+\,+\,+\,+\,+\,+\,+\,+\,+\,+\,+\,+}{\underset{-7\;-6\;-5\;-4\;-3\;-2\;-1\;\;0\;\;1\;\;2\;\;3\;\;4\;\;5\;\;6\;\;7}{}}\xrightarrow{\quad}$$

4. $n - 3.4 \ge -2.3$ _____

$$\xleftarrow{\quad}\overset{\displaystyle +\,+\,+\,+\,+\,+\,+\,+\,+\,+\,+\,+\,+\,+\,+}{\underset{-7\;-6\;-5\;-4\;-3\;-2\;-1\;\;0\;\;1\;\;2\;\;3\;\;4\;\;5\;\;6\;\;7}{}}\xrightarrow{\quad}$$

OBJECTIVE 2

Solve and graph the solution set for each inequality.

5. $3a > 15$ _____

$$\xleftarrow{\quad}\overset{\displaystyle +\,+\,+\,+\,+\,+\,+\,+\,+\,+\,+\,+\,+\,+\,+}{\underset{-7\;-6\;-5\;-4\;-3\;-2\;-1\;\;0\;\;1\;\;2\;\;3\;\;4\;\;5\;\;6\;\;7}{}}\xrightarrow{\quad}$$

6. $-2x < 6$ _____

$$\xleftarrow{\quad}\overset{\displaystyle +\,+\,+\,+\,+\,+\,+\,+\,+\,+\,+\,+\,+\,+\,+}{\underset{-7\;-6\;-5\;-4\;-3\;-2\;-1\;\;0\;\;1\;\;2\;\;3\;\;4\;\;5\;\;6\;\;7}{}}\xrightarrow{\quad}$$

7. $\frac{n}{-2} < -1$ _____

$$\xleftarrow{\quad}\overset{\displaystyle +\,+\,+\,+\,+\,+\,+\,+\,+\,+\,+\,+\,+\,+\,+}{\underset{-7\;-6\;-5\;-4\;-3\;-2\;-1\;\;0\;\;1\;\;2\;\;3\;\;4\;\;5\;\;6\;\;7}{}}\xrightarrow{\quad}$$

8. $\frac{2}{3}x \ge -2$ _____

$$\xleftarrow{\quad}\overset{\displaystyle +\,+\,+\,+\,+\,+\,+\,+\,+\,+\,+\,+\,+\,+\,+}{\underset{-7\;-6\;-5\;-4\;-3\;-2\;-1\;\;0\;\;1\;\;2\;\;3\;\;4\;\;5\;\;6\;\;7}{}}\xrightarrow{\quad}$$

OBJECTIVE 3

Solve and graph the solution set for each inequality.

9. $2x > 4 + x$ _____

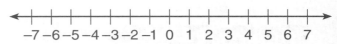

10. $-4x \le 6 - x$ _____

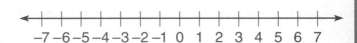

OBJECTIVE 3 *(continued)*

11. $14 - x \geq 9$ _____

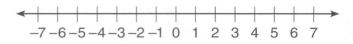

12. $\frac{1}{2}x - 5 \geq x - 3$ _____

OBJECTIVE 4

Solve and graph the solution set for each inequality.

13. $x + 2 > 3$ and $x - 1 < 3$

_____

14. $\frac{x}{2} < -1$ or $4x > 20$

_____

15. $|x| > 3$

_____

16. $6 - x > 5$ and $2x > -12 - x$

_____

OBJECTIVE 5

Graph the linear inequalities on the coordinate planes.

17. $x + y \geq 4$

18. $x < 3 + 2y$

19. $x = y - 3$

20. $2y \geq 3x$

Inside Algebra

Solving Systems of Linear Equations and Inequalities

In this chapter, we use what we know about linear equations and inequalities to graph systems of equations and inequalities. We learn to recognize systems that have no solutions, one solution, or infinite solutions. We also explore different ways to solve systems of equations, and recognize the solution to a system of inequalities.

Objective 1
Solve systems of equations by graphing.

Objective 2
Determine whether a system of equations has one solution, no solutions, or infinitely many solutions.

Objective 3
Solve systems of equations using the substitution method.

Objective 4
Solve systems of equations by eliminating one variable.

Objective 5
Solve systems of inequalities by graphing.

Chapter 7
VOCABULARY

consistent A system of equations that is always true

$$2x - y = 3$$
$$\underline{4x - 2y = 6}$$
$$0 = 0$$

---

elimination Removing one variable from a system of equations by adding or subtracting like terms with the same coefficients

$$x + 2y = 8 \qquad -3 + 2y = 8$$
$$\underline{-2x - 2y = -5} \qquad y = \frac{11}{2}$$
$$-x + 0 = 3$$
$$x = -3$$

---

inconsistent A system of equations that is never true

$$3x - 2y = 0$$
$$\underline{3x - 2y = -2}$$
$$0 = -2$$

substitution Removing one variable from a system of equations by rewriting the system in terms of the other variable

$$x = 2y + 8 \text{ and } 2x + 2y = 4$$
$$2(2y + 8) + 2y = 4$$
$$4y + 16 + 2y = 4$$
$$6y = -12 \qquad x = 2(-2) + 8$$
$$y = -2 \qquad x = 4$$

---

system of equations A set of two or more equations that use the same variables

$$y = 2x - 3 \text{ and } 3y + 6 = x$$

---

system of inequalities A set of two or more linear inequalities that use the same variables

$$y \leq 2x - 3 \text{ and } 3y + 6 \leq x$$

Name_____ Date_____

APPLY SKILLS 1

- Graph each system of equations by either using an *x/y* table of values and plotting the corresponding ordered pairs or by using the slope/*y*-intercept form of the equations.

- Determine the point of intersection of the system.

- Verify that the point of intersection is a solution to the system by substituting the ordered pair back into both equations and determining that both equations form true statements.

Example:

$y = 3x - 3$
$y = -x + 5$

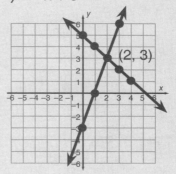

(2, 3)

Intersection at (2, 3)

$y = 3x - 3$	$y = -x + 5$
$3 = 3(2) - 3$	$3 = -(2) + 5$
$3 = 3$	$3 = 3$

1. $y = 3x - 1$
  $y = -2x + 4$

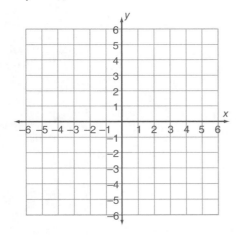

_____

2. $x - 3y = -9$
  $2x + y = -4$

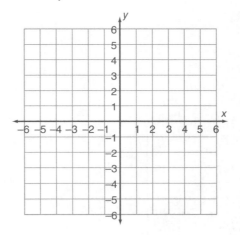

_____

APPLY SKILLS 1 (*continued*)

3. $2x - y = 9$
$x + y = 3$

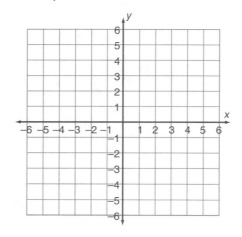

4. $y = 4x - 1$
$y = -2x - 7$

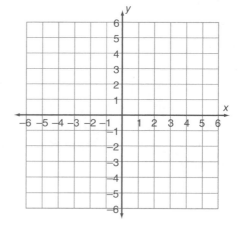

5. $y = x + 3$
$x + y = 1$

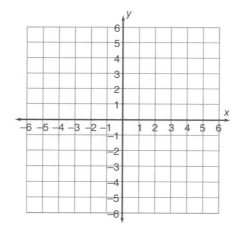

6. $2x + y = -2$
$y = x + 7$

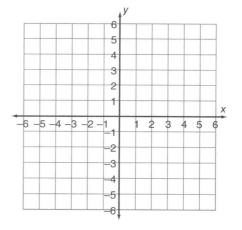

Name _____ **Date** _____

APPLY SKILLS 2

- Graph each system of equations by either using an x/y table of values and plotting the corresponding ordered pairs or by using the slope/y-intercept form of the equations.

- Determine the point of intersection of the system.

- Verify that the point of intersection is a solution to the system by substituting the ordered pair back into both equations and determining that both equations form true statements.

Example:

$x + 2y = 4$
$2x - y = -2$

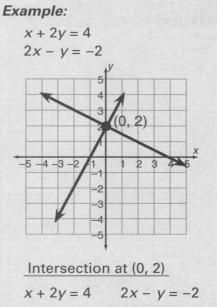

Intersection at (0, 2)

$x + 2y = 4$	$2x - y = -2$
$0 + 2(2) = 4$	$2(0) - 2 = -2$
$4 = 4$	$-2 = -2$

1. $y = 2x + 1$
$y = -x + 4$

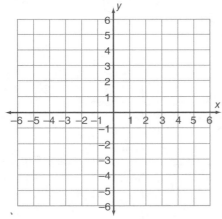

_____

2. $x - 3y = 6$
$x + y = 2$

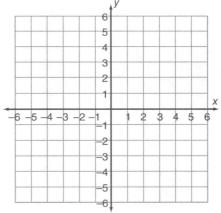

_____

APPLY SKILLS 2 (*continued*)

3. $x - 1 = y$
$4x + 2 = y$

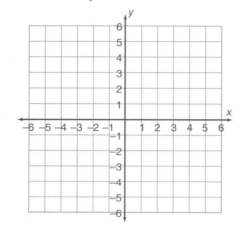

_____

4. $y = 2x - 3$
$x + 3y = 12$

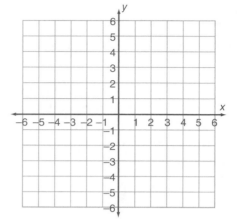

_____

5. $y = \frac{1}{2}x - 3$
$x + y = 3$

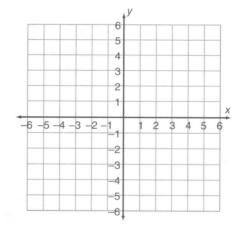

_____

6. $y = 2x$
$y + 4x = 3$

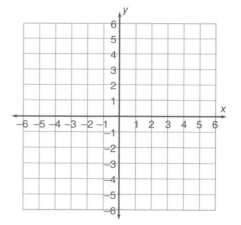

_____

COMPARING EARNINGS

Graph both of the income equations on the graph below and determine their point of intersection.

- Suppose you have a job that pays $12 for travel expenses plus $8 per hour worked. Your potential income can be calculated by the equation:
Income = $8 • (number of hours worked) + $12, or $y = 8x + 12$.

- Now suppose your best friend has a job that pays $6 for travel expenses plus $10 per hour worked. That potential income can be calculated by the equation:
Income = $10 • (number of hours worked) + $6, or $y = 10x + 6$.

You may construct the graphs by completing x/y tables or by using the slope/y-intercept method.

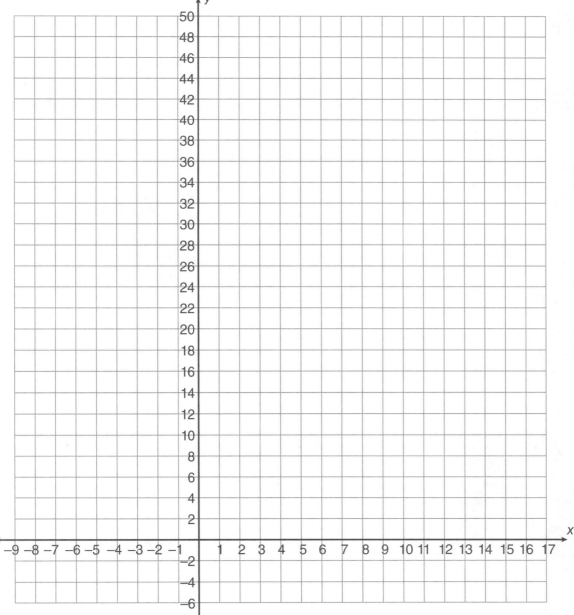

COMPARING EARNINGS *(continued)*

Answer the questions based on your graph.

1. How many hours would both you and your best friend work for both of you to receive the same amount of income?

   _____

2. Who makes more money after the first two hours of work?

   _____

3. Who makes more money after the first four hours of work?

   _____

4. If you are going to work 15 hours per week, which pay schedule would you prefer? Why?

   _____

   _____

Name _____   Date _____

APPLY SKILLS 1

Make a table of values and construct the graph to determine the number of solutions for each system of equations. Write each equation in slope/*y*-intercept form and compare the equations to the graphs.

Example:

$y = -2x + 3$

x	y
−1	5
0	3
1	1
$1\frac{1}{2}$	0

$y = x + 6$

x	y
−6	0
−1	5
0	6
1	7

one solution

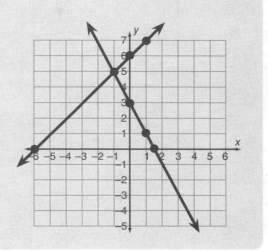

1. $y = 3x - 1$ $y = 2x + 3$

x	y

x	y

_____

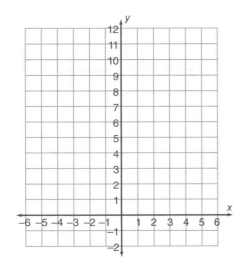

2. $y = -4x + 2$ $4x + y = 6$

x	y

x	y

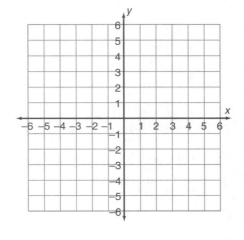

Inside Algebra

Name_____ Date_____

APPLY SKILLS 1 (continued)

3. $4x - 2y = 8$ $2x - y = 4$

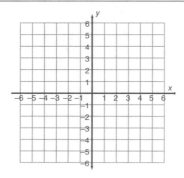

4. $6x + 6y = 18$ $-4x + 2y = 8$

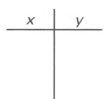

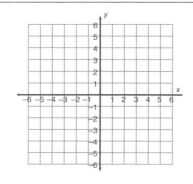

5. $y - 2x = 4$ $4x = 2y + 10$

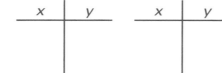

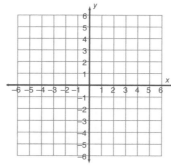

6. $x + y = 5$ $x - y = 7$

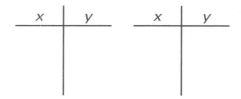

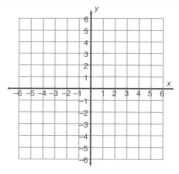

7. What do you notice about the graphs and the equations in the slope/y-intercept form?

_____

_____

_____

_____

APPLY SKILLS 2

Determine how many solutions each system of equations will have. You may use graph paper if you wish.

Example:

$y = 3x + 4$

$-12x + 4y = 8$

___no solution___

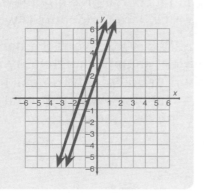

1. $y = 2x + 4$
$y = 3x - 2$

_____

2. $x + y = 3$
$2x + y = 6$

_____

3. $x = 4 - y$
$x + y = 2$

_____

4. $2x - y = 4$
$2y + 8 = 4x$

_____

5. $y = 3x + 1$
$2y - 3x = 4$

_____

6. $x = 2y + 6$
$4y = 2x + 6$

_____

7. $y = 2x + 3$
$y = -x - 6$

_____

8. $x + y = 4$
$y = 3 - x$

_____

9. $2x + y = 3$
$2y = 6 - 4x$

_____

SAILING SHIPS

Solve the problem using a system of equations and graph the solutions.

Two ships are sailing in the same area. Ship A is following a course given by the equation $y = x + 8$. Ship B is following a course given by the equation $y = 2x - 2$. The danger spot for these two ships is where their courses would intersect.

Both ships are heading northeast. Ship B will arrive at the danger point first, but to be safe, it makes a 90° turn (right angle) counterclockwise at the point of intersection. Ship B travels for a short period of time on this new course before it returns to its original path along the course $y = 2x - 2$. Find an equation that represents the course for Ship B during the time it is forced to change direction.

_____

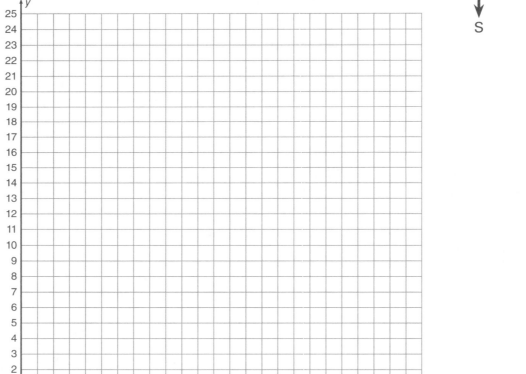

Name_____ **Date**_____

SOLVING PROBLEMS USING SYSTEMS OF EQUATIONS

For each problem, determine the pairs of integers that satisfy both of the conditions. Graph the equations to determine if there is one solution, there are infinite solutions, or there are no solutions. Then answer Problem 4.

1. The sum of 4 times the first number, x, and 2 times the second number, y, is 12.

When 3 times the second number, y, is subtracted from 6 times the first number, x, the result is 12.

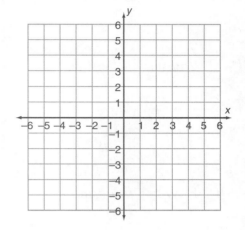

_____

2. The sum of 8 times the first number, x, and 2 times the second number, y, is 16.

When the second number, y, is added to 4 times the first number, x, the result is 8.

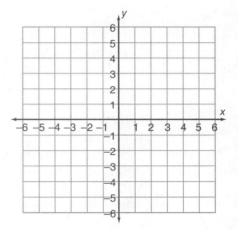

_____

Inside Algebra   **Chapter 7 • Objective 2 • PS 2**   **263**

Name_____ Date_____

SOLVING PROBLEMS USING SYSTEMS OF EQUATIONS
(continued)

3. The sum of 6 times the first number, x, and 3 times the second number, y, is 18.

   When the second number, y, is added to 2 times the first number, x, the result is 4.

   _____

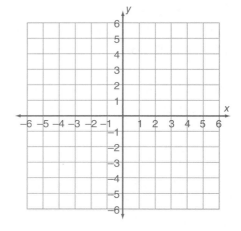

4. How can you tell the number of solutions without constructing a graph?

   _____

   _____

   _____

   _____

   _____

Name_____ Date_____

THE ALGEBRA ALPHABET

Follow the steps below to solve Problems 1–4.

Step 1: Substitute the numerical values below into the equation and write the equation in numerical form.

Step 2: Simplify both sides of the equation.

Step 3: Determine if each comparison is true or false.

$A = 1 + 4$	$B = 2 + 7$	$C = -3 + 4$	$D = -1 + 6$
$E = 4 - (-3)$	$F = 10 - 7$	$G = 9 - 1$	$H = 4 + 2$
$I = 6 + 8$	$J = -6 + (-4)$	$K = (-1) \cdot (-5)$	$L = \frac{16}{2}$
$M = 2 \cdot 7$	$N = \frac{18}{3}$	$O = 5 \cdot (-2)$	$P = (-1) \cdot (-7)$
$Q = 3 \cdot 3$	$R = \frac{12}{12}$	$S = \frac{27}{3}$	

> **Example:**
>
> Given: $Q = S$
>
> $3 \cdot 3 = \frac{27}{3}$
>
> $9 = 9$ true

1. Given: $A = B$

2. Given: $D = A$

3. Given: $E = P$

4. Given: $G = R$

Use the equations above to create two comparisons that are true.
Prove your answer.

5. Given: _____

6. Given: _____

Use the equations above to create two comparisons that are false.
Prove your answer.

7. Given: _____

8. Given: _____

APPLY SKILLS 1

Solve.

WORK SPACE

1. Given $x = 2y - 3$, substitute 4 for y and solve for x. _____

2. Given $x = 6y + 1$, substitute -2 for y and solve for x. _____

3. Given $x - 3 + y = 2x$, substitute 4 for x and solve for y. _____

4. Given $2x + y = 6$, substitute x for y and solve for x. *Note:* This is the same as having two equations, $2x + y = 6$ and $y = x$. _____

5. Given $x - 2y = -1$, substitute $y + 1$ for x and solve for both y and x. *Note:* This is the same as having two equations, $x - 2y = -1$ and $x = y + 1$. Substitute $y + 1$ for x and solve for y _____; then use this value of y in $x - 2y = -1$ and solve for x. _____

6. If $x + y = 4$ and $x = y - 2$, solve for x and y. *Note:* In the equation $x + y = 4$, substitute $y - 2$ for x and solve for y _____; then use this value of y in $x = y - 2$ and solve for x. _____

7. If $x + 2y = 3$ and $x = 2 - y$, solve for x and y. _____ _____

8. If $y = 3 + x$ and $2x + y = 0$, solve for x and y. _____ _____

APPLY SKILLS 2

Follow the steps below for each system of equations.

Step 1: Tell whether it would be easier to isolate a variable in equation a or b.

Step 2: Tell whether equation c shows the correct substitution.

Step 3: Now, solve each system for x and y. If the substitution was done incorrectly, correct it and solve for x and y.

Example:

   a. $3x + y = 4$
   b. $x = y - 4$
   c. $3(y - 4) + y = 4$
   _____b, yes_____

   $3y - 12 + y = 4$
   $\qquad\qquad 4y = 16$

   $y = 4,\ x = 0$

---

1. a. $2x + y = 4$
  b. $y = x + 7$
  c. $2x + (x + 7) = 4$
  _____

2. a. $x = 2y - 3$
  b. $x - y = 6$
  c. $x - (2y - 3) = 6$
  _____

3. a. $x = y + 4$
  b. $y + x = 7$
  c. $y + (y + 4) = 7$
  _____

4. a. $2x = 2y - 3$
  b. $y = 6 + x$
  c. $2x = 2(6 + x) - 3$
  _____

5. a. $2x + 5 = y$
  b. $-3 = x + y$
  c. $2x + 5 = -3$
  _____

6. a. $2x - 3 = y$
  b. $y = 3x + 6$
  c. $2x - 3 = 3x + 6$
  _____

APPLY SKILLS 3

Solve each system of equations by the substitution method.

Example:

$y = x - 4$

$x + y = 6$ (5, 1)

$x + (x - 4) = 6$

$2x - 4 = 6$

$2x = 10$

$x = 5$

$y = 5 - 4$

$y = 1$

1. $2y - 4 = x$

    $x + y = 2$ _____

2. $y + x = 5$

    $y = x + 10$ _____

3. $y + x = 5$

    $x = y - 3$ _____

4. $y = x - 4$

    $y = 6$ _____

5. $x + 2 = y$

    $x + 3y = -2$ _____

6. $y = 3x - 4$

    $x + y = 8$ _____

7. $4x - 3 = y$

    $x + 6 = y$ _____

8. $x = -7$

    $2x + y = 6$ _____

APPLY SKILLS 4

Solve each system of equations by the substitution method.

Example:

$y = x + 4$
$x + y = 6$ ___(1, 5)___

$x + (x + 4) = 6$
$2x + 4 = 6$
$2x = 2$
$x = 1$

$y = 1 + 4$
$y = 5$

1. $2y + 4 = x$
$x - y = 2$ _____

2. $x + 5 = y$
$2x + y = -10$ _____

3. $x + y = 5$
$x = y + 3$ _____

4. $y + x = 4$
$x = 6$ _____

5. $x = y - 1$
$2x + y = 7$ _____

6. $y = 2x - 4$
$x + y = 8$ _____

7. $3x - 3 = y$
$x + 7 = y$ _____

8. $y = 3$
$2x + y = -5$ _____

Name_____ Date_____

MATCHING EQUATIONS

Given equations A through D, use the process of substitution to answer the questions.

A. $y = -3x + 4$ **B.** $y = 2x + 3$ **C.** $y = -3x + 2$ **D.** $-2x + y = 3$

1. Which two equations form a system with exactly one solution? What is the solution?

_____

_____

2. Which two equations form a system that has no solution?

_____

3. Which two equations form a system that has infinite solutions?

_____

4. How did you make decisions for Problems 1, 2, and 3? Write your answer in complete sentences.

_____

_____

_____

_____

_____

_____

_____

Name_____ Date_____

COMPARING EARNINGS

Solve the problems using a system of equations.

Carrie and Cooper are working at the same store selling sporting goods. They have options on earning their salaries. Carrie chose to get paid by straight commission, which is 25% of all her sales per month. The amount (A) that she earns is therefore 0.25 of sales (s), or $A = 0.25s$.

Cooper decided to get paid by having a salary of $600 per month plus 10% of his sales. The amount (A) that he earns is $600 plus 0.10 of sales ($s$), or $A = 600 + 0.10s$.

1. If each of them had $3,000 in sales for one month, who will earn more that month? How much would each earn?

    _____

    _____

    _____

2. If each person had $6,000 in sales for one month, who will earn more that month? How much would each earn?

    _____

    _____

    _____

3. Solve the system of equations by substitution. What does this solution represent?

    _____

    _____

MATCHING

Match the given system to the equation that results when the elimination method is used properly. Write the correct letter next to the matching system.

Systems

1. $x + 3y = 4$
$-x + 4y = 10$ _____

2. $3x - 2y = 6$
$-3x + 6y = 2$ _____

3. $2x + 4y = 8$
$4x - 4y = 10$ _____

4. $-2x - 6y = 4$
$8x + 6y = -16$ _____

5. $-3x - y = 12$
$3x + 5y = 8$ _____

6. $5x - 3y = 2$
$7x - 3y = 12$ _____

7. $11x + y = 14$
$11x + 3y = -2$ _____

8. $14x + 2y = 6$
$14x - y = -3$ _____

9. $4x + y = -10$
$x + y = 2$ _____

10. $x - 7y = -6$
$4x + 7y = -4$ _____

Resulting Equations

a. $-2y = 16$

b. $5x = -10$

c. $4y = 20$

d. $3y = 9$

e. $3x = -12$

f. $2x = 10$

g. $7y = 14$

h. $6x = -12$

i. $6x = 18$

j. $4y = 8$

TIC-TAC-TOE

Find a partner. On your turn, select a square and prove whether the system of equations has zero, one, or infinitely many solutions. If you are correct, place a marker on that square. The first player with three markers in a row wins.

1.

$x + y = 9$ $2x - y = 15$	$x + y = 4$ $-x - y = 1$	$x - y = 3$ $2x - 2y = 6$
$x + y = -4$ $-2x + y = 14$	$x + y = 5$ $-x + y = -3$	$3x - 2y = 4$ $4x + 2y = 10$
$2x + 3y = 5$ $5x + 4y = 16$	$4x + 2y = 12$ $3x - 12y = -18$	$x + y = 9$ $-2x - 2y = -18$

2.

$2x - y = 2$ $x + y = 4$	$x - y = -3$ $3x + y = 3$	$2x + y = 9$ $x - y = 9$
$x + 2y = 7$ $2x + y = 2$	$x + y = -1$ $2x + 3y = 0$	$x + 3y = 1$ $2x - y = -12$
$2x + y = 7$ $2x + y = 3$	$5x + 2y = 11$ $2x - 3y = -7$	$3x + y = 13$ $x - 2y = -12$

Name_____ Date_____

TIC-TAC-TOE (*continued*)

3.

$x - y = 0$ $2x - y = 1$	$2x + 3y = 9$ $x + 2y = 6$	$x - 2y = 0$ $2x + y = 5$
$x + 5y = 23$ $3x - y = 5$	$x - 2y = 8$ $2x - 4y = 16$	$4x - 3y = -2$ $2x + y = -16$
$x - 6y = 13$ $3x + y = 20$	$6x - 4y = -2$ $5x + 2y = 9$	$2x + y = 11$ $x - 2y = 18$

4.

$x + 2y = 12$ $2x - 3y = -4$	$5x + 2y = -9$ $3x + y = -5$	$x - y = 7$ $-2x + 2y = 13$
$2x - 3y = 9$ $3x + y = -3$	$2x + 5y = 67$ $3x - 2y = 15$	$x + 3y = 3$ $3x - 3y = -27$
$2x + 3y = 2$ $3x - 2y = 16$	$5x + 4y = 0$ $2x - 3y = 0$	$x + 5y = -7$ $3x + y = 7$

APPLY SKILLS 1

Solve the systems of equations using the elimination method.

Example:

$$4x + 2y = 12$$
$$\underline{-4x + 1y = -6}$$
$$3y = 6$$

$$y = 2,\ x = 2$$

1. $\quad x - 4y = 1$
$\quad\ -x - y = -6$

2. $\quad x + y = 6$
$\quad\ x - 2y = 3$

3. $\ 2x + 7y = 4$
$\quad 3x - 7y = 6$

4. $\ -3x + 5y = 15$
$\quad\ \ 3x - 5y = 30$

5. $\quad 2x - 7y = 28$
$\quad -2x + 7y = -28$

6. $\quad 4x + 3y = 9$
$\quad -4x - 3y = 4$

7. $\quad x - y = 10$
$\quad 3x + y = 2$

8. $\ 4x + 8y = 9$
$\quad 9x - 8y = 17$

Name_____ Date_____

APPLY SKILLS 1 (*continued*)

9. $-2x + 3y = 5$
$2x - 9y = 1$

10. $x + 2y = 7$
$2x + \ y = 8$

11. $x + y = 3$
$2x + y = 7$

12. $x - 2y = 4$
$2x + 2y = 8$

13. $3x - 4y = \ 5$
$-3x + 4y = -5$

14. $x - 4y = 8$
$-x + \ y = 1$

Name_____ Date_____

APPLY SKILLS 2

Solve the systems of equations using the elimination method.

Example:

$$2x - 3y = 24$$
$$x - 5y = -2$$

$$2x - 3y = 24$$
$$\underline{-2x + 10y = \quad 4}$$
$$7y = 28$$

$$y = 4, \ x = 18$$

1. $\quad 4x + 2y = 12$
$\quad\quad 3y - 12x = -18$

2. $2x + y = -2$
$\quad\ 2x + 4y = 10$

3. $3x + 5y = 8$
$\quad\ 3x + 2y = -1$

4. $\quad 3x - 12y = 3$
$\quad\ -2y - 2x = -12$

5. $5x + 3y = 10$
$\quad\ 2x - 2y = 4$

6. $2x - 4y = 8$
$\quad\ x - 3y = 2$

7. $-3x + 5y = -30$
$\quad\ 9x - 15y = 90$

8. $\quad 2x - 7y = 10$
$\quad\ -4x + 14y = -28$

APPLY SKILLS 2 (*continued*)

9. $x + 5y = 3$
$4x + 14y = 6$

10. $x - y = 10$
$3x + 2y = 5$

11. $2x + 8y = 32$
$6x - 4y = 12$

12. $-3x + 2y = 12$
$3x - 4y = -18$

13. $3x + y = -1$
$x - 2y = -5$

14. $y - 2x = -3$
$x - 2y = -3$

ELIMINATING A VARIABLE

Use elimination of a variable to determine whether there is an ordered pair of integers that satisfies all the conditions in each problem, whether there is no solution, or whether there are infinitely many solutions.

1. The sum of the first number, x, and 2 times the second number, y, is 12.

    When 2 times the second number, y, is subtracted from 3 times the first number, x, the result is 12.

    _____

2. The sum of 8 times the first number, x, and 2 times the second number, y, is 28.

    When the second number, y, is subtracted from 4 times the first number, x, the result is 10.

    _____

3. The sum of the first number, x, and 3 times the second number, y, is 3.

    When 3 times the second number, y, is subtracted from 5 times the first number, x, the result is 15.

    _____

PROBLEM SOLVING

Name_____ Date_____

HOW MANY MEN AND HOW MANY WOMEN?

1. Read the situation, and write a system of equations from the information given. One equation should be based on the number of employees, and one equation should be based on the cost of the food. *Hint:* Items with similar labels (e.g., cost) probably belong together in a single equation.

    Situation: During the past quarter, a manufacturing company earned more profit than the company owner expected. To thank the employees for their hard work, he planned a barbeque. The owner determined that he had around $320 to spend on food, and according to the catering company, the average cost per person would be around $8 per male and $4 per female. The party would be given for all 50 employees of the company. Determine the number of male and female employees.

2. Solve the problem presented by eliminating a variable in the system of equations. Then determine how many employees are male and how many are female.

_____

GRAPH INEQUALITIES

1. Graph the points. Next to each coordinate, tell whether it satisfies the system of inequalities by writing "yes" if it does and "no" if it does not. Then answer the question.

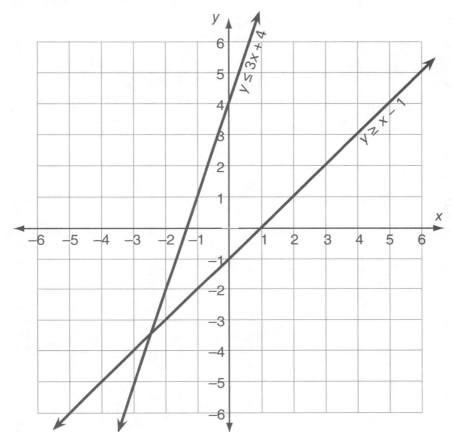

A. (0, 3) _____   B. (−1, −1) _____   C. (1, −1) _____

D. (2, 2) _____   E. (1, 3) _____   F. (−1, 2) _____

G. (3, 4) _____   H. (1, 4) _____   I. (−3, −5) _____

J. (4, 4) _____   K. (0, −2) _____   L. (−1, 1) _____

M. (−1, 0) _____   N. (2, 5) _____   O. (3, 6) _____

P. (−3, −1) _____

2. Do you notice a pattern? Explain.

_____

_____

_____

Name_____ Date_____

GRAPHS

Answer the questions about the graphs.

A.

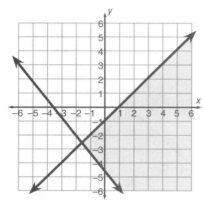

B.

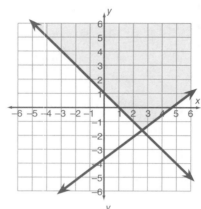

C.

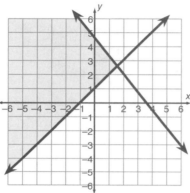

D.

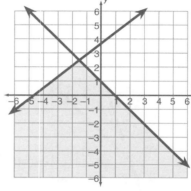

E.

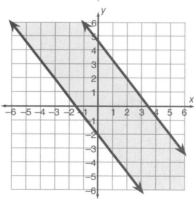

F.

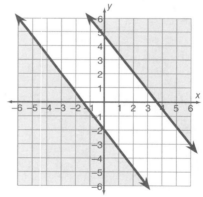

1. Which graphs contain the following points in the solution region?

   (2, 4) _____   (3, −1) _____   (5, 2) _____

   Which graphs contain all three points in the solution region? _____

2. Which graphs contain all three points in the solution region?

   (−1, −3), (3, 0), (4, −5) _____   (0, −3), (−3, 0), (−4, −2) _____

   (−6, −3), (0, −2), (4, 6) _____   (−5, 6), (0, 0), (3, −3) _____

   (1, 2.5), (−4, −1), (−2, 3) _____

APPLY SKILLS 1

Graph the solution for each system of inequalities using the steps.

Step 1: Graph the lines. Think about if the lines should be solid or dashed.

Step 2: Try some points in each region to identify the region of the graph where both inequalities are true.

Step 3: Shade the region where the values are true.

1. Solve $x + y > 2$ and $y < x + 3$.

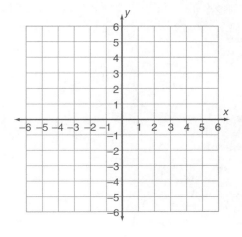

2. Solve $y < 2x - 3$ and $x + y < 5$.

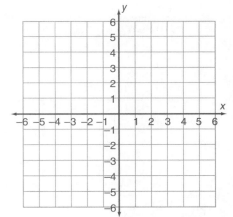

3. Solve $y \leq 4 + x$ and $2x + y < 6$.

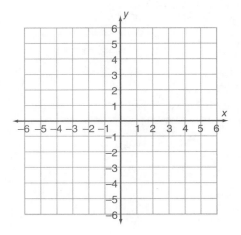

APPLY SKILLS 2

Find the region of points that satisfy the systems of inequalities by graphing them.

Example:

$2x + y > -1$
$-x + y \leq 4$

$2x + y > -1$ $-x + y \leq 4$
$y > -2x - 1$ $y \leq x + 4$

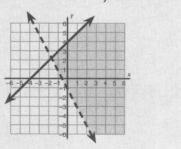

1. $y < x - 2$
    $2x + y \geq 1$

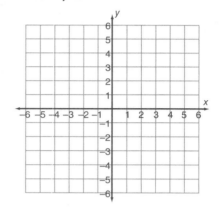

2. $x + y < 3$
    $y \geq 2x - 4$

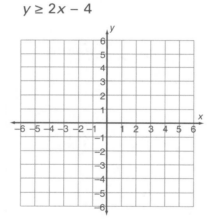

3. $4x + y > 1$
    $-3x + y > -2$

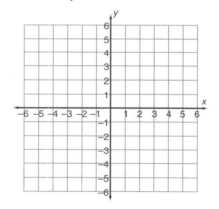

4. $y < -\frac{1}{2}x + 3$
    $y \leq 2x + 5$

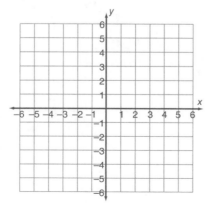

5. $y \geq 5x - 4$
    $y < -x + 1$

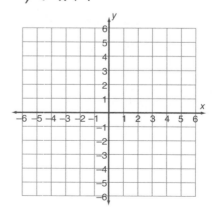

APPLY SKILLS 3

Find the region of points that satisfies each system of inequalities by graphing them.

Example:

$-3x + y > 2$
$y < -x + 3$

$-3x + y > 2$ $y < -x + 3$
$y > 3x + 2$

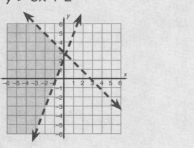

1. $-x + y < -3$
   $4x + y \geq 1$

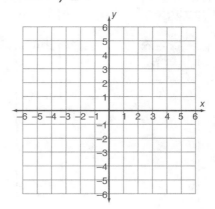

2. $y < -x + 2$
   $-2x + y \geq -3$

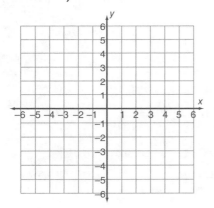

3. $3x + y > 1$
   $y > 4x - 2$

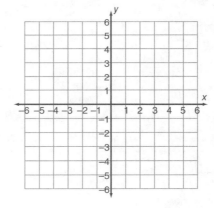

4. $y < -\frac{1}{3}x + 1$
   $y \leq 2x - 4$

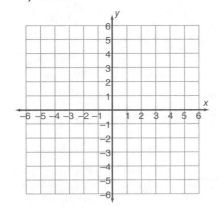

5. $y \geq -x - 4$
   $y < -x + 2$

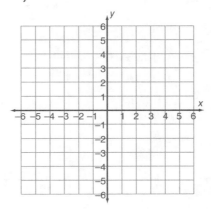

Name_____ Date_____

SATISFYING COMBINATIONS

A street vendor who sells ice cream cones uses inequalities to understand profit and loss. The inequality $y \geq \frac{1}{2}x + 6$ describes the vendor's expenses, or costs of doing business, and the inequality $y \geq 2x$ represents the income from sales for each cone. In each case, x represents the number of cones sold.

Complete the tables for cost and income.

1. Cost: $y \geq \frac{1}{2}x + 6$

x	$\frac{1}{2}x + 6$

2. Income: $y \geq 2x$

x	$2x$

Graph both inequalities below.

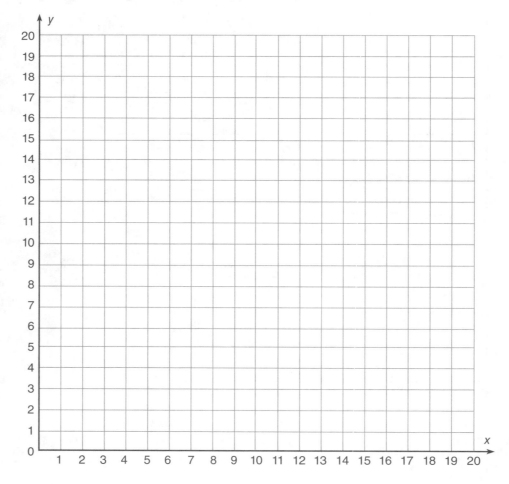

Name_____ Date_____

OBJECTIVE 1

Solve each system of equations by graphing.
Name the intersecting points.

1. $x + y = -2$
$y = 2x - 5$

_____

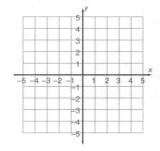

2. $2x + y = -1$
$x + 3y = 7$

_____

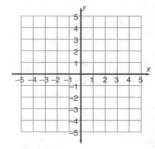

3. $x - y = 2$
$4x + y = -2$

_____

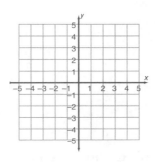

4. $y = 3x - 4$
$x + 2y = 6$

_____

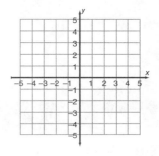

OBJECTIVE 2

Determine whether each system of equations has one solution, no solutions, or infinitely many solutions. A coordinate graph has been provided for you, but you are not required to use it.

5. $2x - y = 2$
$2y = 4x - 4$

_____

_____

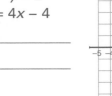

6. $y = 2x - 1$
$x + 3y = 4$

_____

_____

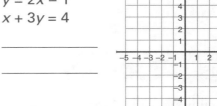

7. $x + 2y = 1$
$y = 2x - 7$

_____

_____

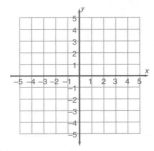

8. $y + 2x = 4$
$2y = 14 - 4x$

_____

_____

OBJECTIVE 3

Solve each system of equations using the substitution method.

9. $x = 8 - y$
   $2y = x + 7$

10. $x + y = 3$
   $2x + 4 = y - 2$

11. $x = 4 - y$
   $x + 2y = 2$

OBJECTIVE 4

Solve each system of equations by eliminating one variable.

12. $2x = y - 1$
   $y - x = 3$

13. $2x + 3y = -4$
   $3x - 2y = 7$

OBJECTIVE 5

Solve each system of inequalities by graphing.

14. $x > 2y - 3$
   $y > 2x + 1$

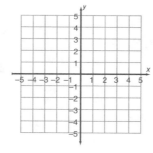

15. $x + 2y < 6$
   $y > x - 3$

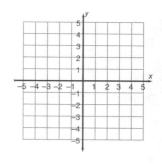

Inside Algebra

Exploring Polynomials

In this chapter, we begin to learn about polynomials by looking at monomials and binomials. We use scientific notation to understand exponents and to introduce binomials. We also combine like terms to add and subtract polynomials, and multiply and divide monomials and binomials.

Objective 1
Multiply and divide monomials and simplify expressions.

Objective 2
Write numbers in scientific notation and find products and quotients of these numbers.

Objective 3
Add and subtract polynomials and express the answer so the powers of the terms are in descending order.

Objective 4
Multiply a polynomial by a monomial and arrange the terms in descending order by powers.

Objective 5
Multiply two binomials and simplify the expressions, including special products of $(a + b)(a + b)$ and $(a + b)(a - b)$.

Chapter 8
VOCABULARY

binomial An expression with two terms

$10 + 6$ or $x - 7$

---

descending order Arranged from largest to smallest; decreasing

98, 87, 52, 31, 16, 4

$2x^5, 2x^3, 7x, 10$

---

exponent The power to which some other quantity is raised

In x^y the exponent is y.

---

like terms Terms that have the same variables and exponents

x^2 and $2x^2$ or $6y$ and $3y$

monomial An expression with only one term

24 or x

---

polynomial An expression with two or more unlike terms

$x^2 + 6x - 7$

---

scientific notation A form of writing numbers as the product of a power of 10 and a decimal number greater than or equal to one and less than 10

2.5×10^4

---

standard notation A form of writing numbers with one digit for each place value

1,238,090

Name _____ Date _____

POWERS

Use your calculator to complete the problems.

1. $5^2 \cdot 5 = (5 \cdot 5) \cdot 5 = $ _____

2. $5^3 \cdot 5^2 = (5 \cdot 5 \cdot 5) \cdot (5 \cdot 5) = $ _____

3. $5^3 \cdot 5^2 \cdot 5 = (5 \cdot 5 \cdot 5) \cdot (5 \cdot 5) \cdot 5 = $ _____

4. $5^4 \cdot 5^2 = (5 \cdot 5 \cdot 5 \cdot 5) \cdot (5 \cdot 5) = $ _____

5. How many times did you use 5 as a factor in Problem 1? _____

6. How many times did you use 5 as a factor in Problem 2? _____

7. How many times did you use 5 as a factor in Problem 3? _____

8. How many times did you use 5 as a factor in Problem 4? _____

9. Use the information in Problems 1–4 to complete the chart.

Problem	Add the exponents on the 5s
1	2 + 1 = _____
2	3 + 2 = _____
3	3 + _____ + _____ = _____
4	_____ + _____ = _____

10. How did your answers to Problem 9 compare with your answers to Problems 5, 6, 7, and 8?

    _____

    _____

11. If you had to calculate $5^3 \cdot 5^2 \cdot 5^4$, how many 5s would you be multiplying?

    _____

12. If you had to calculate $5 \cdot 5^2 \cdot 5^3 \cdot 5^4$, how many 5s would you be multiplying?

    _____ How did you decide how many you would use?

    _____

POWERS (*continued*)

13. Could you calculate Problems 1, 2, 3, and 4 by pushing only four buttons for each problem? _____ What buttons did you push?

_____

_____

14. Use your idea from Problem 12 to find $5^3 \cdot 5^3 \cdot 5^2 \cdot 5$. _____

15. Use your calculator to find $2^3 \cdot 3^2 \cdot 2^2$ by calculating $2 \cdot 2 \cdot 2 \cdot 3 \cdot 3 \cdot 2 \cdot 2$.

_____

16. In Problem 15, how many times did you use the 2 as a factor? _____ The 3? _____

17. Could you use your idea from Problem 12 to find $2^3 \cdot 3^2 \cdot 2^4 \cdot 3$? _____ What would you do?

_____

18. $x^3 \cdot x^2 = x \cdot x \cdot x \cdot x \cdot x = x^?$ _____ Could you use your idea from Problem 12? _____ If so, how would you do it?

_____

19. If you wanted to simplify $x^2 \cdot y^3 \cdot x^2 \cdot y$, could you use your idea from Problem 12? _____ How would you do it?

_____

_____

What is the simplified result? _____

20. Simplify $(a^2 b)(a^3 b^4)$. _____

Name _____ Date _____

DIVIDING MONOMIALS

Solve the problems involving monomials.

1. $\dfrac{2^2}{2} = \dfrac{2 \cdot 2}{2} =$ _____

2. $\dfrac{2^3}{2^2} = \dfrac{2 \cdot 2 \cdot 2}{2 \cdot 2} =$ _____

3. $\dfrac{2^2 \cdot 2^3}{2^4} = \dfrac{2 \cdot 2 \cdot 2 \cdot 2 \cdot 2}{2 \cdot 2 \cdot 2 \cdot 2} =$ _____

4. $\dfrac{2^4 \cdot 2}{2^2 \cdot 2^3} = \dfrac{2 \cdot 2 \cdot 2 \cdot 2 \cdot 2}{2 \cdot 2 \cdot 2 \cdot 2 \cdot 2} =$ _____

5. How many 2s are in the numerator in Problem 3? _____ How many 2s are in the denominator? _____ How many 2s are in the result? _____

6. Complete the table using the information from Problems 1–4.

	Number of 2s in numerator	Number of 2s in denominator	Number of 2s in answer
Problem 1	_____	_____	_____
Problem 2	_____	_____	_____
Problem 3	_____	_____	_____
Problem 4	_____	_____	_____

7. How many 2s are in the answer for $\dfrac{2^9}{2^5}$? _____ How many 2s in $\dfrac{2^5}{2^2}$? _____

   What rule could you make to follow when dividing monomials?

   _____

   _____

   Does this rule work for Problem 6? _____

8. Simplify $\dfrac{2^2 \cdot 3^3}{2 \cdot 3^2}$. _____ Would using your rule provide correct results?

   _____ How did you apply it? _____

   _____

9. If $\dfrac{y^3}{y^2} = \dfrac{y \cdot y \cdot y}{y \cdot y}$, would using your rule provide the same result? _____

10. Use your rule to simplify $\dfrac{a^3 \cdot b^5}{ab^2}$. _____

    What did you do? _____

11. How would you use your rule to simplify $\dfrac{2^3 x^2 y^5}{2^2 xy^3}$? _____

    _____ What was the result? _____

DIVIDING MONOMIALS (*continued*)

Simplify.

Hint: For Problems 15 and 16, use the rules for multiplying monomials by simplifying the numerator first, then simplifying the denominator. Use your rule for dividing monomials.

12. $\dfrac{6x^5y^4}{3x^2y^4} =$ _____

13. $\dfrac{-6x^2}{3x} =$ _____

14. $\dfrac{-2x^3}{-10x} =$ _____

15. $\dfrac{(2x^2)(3y^4)}{(2x)(3xy)} =$ _____

16. $\dfrac{(-4xy^2)(-2xy^4)}{3xy^2} =$ _____

APPLY SKILLS 1

Solve the problems involving monomials.

> *Example:*
> $(3^2 \cdot 5)(3 \cdot 5^2) = (3^2 \cdot 3^1)(5^1 \cdot 5^2) = (3^{2+1})(5^{1+2}) = 3^3 \cdot 5^3 = \underline{3,375}$

1. $(3^2 \cdot 5^3)(3 \cdot 5) = (3^2 \cdot 5^3)(3^1 \cdot 5^1) = (3^2 \cdot 3^1)(5^3 \cdot 5^1) = (3^{2+1})(5^{3+1}) = 3\text{—} \cdot 5\text{—}$

   $= \underline{\quad\quad\quad}$

2. $(2 \cdot 3^3 \cdot 5)(3^4) = (2^1 \cdot 3^3 \cdot 5^1)(3^4) = (2^1)(3^3 \cdot 3^4)(5^1) = 2^1 \cdot 3^{3+4} \cdot 5^1 = 2^1 \cdot 3\text{—} \cdot 5^1$

   $= \underline{\quad\quad\quad}$

3. Write a multiplication problem using monomials that provides the result x^2y^3.

   _____

4. Write the following problem using exponents: $(2xxx)(2 \cdot 2xxxx)$.

   _____

   What is the result?

   _____

5. Find $(3x^2)(3x^2)(3x^2)$ in simplified form.

   _____

6. What is $(3 \cdot x \cdot x \cdot x \cdot y \cdot y)(3 \cdot y \cdot y \cdot y \cdot y)$ in simplified form?

   _____

7. Write a problem involving multiplication of monomials that results in $15ab^2$.

   _____

8. Simplify $(5a^5)(2a^3)$. How did you obtain your result?

   _____

   _____

APPLY SKILLS 1 (*continued*)

9. How would you explain to a friend how to simplify $(3x^5y^3)(3xy^2)$?

    _____

    _____

    _____

    _____

10. Find the value of $(4x^3y^2)(0.375xy^3)$ if $x = 1.5$ and $y = 0.3$. Round your answer to the nearest thousandth.

    _____

11. In Problem 10, if you simplify first, what would be the monomial you would evaluate?

    _____

12. If the area of a square is $A = s^2$ and $s = 3x^2$, what would be the area of the square in terms of x?

    _____

Name _____ **Date** _____

APPLY SKILLS 2

Simplify.

> **Example:**
> $\dfrac{2x^3}{x^2} = \dfrac{2 \cdot x \cdot x \cdot x}{x \cdot x} = 2x$

1. $\dfrac{2^5}{2^2} =$ _____

2. $\dfrac{x^5}{x^2} =$ _____

3. $\dfrac{3^5}{3^2} =$ _____

4. $\dfrac{2x^3y^2}{4xy} =$ _____

5. $\dfrac{4x^4y^4}{8xy^2} =$ _____

Solve the problems involving monomials.

6. Write a monomial division problem that results in a^2b.

_____

7. How would you explain to a friend how to simplify $\dfrac{2^3x^4y^5}{2x^2y^2}$?

_____

_____

_____

_____

_____

8. If you divide $3x^5yz^3$ by $4xyz$, what would be your simplified answer?

_____

Name_____ Date_____

APPLY SKILLS 3

Simplify each problem, find the letter corresponding to the answer in the list below, then write that letter above the problem number at the bottom of the page.

Example:
$(2x^2)(3xy)$
$\underline{6x^3y = S}$

1. $(2x^5y^4) \div (2xy^3)$

_____

2. $(2xy)(2x^3y^4)$

_____

3. $(2x^5)(3x^2y^2)$

_____

4. $(3x^4y)(2x)$

_____

5. $(6x^2y^3) \div (2xy^3)$

_____

6. $(5x^2y^4z) \div (5xy^4z)$

_____

7. $(3xy)^2$

_____

8. $(8x^3y^5) \div (4xy^4)$

_____

$A = x^4y$ $N = x$

$B = x^4$ $R = 2x^5y^9$

$F = 3x$ $S = 6x^3y$

$H = 9x^2y^2$ $T = 6x^5y$

$I = 6x^7y^2$ $U = 4x^4y^5$

$M = 2x^2y$

$\underline{\quad}$ $\underline{\quad}$ $\underline{\quad}$ $\underline{\quad}$ $\underline{\quad}$ $\underline{\ S\ }$ $\underline{\quad}$ $\underline{\quad}$ $\underline{\quad}$
   8   1   4   7   3   ex.   5   2   6

Name _____ Date _____

Simplify the monomial problems.

Example:

$(2xy)(5xy^2) = \underline{10x^2y^3}$

Example:

$(10x^2y^3) \div (2xy) = \underline{5xy^2}$

1. $(2a)(a) = $ _____

2. $(2a)(3a^3) = $ _____

3. $(6a^2) \div (3a) = $ _____

4. $(7b^3)(2b) = $ _____

5. $(6ab)(ab) = $ _____

6. $\frac{4ab}{2a} = $ _____

7. $(ab)(3a) = $ _____

8. $\frac{6a}{a} = $ _____

9. $(2)^2 = $ _____

10. $(3a)^2 = $ _____

11. $(4a)(2ab) = $ _____

12. $(2a) \div (2b) = $ _____

13. $(3xy)(2x^2y) = $ _____

14. $\frac{8x^2y}{4xy} = $ _____

15. $(8x^2y) \div (8xy) = $ _____

16. $(2^2x^2y)(5xy^3) = $ _____

17. $\frac{3xyz}{4xy} = $ _____

18. $\frac{(-2xy)^2}{2x} = $ _____

19. $(2x^2)^2 \div (-3x)^3 = $ _____

20. $(3xy)(x^2)(2x) = $ _____

CALCULATOR EXPERIMENT FOR LARGE NUMBERS

Use a calculator to answer the questions.

1. In expressing numbers in scientific notation, what would be the sign of the exponent for numbers larger than 10?

   _____

2. In expressing numbers in scientific notation, what would be the sign on the exponent for numbers less than 1?

   _____

3. A trillion is a large number. What would 3.5 trillion be in standard notation?

   _____

4. What would 3.5 trillion be in scientific notation?

   _____

5. On your calculator, multiply 650,000 • 5,000,000. What result does your calculator display?

   _____

6. If you use pencil and paper to multiply 650,000 • 5,000,000, what is your result?

   _____

7. How is your result in Problem 6 written in scientific notation?

   _____

8. What do you think your calculator means by its display in Problem 5?

   _____

9. How is your calculator result from Problem 5 written in standard notation?

   _____

CALCULATOR EXPERIMENT FOR LARGE NUMBERS (*continued*)

10. What is the largest number you can display in your calculator in standard notation? Write this number in your calculator.

_____

11. If you add 1 to your result in Problem 10, what does your calculator display?

_____

_____

12. How could you multiply 650,000,000 • 200,000 on your calculator?

_____

What is the result?

_____

13. What would be the result of multiplying 5 billion by 3 million?

_____

CONCEPT DEVELOPMENT

Name_____ Date_____

CALCULATOR EXPERIMENT FOR SMALL NUMBERS

Use a calculator to solve the problems.

1. Write 0.0035 in scientific notation. _____

2. Input 3.5×10^{-3} into your calculator. What does your calculator display?

   _____

3. Write 0.0000065 in scientific notation. _____

4. Input 6.5×10^{-6} into your calculator. What does it display?

   _____

5. Multiply $0.0000002 \cdot 0.0000015$ using paper and pencil.

   _____

6. Write your result for Problem 5 in scientific notation. _____

7. Using your calculator, multiply $0.0000002 \cdot 0.0000015$. What does the calculator display?

   _____

8. What do you think the display means?

   _____

9. Write 0.0000002 in scientific notation and 0.0000015 in scientific notation.

   _____

10. Multiply the results of your answers in Problem 9 without using the calculator.

    _____

CALCULATOR EXPERIMENT FOR SMALL NUMBERS *(continued)*

11. What did you do in Problem 10?

_____

_____

12. Using paper and pencil, divide 0.000006 by 300.

_____

13. Write your result for Problem 12 in scientific notation. _____

14. Write 0.000006 in scientific notation and 300 in scientific notation.

_____

15. Divide. Write your answer in scientific notation. $\frac{6 \times 10^{-6}}{3 \times 10^{2}} =$ _____

16. In Problem 15, what did you do to get the result?

_____

_____

17. Use your calculator to solve 0.000006 ÷ 300. Write the calculator display.

_____

18. How do your answers to Problems 15 and 17 relate?

_____

_____

19. Sulphur dioxide in the air is measured in parts per billion (ppb) as a pollutant. Write 5 ppb as a number in scientific notation.

_____

20. If the sulphur dioxide pollution is 5 ppb and it is doubled, what would the result be in scientific notation?

_____

CONCEPT DEVELOPMENT

Name_____ Date_____

MULTIPLYING AND DIVIDING LARGE AND SMALL NUMBERS

Apply your knowledge of scientific notation to answer the questions.

1. Enter the number 125,000,000 into your calculator. What happened?

   _____

   _____

2. Write the sequence of button pushes to put 1.25×10^8 in your calculator. What does the calculator window display?

   _____

   _____

3. How would your calculator display the number 3,500,000,000,000?

   _____

4. How would your calculator display the number 0.00000035?

   _____

5. If your calculator displays 3.5 10, what is the number in scientific notation? In standard notation?

   _____

6. Multiply 125,000,000 · 200 by using paper and pencil. What is your result in scientific notation?

   _____

7. Multiply 125,000,000 · 200 by using your calculator. What does your calculator display for a result?

   _____

MULTIPLYING AND DIVIDING LARGE AND SMALL NUMBERS (continued)

8. Multiply 125,000 by 2,500,000 on your calculator.

   How did you do it? _____

   Did you need to put the numbers in scientific notation first? _____

   Was the result in scientific notation or standard notation? _____

   Write the result in scientific notation. _____

9. Divide 0.00064 by 200,000 on your calculator.

   What does it display? _____

   What number do you think the result is? _____

10. If your calculator displays 3.2 07, what is the number in standard notation?

    _____

11. If your calculator displays 3.2 −07, what is the number in standard notation?

    _____

12. What is $(3 \times 10^4)(2 \times 10^{-2})$? _____

13. What is $(3 \times 10^4) \div (2 \times 10^2)$? _____

14. What is $(3 \times 10^4)(2 \times 10^2)$? _____

15. What is $(3 \times 10^4) \div (2 \times 10^{-2})$? _____

Name_____ Date_____

STANDARD AND SCIENTIFIC NOTATION

Write the numbers in standard notation.

1. $3 \times 10^3 =$ _____

2. $3 \times 10^{-3} =$ _____

3. $40 \times 10^{-3} =$ _____

4. $40 \times 10^3 =$ _____

Write the numbers in scientific notation.

5. $350 =$ _____

6. $0.0035 =$ _____

7. 5 million $=$ _____

8. $0.0000002 =$ _____

Multiply or divide and write the result in scientific notation.

9. $(3.5 \times 10^2)(2 \times 10^3) =$ _____

10. $(3.5 \times 10^3)(2 \times 10^{-2}) =$ _____

11. $(3.5 \times 10^2)(4 \times 10^3) =$ _____

12. $(6 \times 10^3) \div (2 \times 10^2) =$ _____

13. $(6 \times 10^3) \div (3 \times 10^{-5}) =$ _____

14. $(3.5 \times 10^5) \div (7 \times 10^2) =$ _____

Multiply or divide and write the result in standard notation.

15. $(3.5 \times 10^2)(2 \times 10^3) =$ _____

16. $(3.5 \times 10^3)(2 \times 10^{-2}) =$ _____

17. $(3.5 \times 10^2)(4 \times 10^3) =$ _____

18. $(6 \times 10^3) \div (2 \times 10^2) =$ _____

19. $(6 \times 10^3) \div (3 \times 10^{-5}) =$ _____

20. $(3.5 \times 10^5) \div (7 \times 10^2) =$ _____

Name _____ Date _____

APPLY SKILLS 1

Write the numbers in scientific notation.

Example:
$200 = \underline{\ 2 \times 10^2\ }$

1. $400 = $ _____

2. $5{,}000 = $ _____

3. $0.0004 = $ _____

4. $0.000015 = $ _____

5. $2{,}400{,}000 = $ _____

6. $0.0000356 = $ _____

7. $456{,}000 = $ _____

8. $286{,}451 = $ _____

Write the numbers in standard notation.

Example:
$3 \times 10^2 = \underline{\ 300\ }$

9. $2 \times 10^3 = $ _____

10. $2 \times 10^{-3} = $ _____

11. $4.2 \times 10^5 = $ _____

12. $6.2 \times 10^{-5} = $ _____

13. $4.5 \times 10^2 = $ _____

14. $3.54 \times 10^{-2} = $ _____

APPLY SKILLS 2

Multiply. Write the result in scientific notation.

> **Example:**
> $(2 \times 10^3)(3 \times 10^4) =$
> $\underline{\qquad 6 \times 10^7 \qquad}$

1. $(3 \times 10^2)(2 \times 10^4) =$

_____

2. $(1.1 \times 10^2)(3 \times 10^3) =$

_____

3. $(2.8 \times 10^{-3})(3 \times 10^{-4}) =$

_____

4. $(7 \times 10^8)(2 \times 10^{10}) =$

_____

5. $(1.4 \times 10^3)(5 \times 10^{-2}) =$

_____

Divide. Write the result in scientific notation.

> **Example:**
> $\dfrac{6 \times 10^3}{2 \times 10^1} = \underline{\ 3 \times 10^2\ }$

6. $\dfrac{8 \times 10^3}{2 \times 10^2} =$ _____

7. $\dfrac{8 \times 10^3}{2 \times 10} =$ _____

8. $\dfrac{6 \times 10^5}{2 \times 10^{-3}} =$ _____

9. $\dfrac{2.8 \times 10^5}{7 \times 10^2} =$ _____

10. $(8 \times 10^2) \div (4 \times 10^{-5}) =$ _____

APPLY SKILLS 2 (*continued*)

Multiply or divide as indicated. Write the result in standard notation.

Example:

$(2 \times 10^5)(3 \times 10^3) = 6 \times 10^8$

$600{,}000{,}000$

11. $(4 \times 10^2)(2 \times 10^3) =$

_____

12. $(4 \times 10^2) \div (2 \times 10^3) =$

_____

13. $(5 \times 10^3) \div (4 \times 10^5) =$

_____

14. $(6 \times 10^{13}) \div (2 \times 10^2) =$

_____

15. $7(2.8 \times 10^4) =$

_____

16. $\dfrac{4.2 \times 10^2}{7 \times 10^{-8}} =$

_____

17. $\dfrac{3 \cdot 6 \times 10^7}{2 \times 10^3} =$

_____

Name_____ Date_____

APPLY SKILLS 3

Write the numbers in scientific notation.

Example:
$8{,}420 = \underline{8.42 \times 10^3}$

1. $356 = $ _____

2. $0.356 = $ _____

3. $40 \times 10^3 = $ _____

4. $40 \times 10^{-3} = $ _____

5. $4{,}567{,}000 = $ _____

6. $(3.5 \times 10^3)(2 \times 10^{-3}) = $ _____

7. $\dfrac{450{,}000}{900} = $ _____

8. $(356)(400{,}000) = $ _____

9. $235 \div 500 = $ _____

10. $(-3.5 \times 10^5) \div (7.0 \times 10^{-4}) = $

_____

11. 5 million times 3 thousandths =

_____

MAGIC CHESSBOARD

Suppose you were given a magic chessboard. Each morning, money is placed on a square of the chessboard. The first morning, one penny was on the first square. The second morning, two pennies were on the second square. The third morning, four pennies were on the third square, and so on.

1. A chessboard has 64 squares. When the chessboard is filled, do you think you will get $100? _____ $1,000? _____ $100,000? _____ $1,000,000? _____ If you did not choose one of the above numbers, what is your guess? _____

2. Complete this table, showing how much money would be placed on the board each morning for 32 days.

Day	Money		Day	Money
1	1¢		17	
2	2¢		18	
3	4¢		19	
4	8¢		20	
5	16¢		21	
6	32¢		22	
7	64¢		23	
8			24	
9	$2.56		25	
10			26	
11			27	
12			28	
13			29	
14			30	
15			31	
16			32	

PROBLEM SOLVING

MAGIC CHESSBOARD (*continued*)

3. What will be the first square to have at least one dollar placed on it?

_____

4. What is the first square to have at least $1 million on it?

_____

5. What square will be the first to have $1 billion? Write the amount on squares 31 and 32 in scientific notation.

_____

6. How much money would be on the 64th square? You can use scientific notation if you do not want to know the exact amount.

_____

_____

ADDING AND SUBTRACTING POLYNOMIALS

1. Put the terms in descending order.

> **Example:**
> $2x, 1, x^2$
> $\underline{x^2, 2x, 1}$

   a. b, r, a, z, t, y **b.** $5, 3, 4, -1$

      _____   _____

   c. $5, x, 2x^3, x^2$ **d.** x^2, y^2, xy

      _____   _____

2. Add all the white shoes and black shoes in your class. How would you write the expression?

_____

3. Add the walls and the boards (chalk, white, bulletin) in your classroom. How would you write the expression?

_____

4. Explain why $4x^2$ and $2x$ are not like terms and why $4x^2$ and x^2 are like terms.

_____

_____

_____

5. Put $3x^2 + x^3 + 5 + 2x$ in descending order. How did you determine your answer?

_____

_____

6. Put $3x^2 + x^3 - 2x - 5$ in descending order. How did you determine your answer?

_____

_____

7. Add $(4 + x + x^2)$ and $(3x^2 + 2x + 2)$.

_____

_____

CONCEPT DEVELOPMENT

Name _____ Date _____

ADDING AND SUBTRACTING POLYNOMIALS *(continued)*

8. What is the additive inverse of 4? _____ Of $2x$? _____ Of $x^2 - 3$? _____

9. Subtract $2x^2 + 3$ from $4x^2 + 8$. _____

10. Simplify.

    a. $(5x - 3x^2 + 4) - (5x^2 + 5 - x)$ **b.** $(5x - 3x^2 + 4) + (5x^2 + 5 - x)$

    _____   _____

11. Write in descending order first, then add: $(4 + 3x^2 + x) + (x + 2x^2 - 3)$.

    _____

    _____

12. How would you tell a new student in your class to add polynomials?
    To subtract them?

    _____

    _____

    _____

APPLY SKILLS 1

Write the terms in ascending order.

1. a, c, m, q, d, r **2.** $5, 2, 6, 3, 7$ **3.** x^2, x^3, x^5, x

_____   _____   _____

4. a, a^3, a^2 **5.** $2x^3, 4x^2, 3x$ **6.** $2a, 4a^3, 5a^2$

_____   _____   _____

Write the terms in descending order.

7. a, c, m, q, d, r **8.** $5, 2, 6, 3, 7$

_____   _____

9. x^2, x^3, x^5, x **10.** a, a^3, a^2

_____   _____

11. What does "descending order of a variable" mean?

_____

_____

12. What do you do to order terms with more than one variable?

_____

_____

Write the terms in descending order.

13. a^2b, b^2, a^3 **14.** $3b^3, a^3, b^2a, a^2b$

_____   _____

15. a^3, b^3, a^2b, b^2a **16.** $2x^2y, 3xy, 5y^2$

_____   _____

PROGRESS MONITORING

Name _____   Date _____

APPLY SKILLS 2

Answer the questions about number and variable ordering.

1. Are $3x^2$ and $4x$ like terms? Why or why not?

_____

2. Are $3x^2$ and $5x^2$ like terms? Why or why not?

_____

_____

3. Which terms are like terms in $3x^2$, $4y^2$, $2y$, $3x$, $5x^2$?

_____

4. Are $3x^2y$ and $2x^2y$ like terms? Why or why not?

_____

_____

Group the like terms.

5. $3x$, 4, $6x$, 5, x 6. $3y^2$, $4y^2$, y, $2y$ 7. $2x^2y$, $3xy$, $4yx^2$, $2yx$

_____   _____   _____

_____   _____   _____

Name_____   Date_____

APPLY SKILLS 2 (*continued*)

Add the terms.

8. $3x^2$, $4x$, $5x$, $6x^2$

_____

9. $3y$, $4y^2$, $3y^2$, y

_____

10. 5, $5x^2$, $3x$, 2, $4x$

_____

11. a^2, ab, b^2, $3ab$, $2b^2$

_____

Find the sum or difference.

12. $(a + 2) + (3a - 4) =$

_____

13. $(x^2 + 2x + 1) + (2x^2 - x - 2) =$

_____

14. $(a + 2) - (3a - 4) =$

_____

15. $(x^2 + 2x + 1) - (2x^2 - x - 2) =$

_____

APPLY SKILLS 3

Write the letters that match the solutions in the corresponding blanks at the bottom of the page. You may use a letter more than once.

1. the power of x for $5x^3$

2. the power of x for 7

3. $(3x^2 + x) + (1 - 3x^2 + 2) - x$

4. $(4x^2 + 3x + 3) - (3x^2 + 2x - 2)$

5. $5x^2 + x^3 - 2x + 1$

6. $(5x^2 + 2x + 1) - (5x^2 - 2x + 2)$

7. $(3x^2 + 2x - 1) - (3x^2 + 2x - 1)$

8. $6x^2 + 2xy + y^2 + 3xy - y^2 + x^2$

9. $1 - 2x + 5x^2 + x^3$

10. What is the additive inverse of $3x + 4$?

11. $4x^2 + 3x + 2 - (6 + 2x - x^2)$

12. What is $6x - 5$ minus $2x - 4$?

13. $(3x^2 + 5x + 2) + (4x^2 - 3x + 1) - (7x^2 + 2x)$

14. What is the power of b in $a^3b^2c^4$?

15. $(15x^2 + 7x - 4) - (15x^2 + 7x - 7)$

16. Add the terms: $4x^2, 7x, 4, 3x^2, -8, 5x$.

17. $(3x^2 - 5xy + y^2) - (-4x^2 - 10xy + y^2)$

18. $(7x^2 + 5) + (3x - 2) - (6x^2 + 2x + 3)$

19. $(6 + 5x - x^2) - (6 + 4x - 2x^2)$

20. $(3x^2 + 2xy) + (y^2 + 4) + (2x^2 - xy)$

21. Find the additive inverse of $x^2 - 3x + 2$.

22. $(3x^2 + 2x - 1) - (2x^2 + x - 1)$

23. $3x^2 + 6x - 5x - 8 + 2x^2 + 4$

24. What is the power of x in $3xy^2$?

25. $(4x^3 + 4x^2 + 1) - (3x^3 - x^2 + 2x)$

A. $4x - 1$

B. $-3x - 4$

C. $2a^2 + 3a + 4$

D. $5x^2 + xy + y^2 + 4$

E. $x^3 + 5x^2 - 2x + 1$

F. $-x^2 + 3x - 2$

G. $7x^2 + 5xy$

H. $a^2 + 2ab + b^2$

I. 3

J. $x^5 + x^3 - 2$

K. $x^2 + x + 5$

L. 0

M. 1

N. 7

O. $x^2 + x$

P. $2x - 3$

Q. $17x^3$

R. $5x^2 + x - 4$

S. $7x^2 + 12x - 4$

T. 2

U. $x - 2y$

V. $8x$

W. 4

X. $x^3 - 5x^2 + 2x - 1$

Y. $a^2 + b^2 + 2ab$

$\overline{}$ $\overline{}$ $\overline{}$ $\overline{}$ $\overline{}$ $\overline{}$ $\overline{}$ $\overline{}$ $\overline{}$ $\overline{}$ $\overline{}$ $\overline{}$; $\overline{}$ $\overline{}$ $\overline{}$ $\overline{}$
1 2 3 4 5 6 7 8 9 10 11 12 13 14 15 16

$\overline{}$ $\overline{}$ $\overline{}$ $\overline{}$ $\overline{}$ $\overline{}$ $\overline{}$ $\overline{}$ $\overline{}$!
17 18 19 20 21 22 23 24 25

Name_____ **Date**_____

GEOMETRY

Find the areas of the figures.

1. $b = 4x$
$h = (3x - 5)$

_____

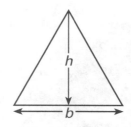

2. $l = 4x - 2$
$w = 3$

_____

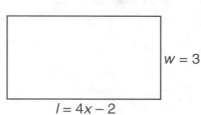

3. $s = x + 5$
$b = 3x + 4$
$h = 4x$

_____

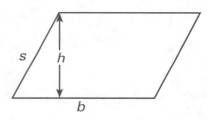

4. $b_1 = 2x - 3$
$b_2 = 4x + 1$
$h = 3x$

_____

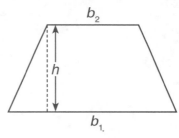

5. A block of steel has a hole drilled in it. Find the area of the piece of steel left. What would the area be if $r = 3$?

_____

_____

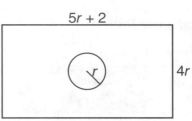

6. At the right is a view of the end of a staircase. What is its area?

_____

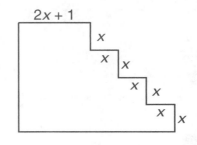

Name_____ Date_____

APPLY SKILLS 1

Use algebra tiles to find each product.

Example:

$x(x + 2) = \underline{x^2 + 2x}$

×	x	1	1
x	x^2	x	x

1. $x(x + 1) =$ _____

2. $x(x - 1) =$ _____

3. $2x(2x + 1) =$ _____

4. $2x(2x - 1) =$ _____

5. $x(2x + 1) =$ _____

6. $x(2x - 2) =$ _____

Express the algebra tile model as a product of a monomial by a polynomial. Find the product.

7.

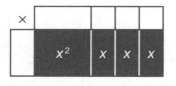

_____

8.

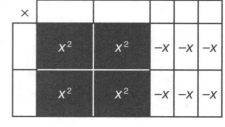

_____

Name _____ Date _____

APPLY SKILLS 2

Find the product and write it in descending order.

Example:

$3(10 + 2) =$ ___36___

$30 + 6$

Example:

$x(3x - 1) =$ ___$3x^2 - x$___

1. $2(30 + 4) =$ _____

2. $2(30 - 4) =$ _____

3. $x(2x + 1) =$ _____

4. $2x(3x - 4) =$ _____

5. $x^2(3x + 1) =$ _____

6. $2x(3x + 1) =$ _____

7. $2x^2(1 + 3x) =$ _____

8. $3x(2x^2 + 2) =$ _____

APPLY SKILLS 2 *(continued)*

9. $3(x^2 + 2x + 3) =$

_____

10. $3x(3 + 2x + x^2) =$

_____

11. $2a(3a^2 + 2a + 4) =$

_____

12. Multiply $(x^2 + 4x + 3)$ by $7x$

_____

13. Find: $3(2x + 4) - 4(x - 1)$

_____

14. Find: $2(x^2 + x - 1) + 3x(1 - 4x)$

_____

APPLY SKILLS 3

Multiply and write the results in the correct order.

Example:
$$ab(a + b) =$$
$$\underline{\hspace{1.5em} a^2b + ab^2 \hspace{1.5em}}$$

1. $xy(xy + 1) =$

_____

2. $ab(2ab + b) =$

_____

3. $xy(2 + xy) =$

_____

4. $2xy(xy + 1) =$

_____

5. $2ab(2ab + b) =$

_____

6. $2xy(2xy + x) =$

_____

7. $2xy(x^2 + xy + y^2) =$

_____

8. $2x^2(y^2 + 2y + 1) =$

_____

9. $(cd + d)2cd =$

_____

10. $6ab(2ab - 3b) =$

_____

11. $6a^2b(2ab - 3b) =$

_____

12. $3x(2x^2y + 3x + 2y) =$

_____

13. $-3d(2c^2d + 4c - 5) =$

_____

14. $(2x)^2(3x^2 - 4) =$

_____

15. $(2ab)^2(a + b) =$

_____

Name_____ Date_____

HUNGRY GOAT

Read each scenario and answer the question.

1. Butter the goat is kept in a pen inside a fenced area. Aside from the pen, the fenced area is covered with grass for grazing. What is the area of grass available to Butter for grazing?

   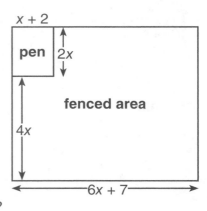

   _____

2. If $x = 4$, what is the area of the grass in Problem 1?

   _____

3. Butter ate all the grass in his fenced area, so he was tied to the corner of Ben's house with a rope $4x$ in length. Ben's house is $4x + 3$ long and $3x$ wide. The yard is covered with grass, and Butter can graze in the area shown in the diagram. Ben is going to mow the lawn, but he won't have to cut the area where Butter grazes. How much grass will Ben still need to cut? Use $\pi = 3.14$ and round answers to the nearest hundredth.

   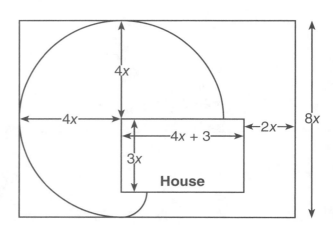

   _____

4. If $x = 4$, what is the area of the grass that Ben needs to cut in Problem 3?

   _____

Name_____ Date_____

APPLY SKILLS 1

Multiply the binomials vertically.

Example:

$$
\begin{array}{rrrr}
 & 10 & + & 2 \\
 & 10 & + & 3 \\
\hline
 & 30 & + & 6 \\
+ 100 & + & 20 & \\
\hline
100 & + & 50 & + & 6 = 156
\end{array}
$$

1.
$$
\begin{array}{rrr}
20 & + & 2 \\
10 & + & 8 \\
\hline
\end{array}
$$

2.
$$
\begin{array}{rrr}
20 & - & 3 \\
10 & + & 2 \\
\hline
\end{array}
$$

3.
$$
\begin{array}{rrr}
10 & - & 3 \\
10 & - & 4 \\
\hline
\end{array}
$$

4.
$$
\begin{array}{rrr}
30 & + & 4 \\
10 & + & 2 \\
\hline
\end{array}
$$

5.
$$
\begin{array}{rrr}
x & + & 1 \\
x & + & 2 \\
\hline
\end{array}
$$

6.
$$
\begin{array}{rrr}
y & - & 3 \\
y & + & 4 \\
\hline
\end{array}
$$

7.
$$
\begin{array}{rrr}
2x & + & 1 \\
3x & + & 2 \\
\hline
\end{array}
$$

8.
$$
\begin{array}{rrr}
2x & - & 3 \\
3x & - & 2 \\
\hline
\end{array}
$$

9.
$$
\begin{array}{rrr}
3x & + & 2 \\
2x & - & 3 \\
\hline
\end{array}
$$

APPLY SKILLS 1 (continued)

Use the Distributive Property to multiply horizontally.

Example:

(10 + 2)(10 + 3)

10(10 + 3) + 2(10 + 3)

100 + 30 + 20 + 6

156

---

10. (10 + 2)(20 + 2)

---

11. (10 − 2)(20 − 2)

12. (x + 2)(x + 3)

---

13. (x + 2)(x − 3)

14. (2x + 1)(3x + 4)

---

15. (2x + 1)(3x − 4)

16. (2x − 3)(3x − 2)

Name_____ Date_____

APPLY SKILLS 2

Use algebra tiles to multiply these binomials. Sketch the resulting product mat and write the result as a polynomial.

Example:

$(x + 1)(x + 2) =$ ___$x^2 + 3x + 2$___

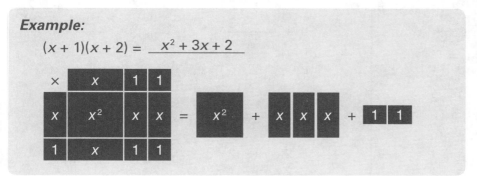

1. $(x + 3)(x + 2) =$ _____

2. $(x - 1)(x + 2) =$ _____

3. $(2x + 1)(x + 1) =$ _____

4. $(2x + 1)(2x + 2) =$ _____

PROGRESS MONITORING

APPLY SKILLS 2 (continued)

Multiply these binomials vertically. Express the result as a polynomial.

Example:

$$
\begin{array}{r}
x + 1 \\
x + 2 \\
\hline
2x + 2 \\
+ x^2 + x \\
\hline
x^2 + 3x + 2
\end{array}
$$

5.
$$
\begin{array}{r}
x + 2 \\
x + 3 \\
\hline
\end{array}
$$

6.
$$
\begin{array}{r}
x + 2 \\
x - 1 \\
\hline
\end{array}
$$

7.
$$
\begin{array}{r}
x + 1 \\
2x + 1 \\
\hline
\end{array}
$$

8.
$$
\begin{array}{r}
2x + 2 \\
2x + 1 \\
\hline
\end{array}
$$

9.
$$
\begin{array}{r}
2x + 1 \\
3x - 4 \\
\hline
\end{array}
$$

Multiply these binomials horizontally. Express the result as a polynomial.

Example:

$(x + 1)(x + 2)$

$x(x + 2) + 1(x + 2)$

$x^2 + 2x + x + 2$

$x^2 + 3x + 2$

10. $(x + 2)(x + 3)$

11. $(x + 1)(2x + 1)$

12. $(x + 2)(x - 1)$

13. $(2x + 1)(2x + 2)$

14. $(2x + 1)(3x - 4)$

APPLY SKILLS 3

Multiply vertically.

Example:

$$
\begin{array}{r}
x \;+\; 1 \\
x \;-\; 1 \\
\hline
-x \;-\; 1 \\
+\, x^2 \;+\; x \\
\hline
x^2 \qquad -\; 1
\end{array}
$$

1.
$$
\begin{array}{r}
x \;+\; 2 \\
x \;-\; 2 \\
\hline
\end{array}
$$

2.
$$
\begin{array}{r}
x \;-\; 2 \\
x \;+\; 2 \\
\hline
\end{array}
$$

3.
$$
\begin{array}{r}
2x \;-\; 3 \\
2x \;+\; 3 \\
\hline
\end{array}
$$

4.
$$
\begin{array}{r}
2a \;+\; b \\
2a \;-\; b \\
\hline
\end{array}
$$

5.
$$
\begin{array}{r}
x \;+\; 2 \\
x \;+\; 2 \\
\hline
\end{array}
$$

6.
$$
\begin{array}{r}
x \;-\; 3 \\
x \;-\; 3 \\
\hline
\end{array}
$$

PROGRESS MONITORING

Name_____ Date_____

APPLY SKILLS 3 *(continued)*

Multiply horizontally.

> **Example:**
> $(x + 1)(x - 1) =$ _____$x^2 - 1$_____
> $x(x - 1) + 1(x - 1)$
> $x^2 - x + x - 1$

7. $(x + 2)(x - 2) =$ _____

8. $(2x - 3)(2x + 3) =$ _____

9. $(x - y)(x + y) =$ _____

10. $(x + 3)^2 =$ _____

11. $(2x - 1)^2 =$ _____

12. $(a + b)^2 =$ _____

13. Explain what we mean by the binomial product of a sum and a difference.

_____

_____

14. Explain how to square a binomial.

_____

_____

APPLY SKILLS 4

Find the products and simplify the answers.

Example:

$(x + 2)(x + 1) =$

$x(x + 1) + 2(x + 1)$

$x^2 + x + 2x + 2$

$x^2 + 3x + 2$

1. $(x + 3)(x + 8) =$

2. $(x + 6)(x - 2) =$

3. $(x - 2)(x - 8) =$

4. $(x + 3)(x - 3) =$

5. $2x(x + 6) =$

6. $(x - 1)(x - 5) =$

7. $(x + 4)^2 =$

8. $(x + 6)(x - 9) =$

9. $(x + 5)(x + 7) =$

APPLY SKILLS 4 (*continued*)

10. $(x - 12)(x + 2) =$

11. $(x + 8)(x - 8) =$

12. $(2x - 1)(x + 5) =$

13. $(x + 6)^2 =$

14. $(x + 1)(x + 0) =$

15. $(x + 11)(x - 11) =$

16. $(2x + 3)(x - 3) =$

17. $(2x + 5)^2 =$

18. $(2x + 4)(2x - 2) =$

19. $(3x + 1)(2x - 3) =$

Name_____ Date_____

OBJECTIVE 1

Simplify.

1. $(2ab)(-3a^2) =$ _____

2. $(x^2y^3)(x^4y) =$ _____

3. $\dfrac{-8x^4y^3}{-2xy^2} =$ _____

4. $\dfrac{a^7b^2c^5}{ab^2c^3} =$ _____

OBJECTIVE 2

Write each number in scientific notation.

5. $6{,}400{,}000 =$ _____

6. $0.000048 =$ _____

7. $(8 \times 10^4)(2.3 \times 10^6) =$ _____

8. $\dfrac{3.3 \times 10^9}{2.2 \times 10^4} =$ _____

OBJECTIVE 3

Add or subtract these polynomials. Express your results in descending order of powers for x.

9. $(x^2 + 2x - 1) + (2x^2 - 3x + 4)$

10. $(2x^2 + 7x + 5) - (x^2 + 3x - 4)$

11. $(3x^3 + x^2 - 2) + (x^2 + 3)$

12. $x^3 + 2x^2 + 5 + 3x^3 - 4x^2 - 3$

Inside Algebra

Name_____ **Date**_____

OBJECTIVE 4

Find each product. Express your results in descending order of powers for *x*.

13. $2x(x - 4)$

14. $ab(a^2 - b^2)$

15. $-5x(x^2 - 3x + 4)$

16. $x^2y(2xy + 3xy^2)$

OBJECTIVE 5

Find each product. Express your results in descending order of powers for *x*.

17. $(x + 1)(x + 4)$

18. $(x + 2)(x - 3)$

19. $(x + 3)(2x - 1)$

20. $(x + 5)(x - 5)$

9

Exploring Polynomials

In this chapter, we learn about polynomials, including quadratic trinomials. We use what we learned about factoring with monomials and polynomials. We also use factoring and models as tools for solving polynomial equations.

Objective 1
Find the greatest common factor through prime factorization for integers and sets of monomials.

Objective 2
Use the greatest common factor and the distributive property to factor polynomials with the grouping technique, and use these techniques to solve equations.

Objective 3
Factor quadratic trinomials of the form $ax^2 + bx + c$, and solve equations by factoring.

Objective 4
Factor quadratic polynomials that are perfect squares or differences of squares, and solve equations by factoring.

Objective 5
Solve quadratic equations by completing the square.

Chapter 9
VOCABULARY

completing the square Adding to or subtracting from a quadratic equation to make it into a perfect square trinomial; a method used to find the solutions of a quadratic equation

$x^2 + 6x + 5 = 0$
$x^2 + 6x + 9 - 4 = 0$
$(x + 3)^2 = 4$
$x = -1$ or -5

---

difference of squares A binomial of the form $a^2 - b^2 = (a + b)(a - b)$

$x^2 - 16 = (x + 4)(x - 4)$

---

factor A monomial that evenly divides a value

Factors of 12: 1, 2, 3, 4, 6, 12

Factors of $2x^2 + 6x$: $2x$ and $x + 3$

---

greatest common factor (GCF) The largest factor that a set of monomials has in common

12: 1, 2, 3, ④ 6, 12
16: 1, 2, ④ 8, 16
The GCF of 12 and 16 is 4.

---

perfect square The product of a monomial with itself

x^2, $16a^2$, or **49**

perfect square trinomial A polynomial of the form $a^2 + 2ab + b^2 = (a + b)^2$ or $a^2 - 2ab + b^2 = (a - b)^2$

$x^2 + 6x + 9 = (x + 3)^2$

---

prime factorization The prime numbers and/or variables whose product is the desired expression, or the process of obtaining those values

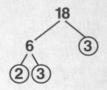

---

quadratic formula

$x = \dfrac{-b \pm \sqrt{b^2 - 4ac}}{2a}$ where $ax^2 + bx + c = 0$

---

quadratic polynomial A polynomial whose greatest power is 2

$x^2 - 4$, $x^2 + 9$, or $x^2 + 3x + 2$

---

quadratic trinomial A polynomial of the form $ax^2 + bx + c$

$x^2 + 4x + 3$

Name_____ Date_____

APPLY SKILLS 1

Find both the common factors and the greatest common factor (GCF) using prime factorization.

1.

Numbers	24	30
Prime Factorization	2 · 3 · 4	2 · 3 · 5
Common Factors		
GCF		

2.

Numbers	18	44
Prime Factorization	$2 \cdot 3 \cdot 3 = 2 \cdot 3^2$	$2 \cdot 2 \cdot 11 = 2^2 \cdot 11$
Common Factors		
GCF		

3.

Numbers	20	36
Prime Factorization	$2 \cdot 2 \cdot 5 = 2^2 \cdot 5$	
Common Factors		
GCF		

4.

Numbers	45	30
Prime Factorization	3 · 3 · 5	
Common Factors		
GCF		

5.

Numbers	60	90
Prime Factorization		2 · 3 · 3 · 5 =
Common Factors		
GCF		

6.

Numbers	16	15
Prime Factorization		3 · 5
Common Factors		
GCF		

7.

Expressions	a^2b	abc
Common Factors		
GCF		

PROGRESS MONITORING

APPLY SKILLS 2

Find the greatest common factor (GCF) of each pair of numbers.

Example:

$12x^2y^3$ and $9x^3y$ ___$3x^2y$___

$12x^2y^3$
$3 \cdot 4 \cdot x \cdot x \cdot y \cdot y \cdot y$
$2 \cdot 2$
$3 \cdot 2 \cdot 2 \cdot x \cdot x \cdot y \cdot y \cdot y$
GCF: $3 \cdot x \cdot x \cdot y$

$9x^3y$
$3 \cdot 3 \cdot x \cdot x \cdot x \cdot y$

1. 42 and 36 _____

2. 12 and 60 _____

3. 9 and 30 _____

4. 45 and 75 _____

5. 27 and 54 _____

6. a^3b^2 and a^4b^5 _____

7. xy^4 and x^2y^5 _____

8. m^5n^4 and m^4n^6 _____

Name_____ **Date**_____

APPLY SKILLS 2 (*continued*)

9. a^6b^4 and a^4b^7 _____

10. m^3np^3 and $m^2n^2p^2$ _____

11. $a^6b^4c^3$ and a^3b^5c _____

12. a^3b^4 and a^2b^6 _____

13. x^4y^3, x^2y^5, and xy^5 _____

14. 12, 24, and 30 _____

15. 32, 48, and 64 _____

APPLY SKILLS 3

Find the greatest common factor (GCF) of each pair of numbers.

Example:

$18a^3b^4$ and $24a^2b^5$

$18a^3b^4$
$9 \cdot 2 \cdot a \cdot a \cdot a \cdot b \cdot b \cdot b \cdot b$
$3 \cdot 3$
$3 \cdot 3 \cdot 2 \cdot a \cdot a \cdot a \cdot b \cdot b \cdot b \cdot b$
GCF: $2 \cdot 3 \cdot a \cdot a \cdot b \cdot b \cdot b \cdot b = 6a^2b^4$

$24a^2b^5$
$2 \cdot 12 \cdot a \cdot a \cdot b \cdot b \cdot b \cdot b \cdot b$
$2 \cdot 6$
$2 \cdot 3$
$2 \cdot 2 \cdot 2 \cdot 3 \cdot a \cdot a \cdot b \cdot b \cdot b \cdot b \cdot b$

1. a^7b^4 and a^4b^3 _____

2. x^5y^4 and x^2y _____

3. m^2n^4 and m^4n^6 _____

4. c^6d^3 and c^3d^5 _____

5. m^5n^7 and m^4n _____

6. $6ab^4$ and $9a^3b^3$ _____

7. $10x^3y^6$ and $25x^2y^8$ _____

Name_____ Date_____

8. $32a^3b^2$ and $20a^4b^5$ _____

9. $27s^3t^4$ and $18st^2$ _____

10. $48m^2n^2p^3$ and $60m^4n^5p^2$ _____

11. $6ab^2$, $15a^2b^2$, and $21a^3b^4$ _____

12. $16x^3y^6z$, $24x^2y^8z^2$, and $32xy^3z$ _____

13. $26m^2n^2p^3$, $12m^2np^2$, and $18m^3n^2p^3$ _____

14. $8ab^2$, $16a^2b^2$, $22a^3b^4$, and $30a^3b^2$ _____

15. $15x^3y^6z$, $45x^2y^8z$, $90xy^3z$, and $25x^2y^8$ _____

APPLY SKILLS 1

Factor the polynomials using the greatest common factor (GCF) and the Distributive Property.

Example:
$2x^2 + 6x =$
$\underline{2x(x + 3)}$

1. $x^2 + 6x =$

_____

2. $x^2 - 4x =$

_____

3. $x^2 + 5x =$

_____

4. $7x - x^2 =$

_____

5. $x^2 + x =$

_____

6. $x^2 - 11x =$

_____

7. $3x^2 + x =$

_____

8. $2x^2 - 4x =$

_____

9. $6x^2 + 8x =$

_____

10. $3x^2 + 9x =$

_____

11. $m^2n^2 + mn^3 =$

_____

12. $m^3n^2 + m^2n^3 =$

_____

13. $2m^2n^2 + 8mn^2 =$

_____

14. $5m^4n - 40m^5n^3 =$

_____

15. $-8m^2n^5 + 32m^2n^3 =$

_____

16. $20a^3b^5 + 50a^5b^3 =$

_____

17. $12a^2b + 18a^3b^3 =$

_____

18. $-8a^4b - 48a^2b^2 =$

_____

19. $2a^5b^3 + 22a^5b^2 =$

_____

20. $14a^3b - 35a^2b^3 =$

_____

Name _____ Date _____

APPLY SKILLS 2

Factor the polynomials using the greatest common factor (GCF) and the Distributive Property.

Example:
$6x^2 + 36x =$
$6x(x + 6)$ _____

1. $-2x^2 + 6x =$

_____

2. $5x^2 - 15x =$

_____

3. $-3x^2 + 12x =$

_____

4. $5x^2 + 25x =$

_____

5. $5m^2n^3 - 35m^5n =$

_____

6. $11mn^2 - 33m^4n =$

_____

7. $-5m^4n - 20m^5n^3 =$

_____

8. $-8m^2n + 24m^2n^2 =$

_____

9. $24a^3b^5 + 48ab^3 =$

_____

10. $16ab^4 + 32ab^2 =$

_____

11. $-9a^4b - 45a^3b^4 =$

_____

12. $13a^3b^2 - 26ab =$

_____

13. $7x^4y^3 + 14x^2y^5 - 28x^3y^2 =$

_____

14. $6x^4y^2 - 24x^3y + 12xy^5 =$

_____

15. $-15x^2y - 5xy^4 - 30xy^4 =$

_____

16. $10x^4y^3 + 16x^2 - 24y^2 =$

_____

17. $-72x^4y + 16x^3y^3 - 20x^2y^2 =$

_____

18. $12a^5b^3 - 3a^4b^3 + 27a^3b^4 + 9a^3b^4 =$

_____

19. $14ab^2 + 35a^3b^2 - 7a^3b + 70ab^4 =$

_____

20. $-32a^4b^3 + 16a^3b^3 - 4a^3b + 24a^2b^2 =$

_____

APPLY SKILLS 3

Factor the polynomials using the greatest common factor (GCF) and the Distributive Property.

Example:

$2x^2 + 10x =$ ___$2x(x + 5)$___

1. $3x^2 + 6x =$ _____

2. $2x^2 - 14x =$ _____

3. $-3x^2 + 12x =$ _____

4. $55x + 5x^2 =$ _____

5. $36x + 9x^2 =$ _____

Factor the polynomials and solve them using the Zero Product Property.

Example:

$3x^2 - 6x = 0$

$3x(x - 2) = 0$

either $3x = 0$ or $x - 2 = 0$

$\frac{3x}{3} = \frac{0}{3}$ or $x - 2 = 0$

$ +2 +2$

$x = 0$ or $x = 2$

$x = 0, 2$

6. $x^2 + 5x = 0$

7. $x^2 - 3x = 0$

8. $4x^2 + 8x = 0$

9. $3x^2 - 12x = 0$

APPLY SKILLS 3 (*continued*)

10. $9x^2 + 27x = 0$

11. $x^2 + 8x = 0$

12. $2x^2 + x = 0$

13. $10x^2 - 5x = 0$

14. $12x^2 + 4x = 0$

15. $27x^2 - 18x = 0$

PROGRESS MONITORING

Name_____ Date_____

APPLY SKILLS 1

Factor each of the quadratic trinomials.

Example:

$x^2 + 6x + 8 = \underline{(x + 2)(x + 4)}$

1. $x^2 + 9x + 20 = $ _____

2. $x^2 + 12x + 20 = $ _____

3. $x^2 - 4x - 32 = $ _____

4. $x^2 + 4x + 3 = $ _____

5. $x^2 + x - 6 = $ _____

6. $x^2 + 8x + 12 = $ _____

7. $x^2 + 6x + 5 = $ _____

8. $x^2 + x - 2 = $ _____

9. $x^2 - 6x + 8 = $ _____

10. $x^2 - 3x - 18 = $ _____

11. $x^2 - 4x + 3 = $ _____

12. $x^2 + 10x + 21 = $ _____

13. $x^2 + x - 12 = $ _____

14. $x^2 - 7x + 12 = $ _____

15. $x^2 + 9x - 10 = $ _____

16. $x^2 - 12x + 32 = $ _____

17. $x^2 - x - 30 = $ _____

18. $x^2 - 8x - 9 = $ _____

19. $2x^2 + 11x + 12 = $ _____

20. $3x^2 + 16x + 5 = $ _____

Inside Algebra

APPLY SKILLS 2

Factor each of the quadratic trinomials.

Example:

$2x^2 - x - 6 = \underline{(2x + 3)(x - 2)}$

1. $x^2 + 3x + 2 = $ _____

2. $5x^2 - 33x - 14 = $ _____

3. $7x^2 + 11x - 6 = $ _____

4. $8x^2 - 19x + 6 = $ _____

5. $14x^2 - x - 4 = $ _____

6. $x^2 + 9x + 20 = $ _____

7. $2x^2 + 3x - 5 = $ _____

8. $3x^2 - 10x - 8 = $ _____

9. $6x^2 + 17x + 10 = $ _____

10. $8x^2 - 2x - 3 = $ _____

11. $16x^2 - 8x - 3 = $ _____

12. $12x^2 - 29x + 15 = $ _____

13. $12x^2 - 16x + 5 = $ _____

14. $32x^2 - 4x - 1 = $ _____

15. $2x^2 - x - 3 = $ _____

16. $20x^2 + 12x + 1 = $ _____

17. $5x^2 - 22x - 15 = $ _____

18. $30x^2 + 1x - 3 = $ _____

19. $6x^2 - 7x - 3 = $ _____

20. $3x^2 - x - 2 = $ _____

Name_____ Date_____

APPLY SKILLS 3

Solve the quadratic trinomials by factoring.

Example:

$2x^2 - x - 6 = 0$

$(2x + 3)(x - 2) = 0$

$2x + 3 = 0$ or $x - 2 = 0$

$x = -\frac{3}{2}, 2$

1. $3x^2 - 10x - 8 = 0$

2. $2x^2 + 3x + 1 = 0$

3. $6x^2 - 7x - 3 = 0$

4. $4x^2 + 4x - 15 = 0$

5. $x^2 + 12x + 20 = 0$

6. $2x^2 - x - 3 = 0$

7. $12x^2 - 16x + 5 = 0$

8. $2x^2 + 3x - 5 = 0$

9. $6x^2 + 17x + 10 = 0$

APPLY SKILLS 3 (*continued*)

10. $8x^2 - 2x - 3 = 0$

11. $16x^2 - 8x - 3 = 0$

12. $2x^2 + 5x - 12 = 0$

13. $x^2 + 3x + 2 = 0$

14. $x^2 - 4x - 32 = 0$

15. $x^2 + 9x + 20 = 0$

16. $14x^2 - x - 4 = 0$

17. $5x^2 - 3x - 2 = 0$

18. $7x^2 + 11x - 6 = 0$

19. $5x^2 - 33x - 14 = 0$

Name_____ Date_____

APPLY SKILLS 4

Solve the quadratic trinomials by factoring.

Example:
$x^2 + 6x + 5 = 0$
$(x + 1)(x + 5) = 0$
$x + 1 = 0$ or $x + 5 = 0$
$x = -1, -5$

1. $x^2 + 12x + 20 = 0$

2. $x^2 + 3x + 2 = 0$

3. $x^2 - 4x - 32 = 0$

4. $x^2 + 9x + 20 = 0$

5. $x^2 - 9x + 14 = 0$

6. $x^2 - 2x - 15 = 0$

7. $x^2 - 6x + 9 = 0$

8. $x^2 + 5x - 6 = 0$

9. $x^2 + 5x + 6 = 0$

APPLY SKILLS 4 *(continued)*

10. $x^2 - 2x - 24 = 0$

11. $x^2 - 8x - 9 = 0$

12. $x^2 - 3x - 18 = 0$

13. $x^2 - 7x + 10 = 0$

14. $x^2 + 2x - 3 = 0$

15. $x^2 + x - 12 = 0$

16. $x^2 - 12x + 32 = 0$

17. $x^2 + 3x - 40 = 0$

18. $x^2 + 10x - 24 = 0$

19. $x^2 - 3x = 0$

PROGRESS MONITORING

APPLY SKILLS 5

Solve the quadratic trinomials by factoring.

Example:

$x^2 - 2x - 8 = 0$

$(x - 4)(x + 2) = 0$

$x - 4 = 0$ or $x + 2 = 0$

$x = 4, -2$

1. $a^2 - 6a - 16 = 0$

2. $b^2 - 9b + 14 = 0$

3. $c^2 - 4c - 21 = 0$

4. $d^2 + 8d - 9 = 0$

5. $x^2 - 9x + 8 = 0$

6. $y^2 - 7y - 30 = 0$

7. $m^2 + 11m + 28 = 0$

8. $c^2 - 20c + 64 = 0$

9. $a^2 + 6a - 27 = 0$

APPLY SKILLS 5 (*continued*)

---

10. $x^2 - x - 30 = 0$

11. $d^2 - 15d + 36 = 0$

---

12. $c^2 + 6c - 40 = 0$

13. $e^2 + e - 20 = 0$

---

14. $g^2 - 9g + 18 = 0$

15. $h^2 - 14h + 33 = 0$

---

16. $x^2 + 15x + 54 = 0$

17. $m^2 - m - 72 = 0$

---

18. $a^2 + 32a + 60 = 0$

19. $p^2 - 21p - 100 = 0$

PROGRESS MONITORING

Name _____ Date _____

APPLY SKILLS 1

Factor each of the perfect square trinomials.

Example:
$x^2 + 22x + 121 =$
$(x + 11)(x + 11) \text{ or } (x + 11)^2$

1. $c^2 + 4c + 4 =$

_____

2. $a^2 + 8a + 16 =$

_____

3. $x^2 + 14x + 49 =$

_____

4. $a^2 + 12a + 36 =$

_____

5. $x^2 - 16x + 64 =$

_____

6. $4x^2 + 4x + 1 =$

_____

7. $16x^2 - 56x + 49 =$

_____

8. $9x^2 + 6x + 1 =$

_____

9. $x^2 - 10x + 25 =$

_____

10. $x^2 + 10x + 25 =$

_____

11. $a^2 - 26a + 169 =$

_____

12. $4x^2 - 12x + 9 =$

_____

13. $16b^2 + 72b + 81 =$

_____

14. $36x^2 - 120xy + 100y^2 =$

_____

15. $25x^2 + 20x + 4 =$

_____

16. $x^2 + 3x + \frac{9}{4} =$

_____

APPLY SKILLS 2

Factor each of the differences of squares.

> *Example:*
> $x^2 - 4 =$
> $\underline{(x + 2)(x - 2)}$

1. $x^2 - 25 =$

_____

2. $a^2 - 169 =$

_____

3. $x^2 - 9 =$

_____

4. $c^2 - 100 =$

_____

5. $y^2 - 36 =$

_____

6. $4x^2 - 9 =$

_____

7. $16b^2 - 81 =$

_____

8. $9x^2 - 16 =$

_____

9. $x^2y^2 - 49 =$

_____

10. $100x^2 - 64 =$

_____

Factor each of the polynomials. This is a review exercise.

11. $3x^2y^2 - 7x^3y =$

_____

12. $x^2 + 7x + 10 =$

_____

13. $x^2 + 16x + 64 =$

_____

14. $6x^2 + 12x + 6 =$

_____

15. $m^3n^4p + m^2n^2p^2 - m^2n^3p^3 =$

_____

16. $x^2 + 2xy + y^2 =$

_____

Name_____ Date_____

APPLY SKILLS 3

Factor and solve each of the perfect square binomials using the Zero Product Property.

Example:
$y^2 - 25 = 0$
$(y + 5)(y - 5) = 0$
$y + 5 = 0$ or $y - 5 = 0$
$y = \pm 5$

1. $c^2 - 4 = 0$

2. $m^2 - 64 = 0$

3. $x^2 - 49 = 0$

4. $a^2 - 1 = 0$

5. $25x^2 - 121 = 0$

6. $36p^2 - 25 = 0$

7. $16m^2 - 9 = 0$

APPLY SKILLS 3 (*continued*)

Factor and solve each of the perfect square trinomials using the Zero Product Property.

Example:

$x^2 + 8x + 16 = 0$

$(x + 4)(x + 4) = 0$

$x + 4 = 0$

$x = -4$

8. $c^2 + 4c + 4 = 0$

9. $m^2 - 16m + 64 = 0$

10. $x^2 + 12x + 36 = 0$

11. $x^2 - 10x + 25 = 0$

12. $9x^2 + 6x + 1 = 0$

13. $16a^2 - 24a + 9 = 0$

14. $25m^2 - 20m + 4 = 0$

APPLY SKILLS 4

Factor and solve each of the quadratic equations using the Zero Product Property and any shortcuts for special quadratics, including GCF, difference of squares, and perfect square trinomials.

1. $c^2 - 2c = 0$

2. $m^2 - 6m = 0$

3. $2z^2 + 6z = 0$

4. $5x^2 - 35x = 0$

5. $4c^2 - 6c = 0$

6. $12v^2 + 8v = 0$

7. $14m^2 - 21m = 0$

8. $a^2 - 16 = 0$

9. $b^2 - 25 = 0$

10. $x^2 - 81 = 0$

APPLY SKILLS 4 (*continued*)

11. $9b^2 - 49 = 0$

12. $c^2 + 18c + 81 = 0$

13. $x^2 + 10x + 25 = 0$

14. $m^2 + 12m + 36 = 0$

15. $d^2 - 16d + 64 = 0$

16. $b^2 - 22b + 121 = 0$

17. $x^2 + 5x + 6 = 0$

18. $x^2 - 3x - 28 = 0$

19. $x^2 + 2x - 8 = 0$

20. $x^2 + 8x + 15 = 0$

APPLY SKILLS 1

Solve the equations using the method of completing the square. Work in pairs or groups.

1. $x^2 + 12x + 5 = 0$

2. $a^2 + 6a + 1 = 0$

3. $x^2 + 8x + 3 = 0$

4. $x^2 + 14x + 5 = 0$

5. $x^2 - 16x + 8 = 0$

6. $x^2 + 2x - 4 = 0$

APPLY SKILLS 2

Solve each of the equations by using the method of completing the square. Work in pairs or groups.

1. $c^2 + 4c + 2 = 0$

2. $x^2 - 12x + 5 = 0$

3. $x^2 + 10x + 12 = 0$

4. $b^2 - 2b - 9 = 0$

5. $x^2 - 6x - 12 = 0$

6. $x^2 + 5x + 2 = 0$

This page intentionally left blank

Name_____ Date_____

OBJECTIVE 1

Find the greatest common factor (GCF) for each pair.

1. 30 and 105

2. 42 and 54

3. $5a^3b^4$ and $12a^3b$

4. $12x^3y^2$ and $9xy^3$

OBJECTIVE 2

Factor the polynomials using the greatest common factor (GCF) and the Distributive Property.

5. $6x^2 + 3x$

6. $a^2b^3c^2 + ab^2c^3 + a^2b^2c^2$

Solve the equations.

7. $x^2 + 4x = 0$

8. $5x^2 - 10x = 0$

OBJECTIVE 3

Factor the quadratic polynomials.

9. $x^2 + 5x + 4$

10. $x^2 - 3x - 10$

Solve the quadratic equations by factoring.

11. $x^2 + 2x - 48 = 0$

12. $x^2 + 2x - 3 = 0$

OBJECTIVE 4

Factor the quadratic polynomials.

13. $x^2 + 4x + 4$

14. $x^2 - 25$

Solve the quadratic equations.

15. $x^2 - 8x + 16 = 0$

16. $x^2 - 1 = 0$

Exploring Quadratic and Exponential Functions

In this chapter, we continue to explore quadratic functions. We learn more about quadratics by graphing quadratic functions and using the graphs and other strategies to solve the equations. We also explore and graph exponential functions.

Objective 1
Graph parabolas, and find the coordinates of the vertex and axis of symmetry.

Objective 2
Estimate the roots of a quadratic equation by graphing the associated function.

Objective 3
Solve quadratic equations by factoring or using the quadratic formula.

Objective 4
Graph exponential functions, and solve problems using the graphs.

Chapter 10
VOCABULARY

axis of symmetry The vertical line through the vertex

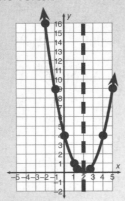

axis of symmetry: $x = 2$

exponential function Any function in which a variable appears as an exponent and may also appear as a base

$y = 2^x$

parabola The graph of a quadratic equation; the shape resembles the letter U

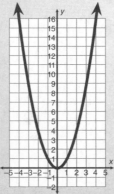

roots The solutions of an equation

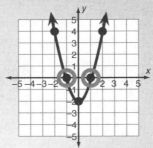

$x = -1$ **and 1**

vertex The turning point of a parabola

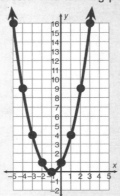

vertex: (−1, 0)

zeros of a function The points at which the function crosses the x-axis

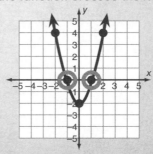

(1, 0) and (−1, 0)

Name_____ **Date**_____

MATCHING GRAPHS

For each equation, give the letter of the matching graph.

Problem Set 1

1. $y = (x - 3)^2 - 4$ _____

2. $y = (x - 1)^2$ _____

3. $y = x^2 + 4x + 3$ _____

4. $y = (x + 2)^2 + 1$ _____

5. $y = x^2 - 1$ _____

6. $y = (x - 1)^2 + 1$ _____

a.

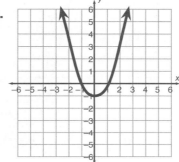

b.

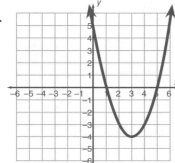

c.

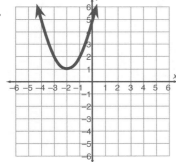

d.

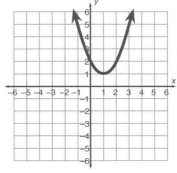

e.

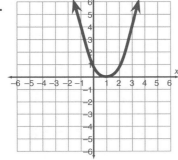

f.

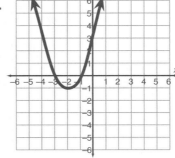

Name_____ Date_____

MATCHING GRAPHS *(continued)*

For each equation, give the letter of the matching graph.

Problem Set 2

1. $y = (x + 3)^2 - 4$ _____

2. $y = (x + 1)^2$ _____

3. $y = x^2 - 4x + 3$ _____

4. $y = (x + 2)^2 - 4$ _____

5. $y = x^2 + 1$ _____

6. $y = (x + 2)^2 + 3$ _____

a.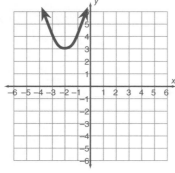

b.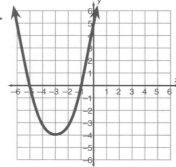

c.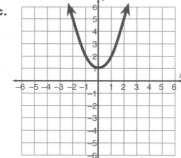

d.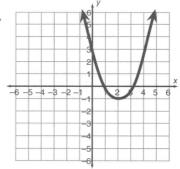

e.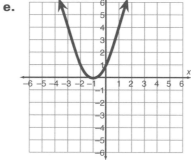

f.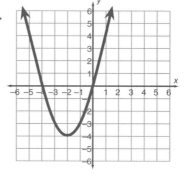

Name_____ Date_____

APPLY SKILLS 1

Construct the graph for each equation.

1. $y = 2x + 1$

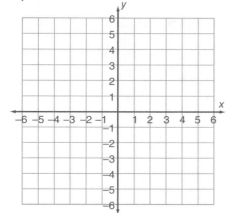

2. $y = x^2$

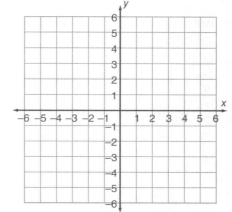

3. $y = 2x^2$

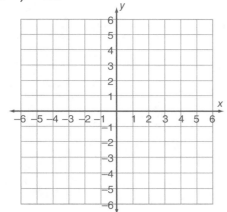

4. $y = x^2 - 3$

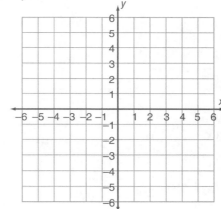

5. $y = 2x^2 - 3$

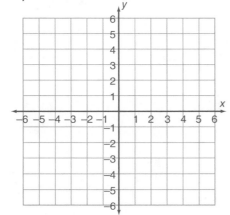

6. $y = (x - 2)^2 - 1$

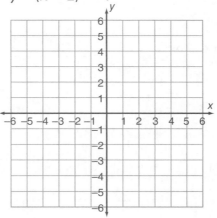

PROGRESS MONITORING

APPLY SKILLS 2

Write the coordinates of the vertex and the equation of the axis of symmetry for the equations. On the page that follows, sketch the graphs of the odd-numbered problems.

Equation	Vertex	Axis of Symmetry
Example: $y = -8x^2$	(0, 0)	$x = 0$
1. $y = x^2 - 4$	_____	_____
2. $y = (x - 5)^2$	_____	_____
3. $y = (x + 2)^2$	_____	_____
4. $y = x^2 + 3$	_____	_____
5. $y = (x - 2)^2 - 5$	_____	_____
6. $y = (x - 1)^2 + 3$	_____	_____
7. $y = (x + 4)^2 + 1$	_____	_____
8. $y = (x + 6)^2 - 8$	_____	_____
9. $y = 4 - x^2$	_____	_____
10. $y = -\frac{1}{2}x^2$	_____	_____

APPLY SKILLS 2 *(continued)*

Use the information from the previous page to graph the odd-numbered problems.

1. $y = x^2 - 4$

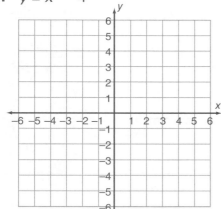

3. $y = (x + 2)^2$

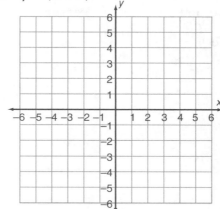

5. $y = (x - 2)^2 - 5$

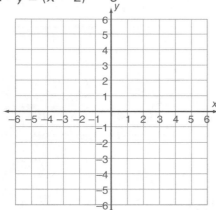

7. $y = (x + 4)^2 + 1$

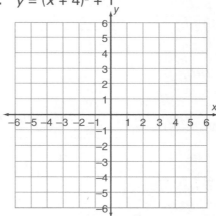

9. $y = 4 - x^2$

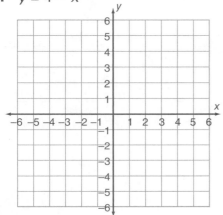

APPLY SKILLS 3

Write the coordinates of the vertex, the equation of the axis of symmetry, and the direction the graph opens—upward or downward—for each equation. On the page that follows, sketch the graphs of the even-numbered problems.

Equation	Vertex	Axis of Symmetry	Direction
Example:			
$y = 5x^2 - 6$	$(0, -6)$	$x = 0$	upward
1. $y = 4x^2$	_____	_____	_____
2. $y = -3x^2$	_____	_____	_____
3. $y = -\frac{1}{3}x^2$	_____	_____	_____
4. $y = \frac{1}{2}x^2$	_____	_____	_____
5. $y = 2x^2 - 5$	_____	_____	_____
6. $y = 4 - \frac{1}{2}x^2$	_____	_____	_____
7. $y = 6 - 5x^2$	_____	_____	_____
8. $y = \frac{1}{4}x^2 + 2$	_____	_____	_____
9. $y = 3x^2$	_____	_____	_____
10. $y = -\frac{1}{2}x^2$	_____	_____	_____

APPLY SKILLS 3 *(continued)*

Use the information from the previous page to graph the even-numbered problems.

2. $y = -3x^2$

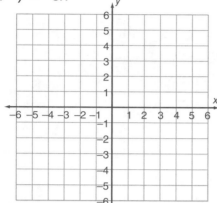

4. $y = \frac{1}{2}x^2$

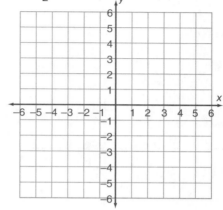

6. $y = 4 - \frac{1}{2}x^2$

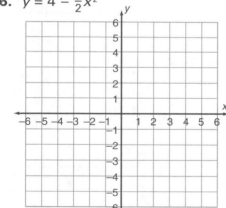

8. $y = \frac{1}{4}x^2 + 2$

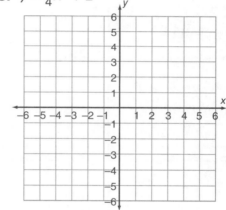

10. $y = -\frac{1}{2}x^2$

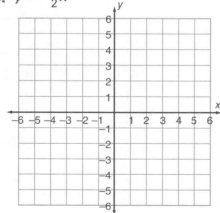

PROGRESS MONITORING

Name_____ Date_____

APPLY SKILLS 4

Write each of the equations in the form $y = (x - b)^2 + c$. Write the coordinates of the vertex and the equation of the axis of symmetry. On the page that follows, sketch the graphs of the odd-numbered problems.

Equation	$y = (x - b)^2 + c$	Vertex	Axis of Symmetry
Example: $y = x^2 - 4x + 5$	$y = (x - 2)^2 + 1$	(2, 1)	$x = 2$
1. $y = x^2 - 6x + 6$			
2. $y = x^2 + 8x + 16$			
3. $y = x^2 + 2x - 3$			
4. $y = x^2 - 4x$			
5. $y = x^2 - 10x + 16$			
6. $y = x^2 + 8x + 12$			
7. $y = x^2 + 6x$			
8. $y = x^2 - 5x - 2$			
9. $y = x^2 - 7x + 3$			
10. $y = x^2 + 10x + 25$			

APPLY SKILLS 4 (*continued*)

Use the information from the previous page to graph the odd-numbered problems.

1. $y = x^2 - 6x + 6$

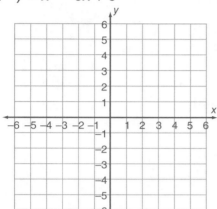

3. $y = x^2 + 2x - 3$

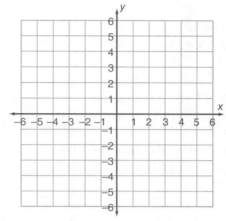

5. $y = x^2 - 10x + 16$

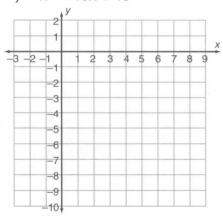

7. $y = x^2 + 6x$

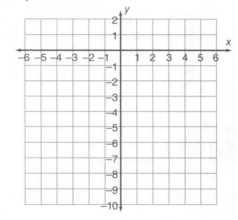

9. $y = x^2 - 7x + 3$

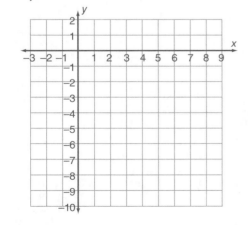

WRITING QUADRATICS

Write the quadratic equation for the description of each graph.

1. The graph that has the same shape as the graph of $y = x^2$ but is shifted to the right by 3

   _____

2. The graph that has the same shape as the graph of $y = 2x^2$ but opens downward and is moved up by 4

   _____

3. The graph that has the same shape as the graph of $y = x^2$ but is moved to the left by 2

   _____

4. The graph that has the same shape as the graph of $y = x^2$ but is shifted to the right by 1 and down by 4

   _____

5. The graph that has the same shape as the graph of $y = x^2$ but is shifted up by 3

   _____

6. The graph that has the same shape as the graph of $y = x^2$ but is shifted to the left by 2 and up by 1

   _____

7. The graph that has the same shape as the graph of $y = x^2$ but is shifted to the right by 1 and opens downward

   _____

8. The graph that is as wide as the graph of $y = \frac{1}{2}x^2$ but is moved down by 4

   _____

9. The graph that has the same shape as the graph of $y = x^2$ but is shifted to the right by 100 and down by 200

   _____

10. The graph that has the same shape as the graph of $y = x^2$ but opens downward and is shifted up by 1.414

   _____

GRAPHING QUADRATIC EQUATIONS

Find the zeros and the vertex of each graph. If you cannot find exact values for the zeros, state the consecutive integers they lie between. Graph the equations.

1. $y = x^2 - 4x + 3$

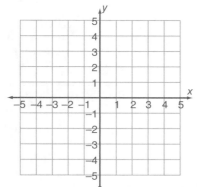

_____

_____

2. $y = x^2 + 4x + 4$

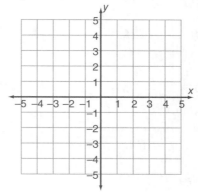

_____

_____

3. $y = x^2 - 6x + 11$

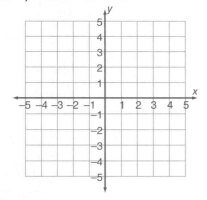

_____

_____

4. $y = 4 - x^2$

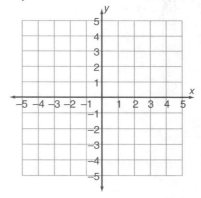

_____

_____

5. $y = x^2 + 2x - 5$

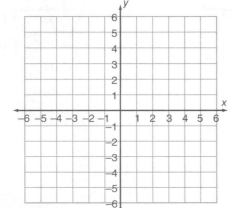

_____

_____

_____

CONCEPT DEVELOPMENT

Name_____ Date_____

APPLY SKILLS 1

Given the graphs of quadratic functions, estimate the zeros. If whole-number zeros cannot be found, estimate the zeros by stating the consecutive integers between which the roots lie.

Example:

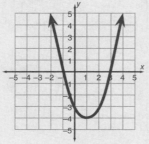

Roots are −1 and 3.

1.

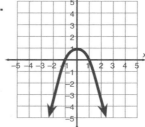

_____

_____

2.

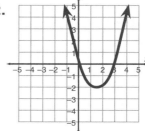

_____

_____

3.

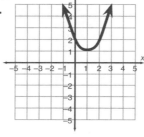

_____

_____

_____

4.

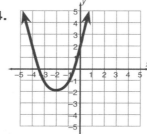

_____

_____

_____

5.

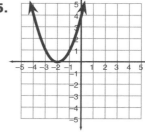

_____

_____

_____

6.

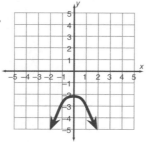

_____

_____

_____

7.

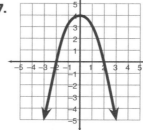

_____

_____

_____

8.

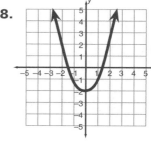

_____

_____

_____

Name_____ Date_____

APPLY SKILLS 2

Find the roots to the quadratic equations by graphing the associated functions. If the roots are not integers, name the consecutive integers between which the roots lie.

Example:

$x^2 - 6x + 4 = 0$

$$y = x^2 - 6x + 4$$

$$y = x^2 - 6x + 9 - 5$$

$$y = (x - 3)^2 - 5$$

Roots are between 0 and 1 and between 5 and 6.

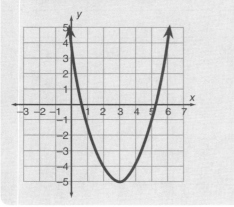

1. $x^2 + 4x + 1 = 0$

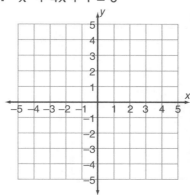

_____

_____

_____

2. $x^2 + 8x + 9 = 0$

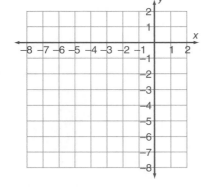

_____

_____

_____

3. $x^2 - 8x + 18 = 0$

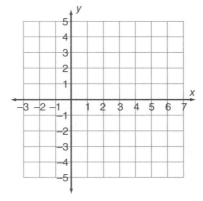

_____

_____

_____

APPLY SKILLS 2 *(continued)*

4. $x^2 - 10x + 20 = 0$

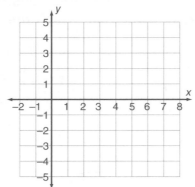

_____

_____

5. $x^2 - 2x - 4 = 0$

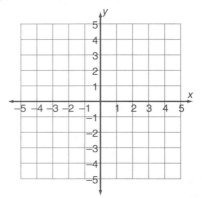

_____

_____

6. $x^2 + 6x + 9 = 0$

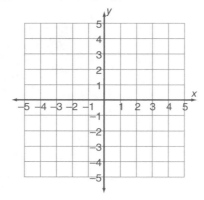

_____

_____

7. $x^2 - 6x + 10 = 0$

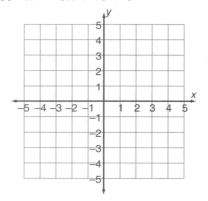

_____

_____

APPLY SKILLS 1

Solve each of the equations by taking the square root of both sides. If the answer is not an integer, round the answer to the nearest hundredth using a calculator.

Example:

$(x - 4)^2 = 7$

$\sqrt{(x - 4)^2} = \sqrt{7}$

$|x - 4| = \sqrt{7}$

$x = 4 \pm \sqrt{7}$

$x = 6.65$ or $x = 1.35$

1. $x^2 = 81$

2. $x^2 = 45$

3. $(x - 1)^2 = 36$

4. $(x + 3)^2 = 64$

5. $(x + 5)^2 = 1$

6. $(x - 4)^2 = 49$

7. $(x - 3)^2 = 10$

8. $(x + 4)^2 = 40$

9. $(x - 7)^2 = 35$

10. $(x + 11)^2 = -5$

11. $(x + 4)^2 = 0$

Name_____ Date_____

APPLY SKILLS 2

Solve each of the equations using the quadratic formula or by factoring. You may use a calculator to find square roots when needed. Round answers to the nearest hundredth using a calculator.

Quadratic formula: $x = \dfrac{-b \pm \sqrt{b^2 - 4ac}}{2a}$

Example:

$x^2 + 6x + 5 = 0$

$(x + 1)(x + 5) = 0$

$x + 1 = 0$ or $x + 5 = 0$

$x = -1$ or $x = -5$

Example:

$x^2 + 6x + 2 = 0$

$a = 1;\ b = 6;\ c = 2$

$x = \dfrac{-6 \pm \sqrt{6^2 - 4 \cdot 1 \cdot 2}}{2 \cdot 1}$

$x = \dfrac{-6 \pm \sqrt{36 - 8}}{2}$

$x = \dfrac{-6 \pm \sqrt{28}}{2}$

$x = \dfrac{-6 + 5.29}{2}$

or $x = \dfrac{-6 - 5.29}{2}$

$x = -0.36$ or $x = -5.65$

1. $x^2 - 6x - 8 = 0$

2. $x^2 + 6x = -9$

3. $x^2 + 8x - 9 = 0$

4. $x^2 - 8x - 4 = 0$

APPLY SKILLS 2 (*continued*)

5. $x^2 - 2x - 8 = 0$

6. $x^2 - 10x - 5 = 0$

7. $x^2 - 4x + 7 = 0$

8. $x^2 + 10x + 20 = 0$

9. $2x^2 - 7x + 4 = 0$

10. $3x^2 + 4x - 4 = 0$

APPLY SKILLS 3

Solve each of the equations using the quadratic formula. In each problem, write the values of *a*, *b*, and *c*, then write the formula and show your work. You may use a calculator to find the square root. Round answers to the nearest thousandth.

Example: $x^2 + 5x + 3 = 0$

$a = 1; b = 5; c = 3$

$x = \dfrac{-b \pm \sqrt{b^2 - 4ac}}{2a}$

$x = \dfrac{-5 \pm \sqrt{5^2 - 4 \cdot 1 \cdot 3}}{2 \cdot 1}$

$x = \dfrac{-5 \pm \sqrt{25 - 12}}{2}$

$x = \dfrac{-5 \pm \sqrt{13}}{2}$

$x = \dfrac{-5 + 3.606}{2}$ or $x = \dfrac{-5 - 3.606}{2}$

$x = -0.697$ or $x = -4.303$

1. $x^2 - 7x - 18 = 0$

2. $x^2 + 3x - 7 = 0$

3. $x^2 + 9x - 11 = 0$

4. $2x^2 + x - 3 = 0$

5. $3x^2 - 8x + 4 = 0$

PROGRESS MONITORING

APPLY SKILLS 3 *(continued)*

6. $4x^2 - 7 = 0$

7. $3x^2 + 5x + 4 = 0$

8. $3x^2 - 12x + 12 = 0$

9. $4x^2 - 7x + 3 = 0$

10. $2x^2 - 7x + 6 = 0$

Name_____ Date_____

GRAPHING EXPONENTIAL FUNCTIONS

Complete the table, and graph the equation.

1. $y = 2^x$

x	y
0	
1	
2	
3	
4	
5	
6	
−1	
−2	
−3	
−4	

2. $y = \left(\dfrac{1}{2}\right)^x$

x	y
0	
1	
2	
3	
4	
5	
6	
−1	
−2	
−3	
−4	
−5	

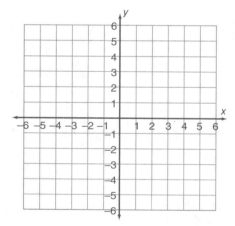

Name_____ Date_____

APPLY SKILLS 1

1. Complete the table of ordered pairs, and graph the exponential function $y = 3^x$.

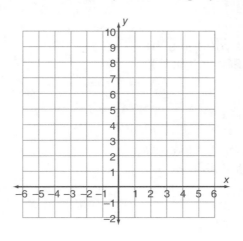

x	y
0	
1	
2	
3	
4	
5	
−1	
−2	
−3	
−4	

2. In Problem 1, what happens when the x values get large (above 5)? What happens when the x values get small (below −4)?

_____

_____

3. Complete the table of ordered pairs, and graph the exponential function $y = \left(\frac{1}{3}\right)^x$.

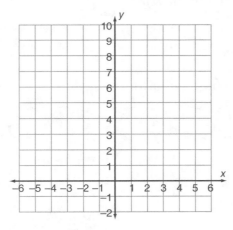

x	y
0	
1	
2	
3	
4	
−1	
−2	
−3	
−4	
−5	

4. In Problem 3, what happens when the x values get large (above 4)? What happens when the x values get small (below −5)?

_____

_____

PROGRESS MONITORING

Name_____ Date_____

APPLY SKILLS 2

Solve each problem using the formula
$A = P\left(1 + \dfrac{r}{n}\right)^{nt}$.

1. How much money would you have after 30 years if you invested $10,000 at 6% compounded quarterly?

   _____

2. How much money would you have after 30 years if you invested $10,000 at 5% compounded monthly?

   _____

3. How much money would you have after 30 years if you invested $10,000 at 5% compounded daily? (Round the number of days in a year to 360.)

   _____

4. How much money would you have after 20 years if you invested $10,000 at 7% compounded quarterly?

   _____

5. How much money would you have after 20 years if you invested $10,000 at 5% compounded monthly?

   _____

WORK SPACE

APPLY SKILLS 2 (*continued*)

Solve each problem using the formula $A = C(1 - r)^t$.

6. Find the value of a $25,000 car after 5 years if it depreciates at the rate of 15% per year.

   _____

7. Find the value of a $24,000 car after 4 years if it depreciates at the rate of 16% per year.

   _____

8. Find the value of a $30,000 car after 3 years if it depreciates at the rate of 15% per year.

   _____

9. Find the value of a $30,000 car after 4 years if it depreciates at the rate of 14% per year.

   _____

10. Find the value of a $30,000 car after 5 years if it depreciates at the rate of 14% per year.

    _____

WORK SPACE

PROGRESS MONITORING

FINDING WHICH ONE IS MORE

For each pair of problems below, guess which problem would amount to more money. Work the problems to see if your guess is correct.

1a. You receive an allowance of $10 the first week of every month, and the amount you receive doubles every week after that. Assume there are four weeks to a month. How much would your allowance be after one month?

1b. You receive an allowance of a penny the first day of the month, and the amount you receive doubles every day for the rest of the month. Assume the month has 30 days. How much would your allowance be after one month?

Day	Allowance	Total Earned
1	1¢	$0.01
2	2¢	
3		
n		
30		

2a. You invest $1,000 at age 21 and receive 8% compounded monthly until age 65. How much money would you have at age 65?

2b. You invest $3,000 at age 40 and receive 8% compounded monthly until age 65. How much money would you have at age 65?

FINDING WHICH ONE IS MORE *(continued)*

3a. You invest $10,000 at 10% interest compounded quarterly 10 years before you retire. How much money would you have when you retire?

3b. You invest $2,000 at 8% interest compounded quarterly 40 years before you retire. How much money would you have when you retire?

4a. You have $10,000 to put into savings. Bank A will pay 6% per year compounded quarterly. How much money will you have at the end of one year? At the end of two years?

4b. You have $10,000 to put into savings. Bank B will pay you 6.5% per year compounded annually. How much money will you have at the end of one year? At the end of two years?

OBJECTIVE 1

Name the coordinates of the vertex and axis of symmetry for each equation and construct the graph in the space provided.

1. $y = (x + 2)^2 - 4$

vertex _____

axis of symmetry _____

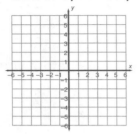

2. $y = x^2 + 6x + 4$

vertex _____

axis of symmetry _____

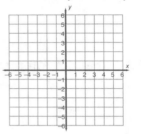

3. $y = x^2 - 4x + 2$

vertex _____

axis of symmetry _____

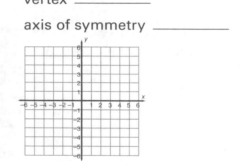

4. $y = 4 - x^2$

vertex _____

axis of symmetry _____

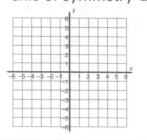

OBJECTIVE 2

Find the roots of the quadratic equations by graphing the associated functions. If the roots are not exact, name the consecutive integers between which the roots lie.

5. $x^2 + 6 = 5x$

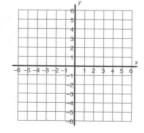

6. $x^2 + 3x - 3 = 0$

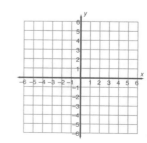

OBJECTIVE 3

Solve the quadratic equations by factoring or using the quadratic formula $x = -b \pm \frac{\sqrt{b^2 - 4ac}}{2a}$. If the answer is not an integer, round the answer to the nearest hundredth, using a calculator.

7. $x^2 + 2x - 3 = 0$

8. $10x = x^2 - 24$

9. $x^2 + 4x + 2 = 0$

10. $x^2 - 2x - 2 = 0$

OBJECTIVE 4

Graph the exponential function.

11. $y = \left(\frac{1}{4}\right)x$

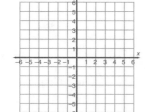

12. $y = 2^x$

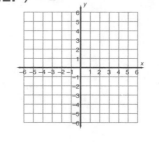

CHAPTER 10 REVIEW

OBJECTIVE 4 *(continued)*

Solve the problems involving compound interest.

13. Using the formula $A = P\left(1 + \frac{r}{n}\right)^{nt}$, find the amount of money you would have after 4 years if you invested \$10,000 at 6% compounded semiannually.

$A = 10,000\left(1 + \frac{0.06}{2}\right)^{2 \cdot 4}$

_____

14. Using the formula $A = P\left(1 + \frac{r}{n}\right)^{nt}$, find the amount of money you would have after 10 years if you invested \$10,000 at 6% compounded semiannually.

$A = 10,000\left(1 + \frac{0.06}{2}\right)^{2 \cdot 10}$

_____

Exploring Rational Expressions and Equations

In this chapter, we use what we know about fractions and rational numbers to explore rational expressions. We multiply and divide rational expressions and find common denominators to add and subtract. We also explore polynomial division and solve equations involving rational expressions.

Objective 1
Simplify rational expressions.

Objective 2
Multiply and divide rational expressions.

Objective 3
Divide a polynomial by a binomial.

Objective 4
Add and subtract rational expressions.

Objective 5
Solve rational expressions.

Chapter 11
VOCABULARY

excluded value A value of a variable that results in a denominator of zero

$$\frac{3x}{9x^2}; \ x \neq 0$$

---

least common denominator (LCD) The lowest value that is a multiple of the denominators of more than one fraction

The LCD of $\frac{3}{5}$ and $\frac{1}{3}$ is 15.

$$\frac{3}{5} \cdot \frac{3}{3} = \frac{9}{15} \text{ and } \frac{1}{3} \cdot \frac{5}{5} = \frac{5}{15}$$

---

rational expression Any expression that can be written as the quotient of two integers or polynomials

$$\frac{1}{2}, \ \frac{1}{3x}, \text{ or } \frac{x+2}{x-1}$$

APPLY SKILLS 1

Simplify the rational expressions.

Example:
$$\frac{x^2 - 9}{x^2 + 5x + 6} = \frac{x - 3}{x + 2}$$
$$\frac{(x - 3)(x + 3)}{(x + 2)(x + 3)}$$

1. $\frac{12}{16}$ = _____

2. $\frac{24}{32}$ = _____

3. $\frac{15}{24}$ = _____

4. $\frac{17a^2}{51a^2b}$ = _____

5. $\frac{3a^2 - 3}{a + 1}$ = _____

6. $\frac{b^2 + 2b + 1}{b + 1}$ = _____

7. $\frac{a^2 - 1}{a^2 - 2a + 1}$ = _____

8. $\frac{x^2 + 5x + 6}{x^2 - 3x - 10}$ = _____

9. $\frac{3x + 3}{4x^2 + 4x}$ = _____

10. $\frac{x^2 + x - 2}{x^2 - 4x + 3}$ = _____

Name_____ Date_____

Write the values of the variables that are excluded for the rational expressions.

> **Example:**
>
> $\dfrac{x+1}{x^2-1} \to x^2-1 = (x-1)(x+1) \neq 0$ so $x \neq -1, 1$

11. $\dfrac{12}{16}$

12. $\dfrac{17a^2}{51a^2b}$

13. $\dfrac{3a^2-3}{a+1}$

14. $\dfrac{b^2+2b+1}{b+1}$

15. $\dfrac{a^2-1}{a^2-2a+1}$

16. $\dfrac{x^2+5x+6}{x^2-3x-10}$

17. $\dfrac{3x+3}{4x^2+4x}$

18. $\dfrac{x^2+x-2}{x^2-4x+3}$

Name_____ Date_____

APPLY SKILLS 2

Solve.

1. Let $x = 3$. Find the value of $\frac{x^2 + 4x + 4}{x^2 + 6x + 8}$.

   _____

2. Let $x = 4$. Find the value of $\frac{x^2 + 2x - 15}{x^2 + x - 12}$.

   _____

3. Simplify $\frac{x^2 + 4x + 4}{x^2 + 6x + 8}$.
   Evaluate your result when $x = 3$.
   Compare your result with that of Problem 1.

   _____

4. Simplify $\frac{x^2 + 2x - 15}{x^2 + x - 12}$.
   Evaluate your result when $x = 3$. Evaluate
   the original problem before simplification.
   Compare your results.

   _____

   _____

5. Simplify $\frac{x^2 + 3x + 2}{x^2 + 5x + 4}$.
   Evaluate your result when $x = -1$.

   _____

6. Evaluate $\frac{x^2 + 3x + 2}{x^2 + 5x + 4}$ without simplifying for
   $x = -1$. Compare this result with the result
   of Problem 5.

   _____

   _____

APPLY SKILLS 2 *(continued)*

Simplify the rational expressions.

WORK SPACE

7. $\dfrac{x^2 + 6x + 9}{2x^2 + 6x} = $ _____

8. $\dfrac{4x^2 + 5x + 1}{x^2 - x - 2} = $ _____

9. $\dfrac{4x^2 - 4}{2x^2 + 4x + 2} = $ _____

10. $\dfrac{x^2 - 1}{(x - 1)^2} = $ _____

11. In Problem 7, what are the excluded values?

_____

APPLY SKILLS 3

Simplify each expression. Identify any excluded values.

Example:

$\dfrac{2x^2y}{4xy^2} = $ _____ $\dfrac{x}{2y}$

$\dfrac{2}{4} \cdot \dfrac{x^2}{x} \cdot \dfrac{y}{y^2} = \dfrac{x}{2y}$

$y \neq 0,\ x \neq 0$

1. $\dfrac{3 \cdot 5}{6 \cdot 7} = $ _____

2. $\dfrac{4x}{2x^2} = $ _____

3. $\dfrac{x^2yz}{xy^2z^3} = $ _____

4. $\dfrac{6x^2y^4}{2xy^2} = $ _____

5. $\dfrac{4a^2b^3c}{12a^2bc} = $ _____

PROGRESS MONITORING

APPLY SKILLS 3 (continued)

Example:

$\dfrac{x+1}{x^2-1} = \dfrac{\dfrac{1}{x-1}}{}$

$x \neq 1, -1$

$\dfrac{(x+1)}{(x+1)(x-1)} = \dfrac{1}{x-1}$

6. $\dfrac{x+2}{x^2+5x+6} =$ _____

7. $\dfrac{x^2+xy}{x^2+4xy+3y^2} =$ _____

8. $\dfrac{a^2-3a}{a^2+a-12} =$ _____

9. $\dfrac{a^2+3a+2}{a^2-a-6} =$ _____

10. $\dfrac{6x+18}{x^2+6x+9} =$ _____

11. $\dfrac{a^2+a-6}{5a-10} =$ _____

MISSING PARTS

Find the missing dimension in each problem. Simplify all rational expressions.

1. A rectangle has an area of $4x^3y^4$, and its length is x^2y^2. What is its width?

   _____

2. A rectangle has an area of $x^2 - 25$. The length is $x^2 + 10x + 25$. Find the width.

   _____

3. A triangle has an area of $x^2 - 9x + 8$. The base is $x^2 - 16x + 64$. Find the height.

   [Hint: $A = \frac{1}{2}bh$]

   _____

4. A trapezoid has an area of $x^2 - 2x - 15$. It has a top base of $4x - 19$ and a bottom base of $x^2 - 5x + 7$. Find the height.

   [Hint: $A = \frac{h(b_1 + b_2)}{2}$]

   _____

Name_____ Date_____

CAN YOU DO IT?

Simplify the rational expressions.

1. $\dfrac{6x^3 + 12x^2 - 18x}{2x^4 - 18x^2}$

2. $\dfrac{x^3y^2 + 3x^2y^3 + 2xy^4}{x^4y + x^3y^2 - 2x^2y^3}$

3. Evaluate Problem 1 if $x = 2$.

4. Evaluate Problem 2 if $x = 3$ and $y = -2$.

APPLY SKILLS 1

Find each product. Assume no denominator has a value of zero.

Example:

$$\frac{x^2 + 2x + 1}{x + 1} \cdot \frac{x - 1}{x + 1}$$

$$\frac{(x + 1)(x + 1)}{(x + 1)} \cdot \frac{x - 1}{x + 1} = x - 1$$

1. $\frac{1}{2} \cdot \frac{4}{5}$

2. $\frac{3}{8} \cdot \frac{1}{2}$

3. $1\frac{1}{2} \cdot 1\frac{1}{3}$

4. $\frac{2x}{3y} \cdot \frac{8y^2}{6x^3}$

5. $\frac{15a^2b^2}{16a^2b^3} \cdot \frac{12a^4b}{30a^3b}$

6. $\frac{2x + 4}{10x^2} \cdot \frac{6x^3}{x^2 - 4}$

7. $(2x + 4) \cdot \frac{(x - 1)}{x^2 + 3x + 2}$

APPLY SKILLS 1 (continued)

8. $\dfrac{4x^2 - 9}{x - 3} \cdot \dfrac{x^2 - 2x - 3}{2x^2 + 5x + 3}$

9. $\dfrac{3}{3 + 2x} \cdot (10x + 15)$

10. $\dfrac{x^2 - x - 6}{x^2 - 2x - 8} \cdot \dfrac{x^2 - 3x - 4}{x^2 + 2x - 15}$

11. $\dfrac{x^2 - 4x - 5}{x^2 - 3x - 10} \cdot \dfrac{x^2 + 5x + 6}{x^2 + 4x + 3}$

APPLY SKILLS 2

1. What special property does a number times its multiplicative inverse have?

   Hint:
   Multiplicative inverse of $\frac{2x}{4}$ is $\frac{4}{2x}$.

   _____

2. Why are we concerned about excluded values for a variable?

   Hint:
   $\frac{2x}{4} \cdot \frac{5}{3x^2}$

   $x \neq 0$

   _____

Find the multiplicative inverse for each of the rational expressions.

3. $\frac{1}{2}$ _____

4. 3 _____

5. $1\frac{1}{2}$ _____

6. $\frac{x}{y}$ _____

7. $\frac{1}{x^2 - 1}$ _____

8. $\frac{2x - 1}{x^2 + 6x + 9}$ _____

Divide and simplify the rational expressions. Assume no denominator has a value of zero.

9. $\frac{3}{4} \div 1\frac{1}{3}$

10. $\frac{4}{5} \div \frac{6}{10}$

11. $\frac{x^2}{y} \div \frac{5x}{2y}$

APPLY SKILLS 2 (continued)

12. $\dfrac{2x}{y} \div \dfrac{3x^2}{y}$

13. $\dfrac{x^2 + 2x + 1}{x + 2} \div \dfrac{x + 1}{x^2 - 4}$

14. $\dfrac{6x^2 - 12x}{x^2 - 9} \div \dfrac{3x^2 - 6x}{x + 3}$

15. $\dfrac{3ab^2}{5xy^4} \div \dfrac{9a^2b^3}{20x^2y^3}$

APPLY SKILLS 3

Find each product. Assume no denominator has a value of zero.

Example:

$$\frac{2}{3a} \cdot \frac{6a^2}{b} = \frac{4a}{b}$$

1. $\frac{3}{8} \cdot \frac{2}{9}$

2. $\frac{2x}{y^2} \cdot xy$

3. $\frac{1}{x^2y} \cdot \frac{x}{y}$

4. $\frac{a^2b^3c^2}{4ab} \cdot \frac{12}{ab^2}$

5. $\frac{x-3}{x+5} \cdot \frac{x^2+6x+5}{x^2-9}$

6. $\frac{x^2+5x+6}{x^2-x-12} \cdot \frac{x-4}{x^2-x-6}$

Name _____ Date _____

APPLY SKILLS 3 (*continued*)

Find each quotient. Assume no denominator has a value of zero.

Example:

$$\frac{2}{3a} \div \frac{6a^2}{b}$$

$$\frac{2}{3a} \cdot \frac{b}{6a^2} = \frac{b}{9a^3}$$

7. $\frac{1}{2} \div \frac{3}{4}$

8. $\frac{3x}{y} \div \frac{x}{y}$

9. $\frac{6x^2 - 12x}{x^2 - 9} \div \frac{3x^2 - 6x}{x + 3}$

10. $\frac{x - 2}{x + 3} \div \frac{x^2 - 4x + 4}{x^2 + x - 6}$

11. $\frac{x^2 + 8x + 7}{x^2 - 3x - 10} \div \frac{x^2 - 3x - 4}{x^2 - 2x - 15}$

12. $\frac{x + 4}{x^2 + 5x + 6} \div \frac{x^2 + 3x - 4}{x^2 + 7x + 12}$

APPLY SKILLS 1

Find the quotient using algebra tiles. Draw the resulting product mat.

Example:

$(x^2 + 3x + 2) \div (x + 1) = x + 2$

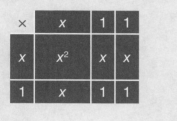

1. $(x^2 + 5x + 4) \div (x + 1) =$

2. $(x^2 + 5x + 6) \div (x + 3) =$

3. $(x^2 + 5x + 8) \div (x + 2) =$

APPLY SKILLS 2

Find each quotient. Assume no denominator has a value of zero.

Example:

$$\begin{array}{r} x + 2 \\ x + 1\overline{)x^2 + 3x + 2} \\ \underline{-(x^2 + x)} \\ 2x + 2 \\ \underline{-(2x + 2)} \\ 0 \end{array}$$

1. $x - 8\overline{)x^2 - 2x - 48}$

2. $2x + 3\overline{)6x^2 + 5x - 6}$

3. $4x - 1\overline{)4x^3 + 7x^2 - 2x}$

4. $x - 3\overline{)3x^2 - 2x - 21}$

5. $x + 2\overline{)x^2 - 3x + 6}$

6. $x - 1\overline{)x^2 - 7}$

7. $3x - 1\overline{)3x^2 + 5x - 1}$

APPLY SKILLS 2 (*continued*)

8. $x + 2 \overline{)x^3 - x - 1}$

9. $2x \overline{)4x^3 + 8x^2 + 6x}$

10. $x + 5 \overline{)x^3 + 7x^2 + 7x - 15}$

11. $n + 3 \overline{)n^2 + 10n + 20}$

12. $y - 9 \overline{)2y^2 - 14y - 30}$

Name _____ Date _____

APPLY SKILLS 1

Find the LCD for the denominators.

> *Example:*
> $2x, 3x^2$
> _____ $6x^2$ _____

1. 2, 3

_____

2. 4, 6

_____

3. 3, 6

_____

4. 5, 6

_____

5. 3, 4

_____

6. $2x, 3x$

_____

7. $x + 1, x - 1$

_____

8. $x^2 + 2x + 1, x + 1$

_____

9. $3x - 2, x + 1$

_____

Rename each rational expression so the denominators are alike.

> *Example:*
> $\dfrac{6}{x^2}, \dfrac{5}{2x}$
> $\dfrac{12}{2x^2}$ and $\dfrac{5x}{2x^2}$

10. $\dfrac{1}{2}, \dfrac{3}{4}$

11. $\dfrac{2}{3}, \dfrac{3}{5}$

12. $\dfrac{1}{x}, \dfrac{2}{3x}$

13. $\dfrac{x}{x + 1}, \dfrac{2}{x - 2}$

14. $\dfrac{3}{2x + 2}, \dfrac{x}{x + 1}$

15. $\dfrac{2}{a^2 b}, \dfrac{3}{ab^2}$

16. $\dfrac{1}{x^2 - 9}, \dfrac{2}{x + 2}$

APPLY SKILLS 2

Find the least common denominator for the pairs of rational expressions.

Example:
$\frac{1}{2x}$ and $\frac{2}{3x^2}$
$6x^2$

1. $\frac{1}{3xy}$ and $\frac{2}{3x}$

2. $\frac{1}{x+1}$ and $\frac{2}{x-1}$

3. $\frac{1}{x^2-x-6}$ and $\frac{2}{x^2-3x}$

4. $\frac{x}{2-x}$ and $\frac{3}{x^2-x-2}$

5. $\frac{2x}{x^2+2x+1}$ and $\frac{y}{x^2-1}$

Rename these rational expression pairs using the least common denominator.

Example:
$\frac{1}{2x}$ and $\frac{2}{3x^2}$
$\frac{3x}{6x^2}$ and $\frac{4}{6x^2}$

6. $\frac{1}{3xy}$ and $\frac{2}{3x}$

7. $\frac{1}{x+1}$ and $\frac{2}{x-1}$

8. $\frac{1}{x^2-x-6}$ and $\frac{2}{x^2-3x}$

9. $\frac{x}{2-x}$ and $\frac{3}{x^2-x-2}$

10. $\frac{2x}{x^2+2x+1}$ and $\frac{y}{x^2-1}$

APPLY SKILLS 3

Add or subtract these rational expressions. Simplify the results.

Example:

$\dfrac{x + 2}{x - 1} + \dfrac{x}{x + 1}$

$\dfrac{(x + 2)(x + 1)}{(x - 1)(x + 1)} + \dfrac{x(x - 1)}{(x + 1)(x - 1)}$

$\dfrac{x^2 + 3x + 2}{(x - 1)(x + 1)} + \dfrac{x^2 - x}{(x + 1)(x - 1)}$

$\dfrac{2x^2 + 2x + 2}{(x - 1)(x + 1)}$

1. $\dfrac{m + 2}{3m} + \dfrac{2m + 1}{3m}$

2. $\dfrac{a}{b} + \dfrac{b}{a}$

3. $\dfrac{x + 2}{3x} - \dfrac{4x - 1}{3x}$

4. $\dfrac{2}{x - 2} - \dfrac{x}{x - 2}$

5. $\dfrac{x - 2}{3} - \dfrac{x + 4}{3}$

6. $\dfrac{2}{x - 1} - \dfrac{1}{x + 1}$

7. $\dfrac{2}{x + 1} + \dfrac{1}{x + 2}$

Name_____ Date_____

APPLY SKILLS 3 (*continued*)

8. $\dfrac{x+2}{x^2+4x+3}+\dfrac{3}{x+3}$

9. $\dfrac{x}{1-x}-\dfrac{2}{x-1}$

10. $\dfrac{x}{x^2+3x+2}+\dfrac{1}{x+2}$

11. $\dfrac{2x}{2x-2}-\dfrac{3}{3x-3}$

12. $\dfrac{1}{3x}+\dfrac{4}{x}$

Name_____ Date_____

FINDING RATIONAL EXPRESSIONS

1. What is the second rational expression if two rational expressions added together yield $\frac{3x^2 - 2x + 8}{(x + 2)(x - 2)}$ and the first rational expression is $\frac{3x}{x + 2}$?

2. Find at least two pairs of rational expressions whose sum is $\frac{3x^2 - 10x + 3}{x^2 - 1}$.

3. A rancher wants to fence a pasture into three lots. She wants to determine the lot sizes depending on the total amount of fencing used. The dimensions are shown below.

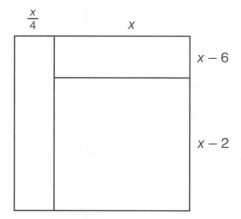

Write a formula to determine the total amount of fence (F). What are the dimensions if the rancher has 546 feet of fence? What are the dimensions if she has 926 feet of fence?

APPLY SKILLS 1

Determine the least common denominator you would use to multiply each term in these rational equations to find a solution.

1. $\frac{1}{2} + \frac{1}{x} = \frac{1}{4}$

2. $\frac{1}{2x} + \frac{1}{x^2} = \frac{1}{x+1}$

3. $\frac{1}{x-3} + \frac{1}{x+3} = 3$

4. $-x + 1 + \frac{1}{x^2 + 3x + 2} = \frac{1}{x+1}$

Solve the rational equations.

Example:
$$\frac{1}{3} + \frac{1}{x} = \frac{1}{2}$$
$$\frac{1}{3}(6x) + \frac{1}{x}(6x) = \frac{1}{2}(6x)$$
$$2x + 6 = 3x$$
$$6 = x \text{ or } x = 6$$

5. $\frac{1}{2} + \frac{1}{x} = \frac{1}{4}$

6. $\frac{5}{3y} + \frac{4}{2y} = \frac{1}{6}$

7. $\frac{1}{2} + \frac{1}{4} = \frac{1}{x}$

8. $\frac{x}{2} + \frac{1}{4} = \frac{4x}{5}$

9. $\frac{3}{x+2} = \frac{4}{x-3}$

10. $\frac{x-2}{x} = \frac{x-2}{x-4}$

11. $x + 3 - \frac{2x}{x-1} = 1$

12. $\frac{3x}{x-2} - \frac{4}{x-1} = 3$

APPLY SKILLS 2

Solve each rational expression. Simplify the results.

1. $\frac{1}{2} + \frac{2}{x} = \frac{1}{x}$

2. $\frac{y}{5} = \frac{3}{y+2}$

3. $\frac{x+1}{x-1} = \frac{x+1}{x}$

4. $\frac{3}{x+3} = \frac{2}{2(x+2)}$

5. $\frac{3}{x} + \frac{x}{x-2} = 1$

6. $x + 2 = -\frac{1}{x}$

7. $\frac{x}{x+2} + \frac{5}{x+1} = \frac{1}{x^2+3x+2}$

8. $\frac{3}{x} - \frac{4}{x+1} = 1$

9. $\frac{3}{x+1} - \frac{x+1}{x-1} = -1$

10. $\frac{x}{x+2} + \frac{4}{x+3} = \frac{2}{x^2+5x+6}$

GEOMETRY WITH RATIONAL NUMBERS

1. An isosceles triangle has a base of $\frac{5}{2y}$ units and a side of $\frac{5}{3y}$ units. The perimeter is $1\frac{1}{6}$ units. What would y be? _____ How long is each side?

_____

_____

WORK SPACE

2. A parallelogram has a base of $\frac{2x+3}{5}$ units and a side of $\frac{x+3}{x}$ units. If the perimeter is $\frac{42}{x}$ units, what is the length of the base and the length of a side?

_____

_____

3. A triangle has sides of $\frac{2x+1}{2x}$, 3, and $\frac{2x+1}{x}$ units. The perimeter is $\frac{27}{x+2}$. What is the length of each side?

_____

_____

This page intentionally left blank

OBJECTIVE 1

Simplify each rational expression.

1. $\dfrac{4x^3y^2}{-2xy^2}$

2. $\dfrac{x^2 + 2x - 8}{x - 2}$

3. $\dfrac{2x + 10}{x^2 + 2x - 15}$

4. Find the excluded values for
$\dfrac{x - 7}{x^2 + 7x + 12}.$

OBJECTIVE 2

Multiply or divide and simplify each rational expression.

5. $\dfrac{3a^2b}{ab^2} \cdot \dfrac{4a^2b}{6a^2b}$

6. $\dfrac{3xy^4}{2a^2b} \div \dfrac{2x^3y^2}{ab^3}$

7. $\dfrac{x^2 + 2x - 3}{x^2 + 5x + 6} \cdot \dfrac{x^2 + 4x + 4}{x - 1}$

8. $\dfrac{x^2 - 2x - 8}{x^2 + x - 6} \div \dfrac{x^2 - 4}{x^2 + 2x - 3}$

CHAPTER 11 REVIEW

Name_____ Date_____

OBJECTIVE 3

Find each quotient.

9. $x + 6 \overline{)x^2 + 9x + 18}$

10. $3x - 1 \overline{)3x^2 + 11x - 4}$

OBJECTIVE 4

Find the sum or difference.

11. $\dfrac{x + 6}{x} + \dfrac{2x + 1}{2x}$

12. $\dfrac{x - 7}{x^2 - x - 6} - \dfrac{3}{x + 2}$

OBJECTIVE 5

Solve each equation for x.

13. $\dfrac{1}{4} + \dfrac{1}{x} = \dfrac{1}{2}$

14. $\dfrac{-4}{x - 2} = \dfrac{8}{x + 1}$

15. $\dfrac{2}{x} + \left(-\dfrac{6}{2x}\right) = \dfrac{x}{-4}$

16. $\dfrac{x - 6}{x^2 - 3x - 4} + \dfrac{3}{x + 1} = \dfrac{2}{x - 4}$

Inside Algebra

Exploring Radical Expressions and Equations

In this chapter, we learn about expressions and equations that use square roots, or radicals. We simplify radical expressions and use radicals to solve problems involving the Pythagorean theorem and the distance formula. We also use what we know about radicals and proportions to solve problems involving similar triangles.

Objective 1
Simplify and perform operations with radical expressions.

Objective 2
Solve equations with radical expressions.

Objective 3
Use the Pythagorean theorem to solve problems.

Objective 4
Find the distance between two points in the coordinate plane.

Objective 5
Find the unknown measures of the sides of similar triangles.

Chapter 12
VOCABULARY

binary operation An operation that is applied to two operands; addition, subtraction, multiplication, and division are binary operations

$$\sqrt{x} \cdot \sqrt{y} = \sqrt{x \cdot y}$$

---

congruent Two angles that have the same measure

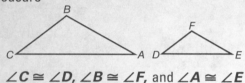

$$\angle C \cong \angle D,\ \angle B \cong \angle F,\ \text{and}\ \angle A \cong \angle E$$

---

constant of proportionality The ratio between the lengths of the sides of two similar triangles

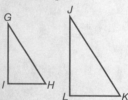

$$\triangle GIH \sim \triangle JLK$$

ratio ≈ 0.65 or 1.5

---

extraneous root A root that is a solution to the derived equation but not the original equation

$$\sqrt{x + 2} + 4 = x$$

$$\boxed{x = 2}\ \text{or}\ x = 7$$

hypotenuse The longest side of a right triangle, opposite the right angle

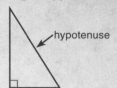

Pythagorean theorem Formula relating the lengths of the sides of a right triangle, telling us that the sum of the squares of the legs is equal to the square of the hypotenuse

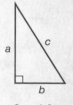

$$a^2 + b^2 = c^2$$

similar Triangles with congruent angles and proportional sides

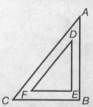

Name_____ **Date**_____

APPLY SKILLS 1

Simplify.

Example:
$\sqrt{18a^3}$
$\sqrt{9} \cdot \sqrt{2} \cdot \sqrt{a^2} \cdot \sqrt{a}$
$3a\sqrt{2a}$

1. $\sqrt{98}$

2. $\sqrt{63}$

3. $\sqrt{x^3 y^2}$

4. $\sqrt{a^4 b^5}$

5. $\sqrt{54}$

6. $-\sqrt{90}$

7. $-\sqrt{50p^2}$

8. $\sqrt{108}$

9. $\sqrt{300}$

10. $\sqrt{96}$

Name _____   Date _____

APPLY SKILLS 2

Simplify.

Example:
$\sqrt{28} \cdot \sqrt{42}$
$\sqrt{4 \cdot 7} \cdot \sqrt{7 \cdot 6}$
$\sqrt{4 \cdot 7 \cdot 7} \cdot \sqrt{6}$
$2 \cdot 7\sqrt{6}$
$14\sqrt{6}$

1. $\dfrac{\sqrt{39}}{\sqrt{3}}$

2. $\sqrt{6} \cdot \sqrt{15}$

3. $\sqrt{15} \cdot \sqrt{18}$

4. $(2\sqrt{7})^2$

5. $\dfrac{\sqrt{x^4 y}}{\sqrt{x}}$; $x, y > 0$

6. $\sqrt{\dfrac{75}{3}}$

7. $\dfrac{\sqrt{28a^2}}{\sqrt{7}}$

8. $\sqrt{50} \cdot \sqrt{147}$

9. $\sqrt{\dfrac{2}{3}} \cdot \sqrt{\dfrac{9}{8}}$

APPLY SKILLS 3

Simplify by rationalizing the denominator.

Example:

$$\frac{\sqrt{7}}{\sqrt{12}}$$

$$\frac{\sqrt{7}}{\sqrt{12}} \cdot \frac{\sqrt{3}}{\sqrt{3}}$$

$$\frac{\sqrt{21}}{\sqrt{36}}$$

$$\frac{\sqrt{21}}{6}$$

1. $\dfrac{\sqrt{5}}{\sqrt{3}}$

2. $\dfrac{\sqrt{15}}{\sqrt{6}}$

3. $\dfrac{2}{\sqrt{5}}$

4. $\dfrac{1}{\sqrt{2}}$

5. $\sqrt{\dfrac{7x^2}{9}}$

6. $\sqrt{\dfrac{20}{12}}$

7. $\sqrt{\dfrac{1}{12}}$

8. $\dfrac{6}{\sqrt{3}}$

9. $\sqrt{\dfrac{3}{8}}$

10. $\dfrac{8}{\sqrt{18}}$

11. $\dfrac{7}{\sqrt{12}}$

PROGRESS MONITORING

APPLY SKILLS 4

Rationalize the denominator in each expression.

Example:

$$\frac{t}{5 - \sqrt{t}}$$

$$\frac{t(5 + \sqrt{t})}{(5 - \sqrt{t})(5 + \sqrt{t})}$$

$$\frac{t(5 + \sqrt{t})}{25 - t}$$

1. $\dfrac{6}{2 + \sqrt{3}}$

2. $\dfrac{-2}{5 - \sqrt{6}}$

3. $\dfrac{4}{\sqrt{3} + 2}$

4. $\dfrac{5}{\sqrt{5} + \sqrt{3}}$

5. $\dfrac{-3}{\sqrt{7} - 2}$

6. $\dfrac{\sqrt{3}}{\sqrt{x} + 2}$

7. $\dfrac{\sqrt{7}}{4 - \sqrt{x}}$

8. $\dfrac{x}{2\sqrt{3} + \sqrt{5}}$

9. $\dfrac{x}{2 + \sqrt{x}}$

10. $\dfrac{w}{\sqrt{w} - 11}$

11. $\dfrac{y}{3 - \sqrt{y}}$

APPLY SKILLS 5

Simplify.

Example:

$5\sqrt{3} - 4\sqrt{x} + 9\sqrt{x}$

$5\sqrt{3} + 5\sqrt{x}$

1. $5\sqrt{7} - 2\sqrt{3} + 3\sqrt{7}$

2. $13\sqrt{5} - 5\sqrt{5}$

3. $\sqrt{18} + \sqrt{12}$

4. $\sqrt{10} + 3\sqrt{10} - \sqrt{5}$

5. $\sqrt{20} + \sqrt{80} - \sqrt{45}$

6. $7\sqrt{y} - 2\sqrt{y} + 3\sqrt{x}$

7. $18\sqrt{x} + 3\sqrt{y} - 4\sqrt{x}$

8. $5\sqrt{50} - 4\sqrt{32}$

9. $\sqrt{200a^2} - \sqrt{98a^2}$

10. $\sqrt{\frac{2}{3}} - \sqrt{\frac{1}{6}}$

11. $\sqrt{\frac{1}{5}} - \sqrt{\frac{1}{10}}$

Name _____ Date _____

APPLY SKILLS 5 (continued)

Multiply as indicated and simplify the answers.

Example:
$(4 - \sqrt{7})(4 + \sqrt{7})$
$16 - \sqrt{49}$
$16 - 7$
9

12. $7(3 - \sqrt{2})$

13. $\sqrt{6}(2 - \sqrt{12})$

14. $4(\sqrt{7} + 3)$

15. $(11 + 6\sqrt{2})x$

16. $(9 - 3\sqrt{3})y$

17. $(6 + \sqrt{3})(4 - \sqrt{3})$

18. $(9 - \sqrt{2})(2 + 2\sqrt{2})$

19. $(\sqrt{5} - 3)(2\sqrt{5} + 1)$

20. $(3\sqrt{x} - 4)(2\sqrt{x} + 7)$

21. $(5 - 4\sqrt{y})(13 - 2\sqrt{y})$

22. $(3 + 2\sqrt{x})(7 - 3\sqrt{x})$

APPLY SKILLS 6

Simplify.

Example:
$\sqrt{2}(7 - \sqrt{8})$
$7\sqrt{2} - \sqrt{2}\sqrt{8}$
$7\sqrt{2} - \sqrt{16}$
$7\sqrt{2} - 4$

1. $\sqrt{128y} - \sqrt{2y}$

2. $\sqrt{75}$

3. $(7\sqrt{3})^2$

4. $\sqrt{12}$

5. $4\sqrt{3} \cdot \sqrt{18}$

6. $\dfrac{5}{\sqrt{7}}$

7. $3(\sqrt{5} - \sqrt{3})$

8. $\dfrac{14(3 + \sqrt{5})}{(3 - \sqrt{5})(3 + \sqrt{5})}$

9. $(3 - \sqrt{2})(5 + 2\sqrt{2})$

10. $\sqrt{867}$

11. $\sqrt{2} + \dfrac{1}{\sqrt{2}}$

PROGRESS MONITORING

Name_____ Date_____

APPLY SKILLS 6 (continued)

12. $3\sqrt{2}(\sqrt{8} - \sqrt{2})$

13. $5\sqrt{6c} \cdot \sqrt{2c}$

14. $\dfrac{\sqrt{12}}{\sqrt{18}}$

15. $5\sqrt{3} - \sqrt{75}$

16. $a(5a - 3\sqrt{a})$

17. $\sqrt{8w^2} + \sqrt{2w^2}$

18. $\dfrac{4}{\sqrt{x} - 3}$

19. $(3\sqrt{x} - 2)(7 + 5\sqrt{x})$

20. $\sqrt{8n + 8} + \sqrt{2n + 2}$

APPLY SKILLS 1

Solve each equation. Check your answer.

Example:

$\sqrt{2x + 5} = 7$

$(\sqrt{2x + 5})^2 = 7^2$

$2x + 5 = 49$

$2x = 44$

$x = 22$

Check:

$\sqrt{2(22) + 5} = 7$

$\sqrt{44 + 5} = 7$

$\sqrt{49} = 7$

$7 = 7$

1. $\sqrt{3x} = 6$

2. $6 - \sqrt{c} = 4$

3. $\sqrt{x - 3} = 5$

4. $10 = \sqrt{-5x}$

5. $\sqrt{\dfrac{x}{7}} = 13$

6. $\dfrac{\sqrt{x}}{4} = 8$

7. $2\sqrt{h} + 3\sqrt{h} = 8$

8. $56 = \sqrt{128a} - \sqrt{2a}$

9. $12 = \sqrt{4a}$

10. $\sqrt{x} - 5 = 0$

APPLY SKILLS 1 (*continued*)

11. $\sqrt{-c} = 2$

12. $\sqrt{4x + 1} = 7$

13. $\sqrt{x + 7} = \sqrt{21}$

14. $\sqrt{\frac{1}{9}x + 1} = \frac{7}{3}$

15. $\sqrt{3x + 4} - 2 = 5$

16. $\sqrt{2x - 3} + 5 = 7$

Name_____ Date_____

APPLY SKILLS 2

Solve each equation. Check your answer.

Example:
$$\sqrt{x-2} + 3 = 7$$
$$\sqrt{x-2} = 4$$
$$(\sqrt{x-2})^2 = 4^2$$
$$x - 2 = 16$$
$$x = 18$$

Check:
$$\sqrt{18-2} + 3 = 7$$
$$\sqrt{16} + 3 = 7$$
$$4 + 3 = 7$$
$$7 = 7$$

1. $2 = \sqrt{4x + 7}$

2. $\sqrt{2h} + 4 = 7$

3. $\sqrt{5x} = 10$

4. $6 - \sqrt{7x - 9} = 3$

5. $\sqrt{y + 6} = 7$

6. $\sqrt{t + 2} + 5 = 11$

7. $\sqrt{2x - 1} = 2$

8. $9 = \sqrt{5x + 6} - 2$

9. $\sqrt{2x} + 4 = 0$

10. $\sqrt{2x - 3} + 5 = -2$

APPLY SKILLS 2 (*continued*)

Solve each equation. Check your answer.

Example:

$$\sqrt{12 + t} = 5\sqrt{t}$$
$$(\sqrt{12 + t})^2 = (5\sqrt{t})^2$$
$$12 + t = 25$$
$$12 = 24t$$
$$t = \frac{1}{2}$$

Check:

$$\sqrt{12 + \frac{1}{2}} = 5\sqrt{\frac{1}{2}}$$
$$\sqrt{\frac{24}{2} + \frac{1}{2}} = 5\sqrt{\frac{1}{2}}$$
$$\sqrt{\frac{25}{2}} = 5\sqrt{\frac{1}{2}}$$
$$\sqrt{25}\sqrt{\frac{1}{2}} = 5\sqrt{\frac{1}{2}}$$
$$5\sqrt{\frac{1}{2}} = 5\sqrt{\frac{1}{2}}$$

11. $\sqrt{14 - d} = 2\sqrt{d}$

12. $\sqrt{25} = \sqrt{x - 3}$

13. $\sqrt{2a^2 + 5} - \sqrt{2a^2 - a} = 0$

Example:

$$2h = \sqrt{-13h - 10}$$
$$(2h)^2 = (\sqrt{-13h - 10})^2$$
$$4h^2 = -13h - 10$$
$$4h^2 + 13h + 10 = 0$$
$$(4h + 5)(h + 2) = 0$$
$$h = -\frac{5}{4}, \; h = -2$$

Check:

$$2\left(-\frac{5}{4}\right) = \sqrt{-13\left(-\frac{5}{4}\right) - 10}$$
$$-\frac{5}{2} = \sqrt{\frac{65}{4} - 10}$$
$$-\frac{5}{2} = \sqrt{\frac{25}{4}}$$

no solution

Check:

$$2(-2) = \sqrt{-13(-2) - 10}$$
$$-4 = \sqrt{26 - 10}$$
$$-4 = \sqrt{16}$$

no solution

14. $x = \sqrt{24 - 5x}$

15. $\frac{1}{2}x = \sqrt{x + 3}$

16. $x - 3 = \sqrt{x + 17}$

PYTHAGOREAN THEOREM PROBLEMS

PRACTICE

1. Find *x*.

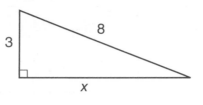

2. Find *a*.

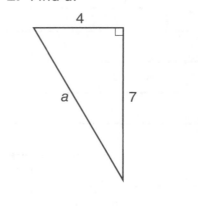

3. Find the length of the hypotenuse of a right triangle in which leg 1 = 12 units and leg 2 = 12 units.

4. Find *c*.

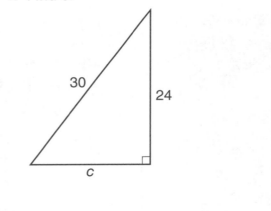

5. Find *t*.

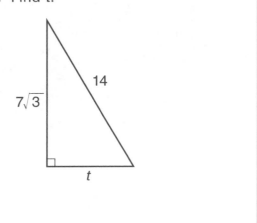

6. Find *b*.

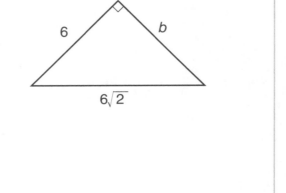

APPLY SKILLS 1

Complete the chart for the sides of right triangles.

	Leg 1	Leg 2	Hypotenuse
Example:	2	4	$\sqrt{2^2+4^2}=\sqrt{20}=2\sqrt{5}$
1.	3	4	
2.	4	6	
3.		11	15
4.	8		17
5.		40	41
6.	9		12

Find the missing sides of the given right triangles.

Example:

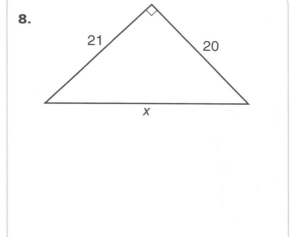

$$12^2 - 6^2 = t^2$$
$$t = \sqrt{108}$$
$$= \sqrt{36 \cdot 3}$$
$$= 6\sqrt{3}$$

7.

2.5
x
1.5

8.

21
20
x

APPLY SKILLS 1 (*continued*)

9.

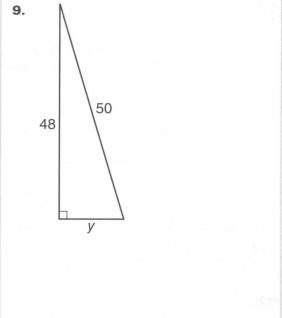

10.

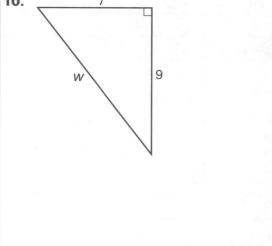

11.

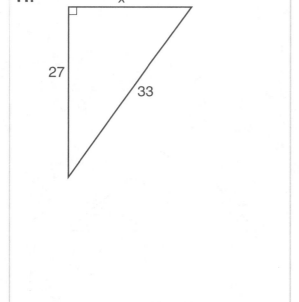

12.

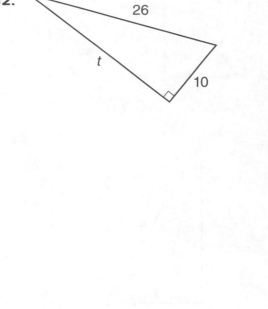

Name_____ Date_____

Complete the chart for the sides of right triangles.

	Leg 1	Leg 2	Hypotenuse
Example:	5	$3\sqrt{2}$	$\sqrt{5^2 + (3\sqrt{2})^2} = \sqrt{43}$
1.		6	$2\sqrt{13}$
2.	14		26
3.		24	25
4.	3		6
5.	$\frac{9\sqrt{3}}{2}$		9
6.	$8\sqrt{2}$	$8\sqrt{2}$	

Find the missing sides of the given right triangles.

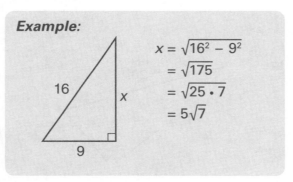

Example:

$$x = \sqrt{16^2 - 9^2}$$
$$= \sqrt{175}$$
$$= \sqrt{25 \cdot 7}$$
$$= 5\sqrt{7}$$

7.

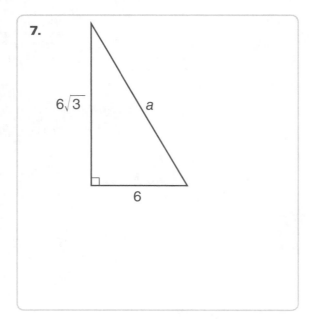

8.

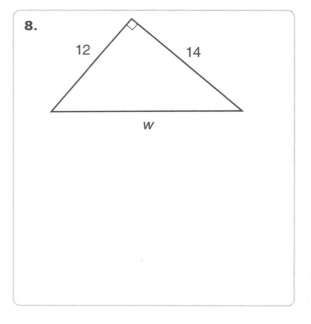

APPLY SKILLS 2 *(continued)*

9.

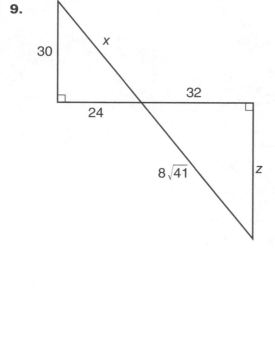

10.

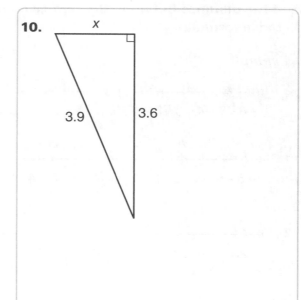

Determine whether the given lengths are sides of a right triangle.

Example:
27, 45, 36 $45^2 = 36^2 + 27^2$
$2,025 = 1,296 + 729$
$2,025 = 2,025$
Yes, this is a right triangle.

11. 22, 14, 26

12. 20, 12, 16

13. 1, 3, 2

14. 91, 84, 35

15. 1.2, 0.6, 1

Name _____ Date _____

APPLY SKILLS 1

Find the distance between the two given points, first visually, then using the distance formula.

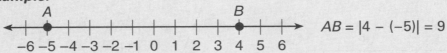

Example:

$AB = |4 - (-5)| = 9$

1.

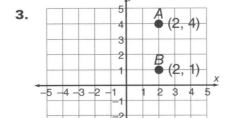

2.

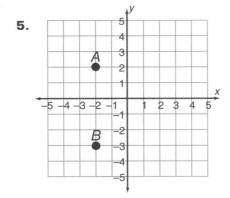

3.

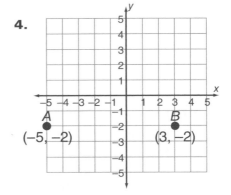

4.

5.

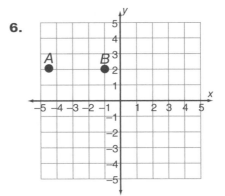

6.

Name_____ Date_____

APPLY SKILLS 1 (*continued*)

Calculate the distance between the given points.

$$d = \sqrt{(x_1 - x_2)^2 + (y_1 - y_2)^2}$$

Example:

   Find *BD*.

   $BD = \sqrt{(5 - -1)^2 + (-2 - -2)^2} = \sqrt{36 + 0} = 6$

7. Find *AC*.

8. Find *AB*.

9. Find *BC*.

10. Find *DC*.

11. Find *AD*.

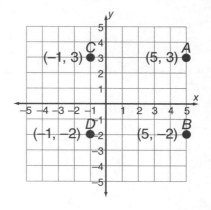

Example:

   Find *AD*.

   $AD = \sqrt{(5 - 1)^2 + (1 - -3)^2} = \sqrt{16 + 16} = 4\sqrt{2}$

12. Find *AC*.

13. Find *BD*.

14. Find *CD*.

15. Find *AB*.

16. Find *BC*.

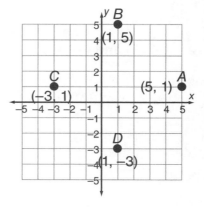

Name _____ Date _____

APPLY SKILLS 2

Plot the points on the coordinate graph, and find the distance between them.

$d = \sqrt{(x_1 - x_2)^2 + (y_1 - y_2)^2}$

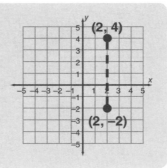

Example:

   (2, 4) and (2, −2)

   $d = \sqrt{(2 - 2)^2 + (4 - -2)^2} = 6$

1. (4, 3) and (10, 3)

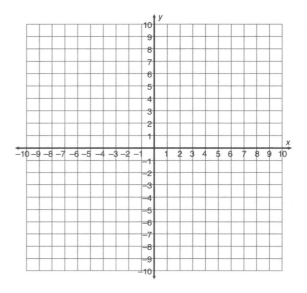

2. (−2, 8) and (−2, −5)

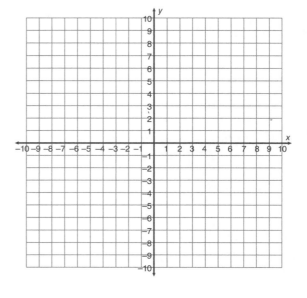

APPLY SKILLS 2 *(continued)*

3. (5, 10) and (5, −8)

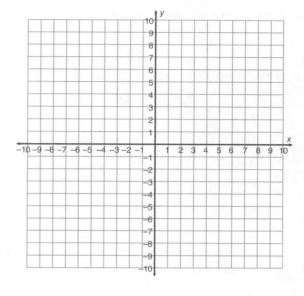

4. (−8, 6) and (7, 6)

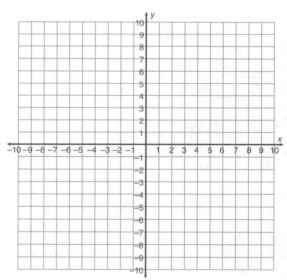

Name_____ Date_____

APPLY SKILLS 2 (*continued*)

Find the distance between the two given points.

$$d = \sqrt{(x_1 - x_2)^2 + (y_1 - y_2)^2}$$

Example: (12, −7) and (−2, 13)

$$d = \sqrt{(12 - -2)^2 + (-7 - 13)^2}$$
$$= \sqrt{14^2 + (-20)^2}$$
$$= \sqrt{196 + 400}$$
$$= \sqrt{596}$$
$$= \sqrt{4 \cdot 149}$$
$$= 2\sqrt{149}$$

5. (−8, 6) and (−1, 7)

6. (5, 4) and (5, −2)

7. (9, −2) and (3, −6)

8. (0.8, −1) and (2, −0.5)

9. (4, 8) and (6, 2)

10. (2, −3) and (7, −3)

11. (2, *a*) and (5, *b*)

APPLY SKILLS 3

Find the missing coordinate if the two points are *d* units apart.

Example:

    (3, *a*) and (6, 7)

$$d = \sqrt{45}$$
$$45 = 9 + (7 - a)^2$$
$$(7 - a)^2 = 36$$
$$|7 - a| = 6$$

$$7 - a = 6 \quad\quad 7 - a = -6$$
$$a = 1 \quad \text{or} \quad a = 13$$

1. (0, *a*) and (4, 9)

$$d = \sqrt{97}$$

2. (*a*, 2) and (4, 17)

$$d = 17$$

3. (12, 10) and (6, *a*)

$$d = 10$$

PROGRESS MONITORING

APPLY SKILLS 1

Write the matching relationship for each pair of triangles that are similar. If they are not similar, tell why they are not.

Example:

Matching relationship:
△EFG ~ △TRW

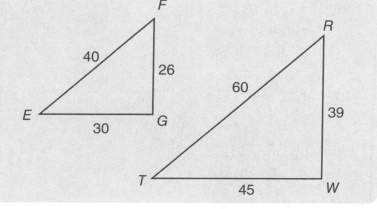

1.

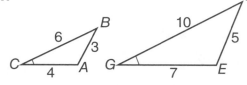

2.

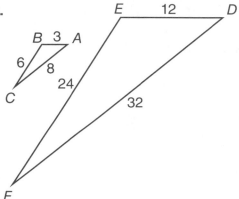

3.

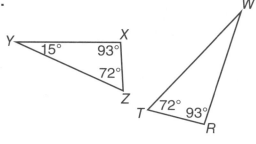

4.

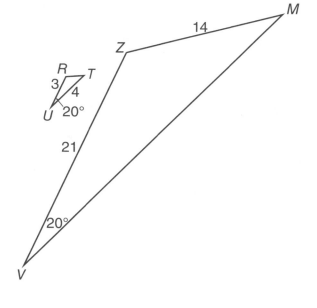

Name_____ Date_____

APPLY SKILLS 1 (*continued*)

Find the missing measures for each pair of similar triangles.

Example:

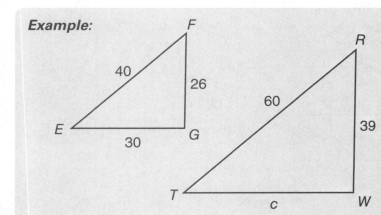

$$\frac{40}{60} = \frac{30}{c}$$

$$c = \frac{60 \cdot 30}{40}$$

$$c = 45$$

5.

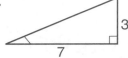 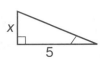

6.

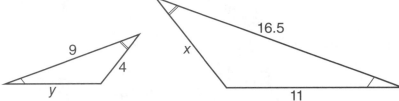

7.

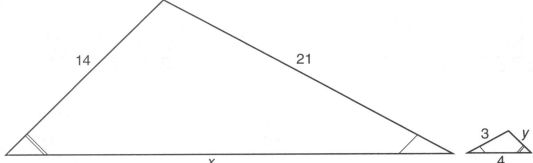

8.

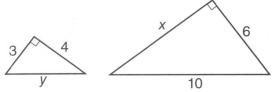

APPLY SKILLS 2

Write a matching relationship for each pair of triangles that are similar. If they are not similar, explain why they are not.

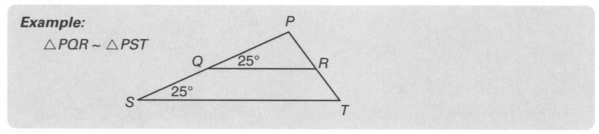

Example:

△PQR ~ △PST

1.

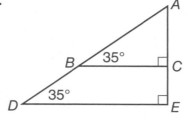

2.

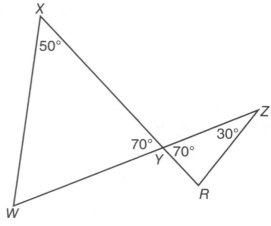

3.

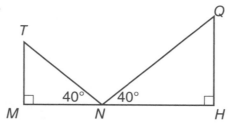

4.

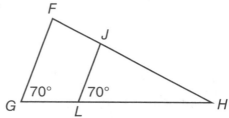

Example:

$AC = 8$, $AB = 6$, $BC = 9$, $CE = 10$

Find CD and DE.

$\triangle ABC \sim \triangle EDC$

$\dfrac{AB}{DE} = \dfrac{BC}{CD} = \dfrac{AC}{CE}$

$\dfrac{6}{DE} = \dfrac{9}{CD} = \dfrac{8}{10}$

$DE = \dfrac{6 \cdot 10}{8} = \dfrac{15}{2}$

$CD = \dfrac{9 \cdot 10}{8} = \dfrac{45}{4}$

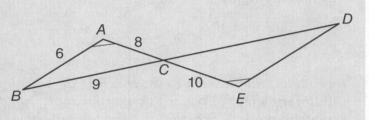

5.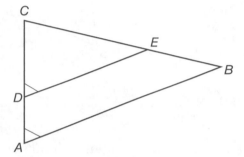

$AC = 12$, $CD = 4$, $BC = 24$ Find CE.

$AC = 15$, $AD = 3$, $BC = 25$ Find BE.

$CD = 16$, $AD = 4$, $DE = 25$ Find AB.

6.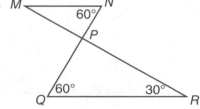

$MN = 2\sqrt{7}$, $NP = \sqrt{7}$, $PQ = 16$
Find:

$\angle MPN$

$\angle M$

MP

QR

PR

7.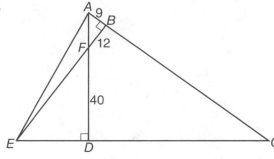

$AB = 9$, $BF = 12$, $DF = 40$
Find:

DE

EF

AF

APPLY SKILLS 3

Solve.

1. Write a matching relationship for the similar triangles.

   Hint: You might want to draw △*RST* on a different sheet of paper to help make the matching relationships.

2. If *RT* = 12, *TQ* = 3, and *RP* = *RS* + 8, find *RS*.

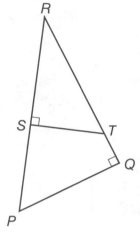

3. If you know that ∠1 ≅ ∠3, find as many pairs of similar triangles as you can. Write the matching for each pair you find.

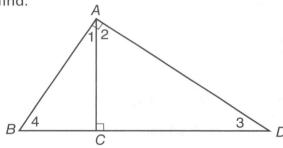

4. If *BC* = 4 and *AC* = 6, find *CD*, *AB*, and *AD*.

OBJECTIVE 1

Simplify.

1. $\sqrt{27}$

2. $\sqrt{x^3 y^7}$

3. $\sqrt{3}(2\sqrt{5} - 2\sqrt{3})$

4. $\sqrt{32} + \sqrt{18}$

Rationalize the denominators.

5. $\dfrac{4}{6 - \sqrt{5}}$

6. $\dfrac{\sqrt{8}}{\sqrt{12}}$

OBJECTIVE 2

Simplify each equation and check for extraneous roots.

7. $\sqrt{3x} = 6$

8. $2 = \sqrt{x + 9}$

9. $x = \sqrt{4 - 3x}$

10. $\sqrt{x - 5} + 2 = 3$

CHAPTER 12 REVIEW

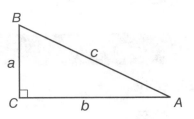

OBJECTIVE 3

Given the right triangle $\triangle ABC$ with $\angle C = 90°$, find the missing lengths of the sides.

11. $a = 3$

$b = 5$

$c = $ _____

12. $a = 2\sqrt{2}$

$b = $ _____

$c = 2\sqrt{11}$

13. $a = $ _____

$b = 12$

$c = 20$

14. Determine whether a triangle with sides with the given lengths is a right triangle, and justify your answer.

$a = 4$ $b = 6$ $c = 9$

OBJECTIVE 4

Find the distance between the given points.

15. $(-1, 3)$ and $(-4, 7)$

16. $(-1, -3)$ and $(4, 1)$

17. $(6, -2)$ and $(0, -2)$

18. $(4, 1)$ and $(6, 7)$

Name_____   Date_____

OBJECTIVE 5

Find the unknown measures of the sides of these similar triangles.

19.

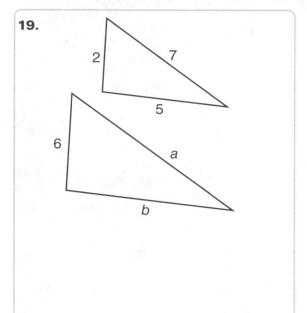

20.

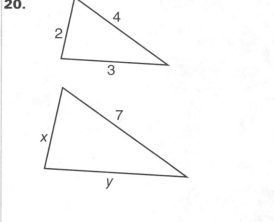

21.

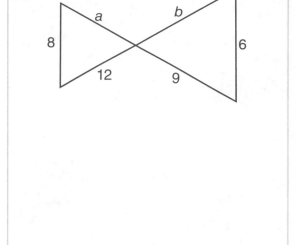

This page intentionally left blank

A

absolute value The distance of a number from zero on the number line; it is always a positive number

$|{-3}| = 3$ or $|9| = 9$

acute triangle A triangle whose angles are all acute, or less than 90°

algebraic expression An expression that includes variables

$9 - 2y$

and All conditions must be true for the statement to be true

$x \geq -1$ and $x \leq 3$

average The sum of the values in a set, divided by the number of values in the set

The average of the numbers 7, 19, 26, 31, and 42 is 25.

axis of symmetry The vertical line through the vertex

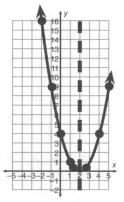

axis of symmetry: $x = 2$

B

best-fit line The line on a graph that will best connect the data or points

binary operation An operation that is applied to two operands; addition, subtraction, multiplication, and division are binary operations

$\sqrt{x} \cdot \sqrt{y} = \sqrt{x \cdot y}$

binomial An expression with two terms

$10 + 6$ or $x - 7$

C

coefficient A number or quantity placed before a variable, which indicates multiplication of that variable

In $8x$, the coefficent of x is 8.

completing the square Adding to or subtracting from a quadratic equation to make it into a perfect square trinomial; a method used to find the solutions of a quadratic equation

$x^2 + 6x + 5 = 0$
$x^2 + 6x + 9 - 4 = 0$
$(x + 3)^2 = 4$
$x = -1$ or -5

compound inequality Two inequalities connected by *and* or *or*

$x > 0$ and $x \leq 7$
$x < 3$ or $x > 13$

congruent Two angles that have the same measure

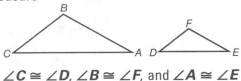

$\angle C \cong \angle D$, $\angle B \cong \angle F$, and $\angle A \cong \angle E$

---

consistent A system of equations that is always true

$2x - y = 3$
$\underline{4x - 2y = 6}$
$0 = 0$

---

constant of proportionality The ratio between the lengths of the sides of two similar triangles

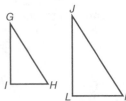

$\triangle GIH \sim \triangle JLK$
ratio ≈ 0.65 or 1.5

---

coordinate plane The plane determined by a horizontal number line, called the *x*-axis, and a vertical number line, called the *y*-axis, intersecting at a point called the origin

---

cube A number or variable raised to the third power

x^3 or 2^3

---

dependent variable A variable whose value is dependent upon the value of another variable

> **If you are traveling by car on a long stretch of highway with no gas stations, the distance you are able to travel is the dependent variable because it depends on the amount of gas you previously put in the car.**

---

descending order Arranged from largest to smallest; decreasing

98, 87, 52, 31, 16, 4

$2x^5, 2x^3, 7x, 10$

---

difference of squares A binomial of the form $a^2 - b^2 = (a + b)(a - b)$

$x^2 - 16 = (x + 4)(x - 4)$

---

domain The possible values for *x* in a relation

$y = 2x + 5$	
x	*y*
−1	3
0	5
3	11

---

elimination Removing one variable from a system of equations by adding or subtracting like terms with the same coefficients

$x + 2y = 8$ $-3 + 2y = 8$
$\underline{-2x - 2y = -5}$ $y = \dfrac{11}{2}$
$-x + 0 = 3$
$x = -3$

---

equation A statement that two quantities or mathematical expressions are equal

$x + 1 = 8$

    Inside Algebra

equilateral triangle A triangle whose three sides are equal in length and three angles are equal in measure; the angles are each 60°

equivalent Equal in value

$3 = 3$

$x + 1 = x + 1$

$\frac{7}{7} = 1$

excluded value A value of a variable that results in a denominator of zero

$\frac{3x}{9x^2}; \; x \neq 0$

exponent The power to which some other quantity is raised

In x^y the exponent is y.

exponential function Any function in which a variable appears as an exponent and may also appear as a base

$y = 2^x$

extraneous root A root that is a solution to the derived equation but not the original equation

$\sqrt{x + 2} + 4 = x$

$x = 2$ or $x = 7$

F

factor A monomial that evenly divides a value

Factors of 12: 1, 2, 3, 4, 6, 12

Factors of $2x^2 + 6x$: $2x$ and $x + 3$

false The statement is always incorrect

Five added to six is ten.

or $3 \cdot 8 = 16$

finite A set that contains a specific number of values

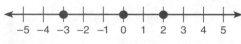

{−3, 0, 2}

function A relation in which every element in the domain is paired with exactly one element in the range

$f(x) = x + 3$

G

greatest common factor (GCF) The largest factor that a set of monomials has in common

12: 1, 2, 3, ④ 6, 12

16: 1, 2, ④ 8, 16

The GCF of 12 and 16 is 4.

H

hypotenuse The longest side of a right triangle, opposite the right angle

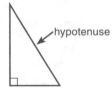
hypotenuse

I

inconsistent A system of equations that is never true

$$3x - 2y = 0$$
$$3x - 2y = -2$$
$$0 = -2$$

independent variable A variable whose value does not depend upon the value of another variable

The length of your hair after a haircut depends on the length that you request to be cut from your hair, for example, 1 inch. The independent variable is the length cut from your hair.

inequality A mathematical sentence that compares two expressions using one of the following symbols:

> Greater than

< Less than

≥ Greater than or equal to

≤ Less than or equal to

$x < 3;\ x \le 7$

infinite A set that goes on forever

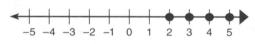

{2, 3, 4, 5...}

integer The set of whole numbers and their opposites

{...−2, −1, 0, 1, 2...}

inverse operations Pairs of operations that undo each other and share an inverse relation

inverse relation The set of ordered pairs obtained from switching the *x*- and *y*-values

The inverse relation for {(5, 8), (6, 9), (7, 10), (8, 11), (9, 12)} is {(8, 5), (9, 6), (10, 7), (11, 8), (12, 9)}.

irrational number A number that cannot be expressed as the ratio of two integers

 $\sqrt{2} = 1.414213...$

isosceles triangle A triangle with two sides of equal length, and the angles opposite the equal sides are also equal

L

least common denominator (LCD) The lowest value that is a multiple of the denominators of more than one fraction

The LCD of $\frac{3}{5}$ and $\frac{1}{3}$ is 15.

$$\frac{3}{5} \cdot \frac{3}{3} = \frac{9}{15} \text{ and } \frac{1}{3} \cdot \frac{5}{5} = \frac{5}{15}$$

like terms Terms that have the same variables and exponents

x^2 **and** $2x^2$ **or** $6y$ **and** $3y$

linear equation The equation of a straight line

$y = 2x + 4$

median The center value in a set when all values are ordered by size

    The median of the numbers 21, 18, 25, 26, and 17 is 21.

mode The value in a set that appears most

    The mode of the numbers 29, 27, 23, 29, 26, and 25 is 29.

monomial An expression with only one term

    24 or _x_

multiplicative inverse Numbers that multiply to equal one

    $3 \cdot \frac{1}{3} = 1$

number line A tool used to represent numbers in graphic form

obtuse triangle A triangle with one obtuse angle, or angle that is greater than 90°; the longest side is always opposite the obtuse angle

open The truth of the statement cannot be determined without further information

    An unknown number multiplied by six is thirty-six.

    or _n_(_n_ + 3) = 40

or If either or both conditions are true, the whole statement is true

    _x_ ≤ −5 or _x_ > −2

ordered pair Two numbers that name the coordinates of a point on a graph, with the horizontal coordinate listed first and the vertical coordinate listed second

    (_x_, _y_) or (5, 8)

P

parabola The graph of a quadratic equation; the shape resembles the letter U

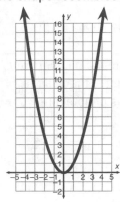

parallel Lines that do not intersect; they are always the same distance apart

percent A ratio whose second term is 100; percent means parts per hundred

    $\frac{56}{100} = 56\%$

perfect square The product of a monomial with itself

x^2, $16a^2$, or 49

perfect square trinomial A polynomial of the form $a^2 + 2ab + b^2 = (a + b)^2$ or $a^2 - 2ab + b^2 = (a - b)^2$

$x^2 + 6x + 9 = (x + 3)^2$

perpendicular Lines that intersect at right angles

point-slope form A linear equation in the form $y - y_1 = m(x - x_1)$

For the points (3, 7) and (0, −2), the point-slope form is $y - 7 = 3(x - 3)$

polynomial An expression with two or more unlike terms

$x^2 + 6x - 7$

power A number or variable that indicates repeated multiplication; x^y is the product of y copies of x

$a^2 = a \cdot a$ or $4^5 = 4 \cdot 4 \cdot 4 \cdot 4 \cdot 4$

prime factorization The prime numbers and/or variables whose product is the desired expression, or the process of obtaining those values

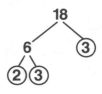

principal square root The positive square root of a number

$\sqrt{81} = \sqrt{9 \cdot 9} = 9$

proportion An equation that states that two ratios are equal

$\dfrac{2}{3} = \dfrac{4}{6}$

Pythagorean theorem Formula relating the lengths of the sides of a right triangle, telling us that the sum of the squares of the legs is equal to the square of the hypotenuse

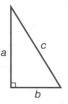

$a^2 + b^2 = c^2$

Q

quadrant One of four regions on a coordinate plane formed by the intersection of the x-axis and the y-axis

quadratic formula

$x = \dfrac{-b \pm \sqrt{b^2 - 4ac}}{2a}$ where $ax^2 + bx + c = 0$

quadratic polynomial A polynomial whose greatest power is 2

$x^2 - 4$, $x^2 + 9$, or $x^2 + 3x + 2$

quadratic trinomial A polynomial of the form $ax^2 + bx + c$

$x^2 + 4x + 3$

R

radical A symbol that indicates that one is to determine the square root

$$\sqrt{}$$

range The possible values for y in a relation

$y = 2x + 5$	
x	y
–1	3
0	5
3	11

ratio A comparison of two numbers

$\frac{2}{3}$, 2:3, or **2 to 3**

rational expression Any expression that can be written as the quotient of two integers or polynomials

$\frac{1}{2}$, $\frac{1}{3x}$, or $\frac{x+2}{x-1}$

rational number A number that can be expressed as the ratio of two integers

$\frac{1}{8}$ or **–0.5**

reciprocal The reciprocal of a number a is a number b such that $a \cdot b = 1$

The reciprocal of $\frac{5}{2}$ is $\frac{2}{5}$.

relation A set of ordered pairs

{(5, 8), (6, 9), (7, 10), (8, 11), (9, 12)}

right triangle A triangle with one right angle, an angle that is exactly 90°

rise The vertical distance traveled

roots The solutions of an equation

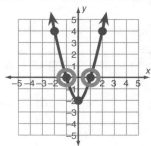

x = –1 and 1

run The horizontal distance traveled

scatter plot A number of coordinate pairs plotted on a graph; used to investigate a possible relationship between two variables

scientific notation A form of writing numbers as the product of a power of 10 and a decimal number greater than or equal to one and less than 10

2.5×10^4

similar Triangles with congruent angles and proportional sides

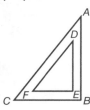

$x = 2(-2) + 8$
$x = 4$

slope The steepness of a line

Slope: $\frac{2}{3}$

slope-intercept form A linear equation in the form $y = mx + b$

$y = 4x + 1$

square A number or variable raised to the second power; the product of two equal factors

b^2 or $49 = 7 \cdot 7$

square root One of two equal factors of a given number

$5 = \sqrt{5 \cdot 5} = \sqrt{25}$

standard form A linear equation in the form $ax + by = c$

$2x - y = -4$

standard notation A form of writing numbers with one digit for each place value

1,238,090

strict inequality An inequality that compares two expressions using only greater than (>) or less than (<)

$x > -2; \ x < 3$

substitution Removing one variable from a system of equations by rewriting the system in terms of the other variable

$x = 2y + 8$ and $2x + 2y = 4$
$2(2y + 8) + 2y = 4$
$4y + 16 + 2y = 4$
$6y = -12$
$y = -2$

system of equations A set of two or more equations that use the same variables

$y = 2x - 3$ and $3y + 6 = x$

system of inequalities A set of two or more linear inequalities that use the same variables

$y \leq 2x - 3$ and $3y + 6 \leq x$